DECEITS OF THE MIND

AND THEIR EFFECTS
ON THE BODY

DECEITS OF THE MIND
AND THEIR EFFECTS
ON THE BODY

Jane G. Goldberg

Transaction Publishers
New Brunswick (U.S.A.) and London (U.K.)

Library of Congress Catalog Number: 90-11233
ISBN: 0-88738-398-X
Printed in the United States of America

Library of Congress Cataloging-in-Publication Data

Goldberg, Jane G. (Jane Gretzner), 1946–
    Deceits of the mind and their effects on the body / Jane G.
Goldberg.
        p.   cm.
    Includes index.
    ISBN 0-88738-398-X
    1. Medicine and psychology. 2. Mind and body. 3. Emotions—
Health aspects. I. Title.
    R726.5.G65 1991
    616.9′8—dc20   90-11233
                                                              CIP

To Eleanore Ament and Cynthia Harter deBlanc
the best buddies a girl could have

Contents

Acknowledgments

I thank my parents for listening to me, as they did, and teaching me Freud's lesson about the creative power of the unconscious long before I had ever heard of Freud.

I thank my sister, Lee, my brother-in-law, Sanford, my nieces, Kim and Lisa, my brother, David, and my aunt and uncle Lulu and Otto, for continuing to give me the feeling of family since my parents' deaths.

I thank my second set of parents, my analysts, Phyllis Meadow and Lou Ormont, for continuing the process that my parents began. I thank Cy Meadow for just being there.

I thank Gregg Lalley, my most ardent fan, who has patiently sat through endless Saturday evenings of oral readings of everything from first drafts to polished versions, and did it with encouragement, sensitivity, good humor, and best of all, love.

I thank Ruth Sackman for her generosity of spirit in sharing her wealth of information, and the love and concern she has shown to me over the years. This book could not have been written were it not for her sensible, intelligent approach to the understanding of the human body which I have come to adopt as my own. I thank Leon Sackman for being married to Ruth, and making it possible for her to carry on with her important and life-saving work.

I thank George Ernsberger for his editorial assistance in bringing the manuscript to its finished form.

I thank Ellen Lack for her case of Angry Andy; Doris Sokosh for her inspirational story of her recovery from cancer; Vera Hirschhorn for her mother's story of a healing crisis; Kathleen Philbin for the story of Carl.

I thank my patients for letting me help them, for letting me be important to them, for letting themselves be important to me, and for the meaning that all that has given to me.

Part One

Why We Get Sick

I

From "It" to "I" to "We"

1

The "It" That Is "I"

In 1984 in the state of Maryland, a man named Michael Stewart was convicted of committing a murder, using as his lethal weapon—words. Some months earlier Stewart had entered the lobby of a motel meaning to commit a simple robbery. He demanded of the desk clerk, Pearl Pizzamiglio, that she fill his brown paper bag with money. In terror, Mrs. Pizzamiglio gave him the $176 that she had at hand. When he had gone, she called the police. At the police station, as she was relating the details of the robbery, she began gasping for breath and clutching at her chest. She was rushed to the hospital exhibiting wildly erratic heart rhythms, and, there, less than two hours after her fateful encounter with Stewart, she was pronounced dead.[1]

Michael Stewart had engaged in no physical action that caused direct damage to Mrs. Pizzamiglio's heart. All he did was talk. Nevertheless it seems clear that his action in terrorizing her *was* what had the effect of stopping her heart, and the finding of guilty felt right—a murder was committed.

The judicial system in Maryland, in rendering the guilty verdict, upheld a concept that we all believe in and observe daily. In a thousand different ways, for good and for ill, we affect each other through our verbal interactions. Our words reflect our feelings toward others, and stimulate feeling responses in them: they feel soothed, hopeful, and understood; agitated, confused, and depressed. We all know that it is not really a mother's kiss to her child's scratched knee that calms the child; it is the tone in her voice that conveys concern for the child's pain and fright. Perhaps a trace of her own sympathetic hurt is also communicated. It is through her ability to use words with feeling that she is able to use herself as an instrument of healing.

3

Stewart's destructive effect on Mrs. Pizzamiglio seems clear enough. His action in terrorizing her makes him responsible for her death. Yet, on a little reflection, some disturbing questions arise. For one thing, many other responses than Mrs. Pizzamiglio's come quickly to mind. A different person might have had a short-lived anxiety attack, another might have taken the whole experience in stride— shrugging it off as just an unpleasant interlude, still another might have sworn a vendetta—pursuing the culprit until he was justly punished.

Mrs. Pizzamiglio was killed, it seems, by that ineffable entity we call *feeling*. Her heart failed, as the Montgomery County jury was told, when bands of heart tissue, overstimulated by a sudden infusion of adrenaline-like substances, ruptured. These chemicals are produced by the hormonal system when intense emotion floods the organism instead of being discharged.[2] But our bodies have ways of preserving our lives in these circumstances. Discharge is usually achieved through translating feeling into action—fight or flight, or the alternatives of the psychological equivalents—word-action (talking) or thought-action (fantasy). Something prevented Mrs. Pizzamiglio from achieving any of these solutions, and that something must have been within her— nothing Michael Stewart did could have accomplished that.

In fact, it's no great strain to imagine an entirely different kind of circumstance triggering this response in Mrs. Pizzamiglio: an auto accident or a fire in the motel, in which she escaped physical injury but felt herself to be in great danger. It seems evident that something particular to Pearl Pizzamiglio's biological and psychological makeup created the responses that culminated in her death.

We may have to ask, at this point, who is the real killer? Michael Stewart may well be seen as merely the happenstance occasion for the enactment by Mrs. Pizzamiglio of her own biological destiny, and we find ourselves in the uncomfortable position of thinking of her death as an odd and surprising variety of suicide instead of a murder.

Mrs. Pizzamiglio's death was not the result of any disease as we commonly think of diseases. Like many victims of sudden heart failure, she had no history of heart disease or hypertension. The process that killed her was sudden and wholly unexpected. So even though she died of a process at work within herself, she was not ill—at least not according to what we have come to understand the word to mean. Might it be that in order to understand a death of this kind, we need a better understanding of the process of disease than contemporary medicine provides? Mrs. Pizzamiglio's death teaches us that our own internal processes can damage us. Feelings can kill. We need, perhaps, a method of classifying diseases—a nosology—where our internal responses are considered to be a distinct form of provocative agent in the formation of disease.

An unwelcome thought surely; we would rather see the agent of destruction as some external entity, some "out-there" thing, rather than something within our own bodies and minds, seemingly involving some sort of participation on our part.

We will see, in the course of this book, that establishing blame—though few of us are free of the compulsion to do it at times, and society probably requires it for its well-being—doesn't get us very far. So, let's satisfy ourselves for now by blaming Pearl Pizzamiglio's death on the relationship—the brief and terrible relationship between the frightful Michael Stewart and the fearful Mrs. Pizzamiglio. Something certainly did go on between them that had the effect of killing her.

Mrs. Pizzamiglio died of, among other things, a bad, a killing relationship. We'll find that does happen, even when, as here, the other meant the victim no such harm. It usually happens, in fact, in much less dramatic ways. Let's consider a relationship the like of which we've all known:

A woman reminds her husband to hold a door for her in a tone that isn't harsh or loud or angry, yet manages to convey an accusation of insensitivity or neglect. Her husband will surely not respond with a deadly heart seizure, but he might clench his jaw for just a moment and his stomach might tighten as, to avoid a scene, he refrains from discharging some quantity of rage—no doubt a small quantity—at being publicly chastised as though he were a thoughtless child. It is by no means farfetched to suppose that regular repetition of such an interactive pattern might lead to an ulcer for this man; it isn't outlandish to imagine, for the sake of our discussion, that ulcer becoming a bleeding ulcer, or even that some resultant hemorrhaging finally causes his death.

Is there a homicide here? Or a suicide? We may be sure of hearing opinions of friends and relations: no wonder, living with that woman—some will say—who wouldn't have developed ulcers; she might as well have put a gun to his head. Others of the same cast of mind, but closer to her, may find otherwise: his neglect provoked only the gentlest response in her, while his own unacknowledged irrational rage was such that had he not killed himself first with his ulcers, he would surely have exploded and destroyed his long-suffering wife.

No court would convict this widow on either of these readings, of course. Nor would we want one to. For just one thing, he (and she) would have had ample opportunity to become aware of the destructive nature of their relationship, and to negotiate a different sort of relationship or, failing that, to separate. (So again, establishing blame is idle, even though understanding the dynamic of this relationship may be very fruitful indeed.)

And now stretch only an inch farther: suppose that the stimulating agent of toxic interactions was applied many years before the manifestation of the disease symptoms. We know this happens where the killing agent is physical: results of exposure to asbestos may not be evident for decades; the drug DES does its damage to the next generation, in the form of cancers in the grown children of women who had taken it. Could it happen when the agent is psychological?

In fact, much impressive research connects certain afflictions occurring in adults—even in middle age and older—to patterns in their relationships in infancy and childhood (when the options of mature negotiating or separation may not be available). For example, studies of cancer patients find a significant incidence of disturbances in their primary nurturing relationship as babies—the mothers of these patients are often characterized as cold or distant. Similarly, cardiac patients show a persistent pattern of radically unsuccessful early relationships with their fathers, marked by intense conflict or disruption by divorce, abandonment, or death.

Can some relationships kill at long distance? We'll see that there is no simple answer to this question—it's rare that a single agent can be identified as *the* killer. Much more work needs to be done in this area, both in carefully designed research and in hard thinking—indeed, this book means to do just a little of this.

Murder and suicide are a part of all of our daily lives, and they are crucial themes in this book, though not in the sense of the acts of violence that the words usually call to mind. Rather, we will be talking about processes that are much less willful or intentional; processes that, for the most part, go unseen, but which are often no less tragic in their consequences. We will be dealing with events that occur on the cellular and biochemical levels of the body. And, in the realm of the mind, we will be looking at entities much more subtle and less tangible than actual behavior; where feelings, thoughts, impulses, and memories hold sway.

This book is about a mother's kisses, as well. It's about health and vitality and love and growth. Most of all, it is about how to use the processes of death and destruction in the service of life. The natural processes of our bodies and minds tell us how to do this.

It's well-known that on the cellular level, murder and suicide take place continuously. Each of us will have entirely new cells in our coat of skin every month; we will replace every cell in our liver every six weeks. Seven years from now, many of the cells in our body at this moment will have been replaced by new cells (with the notable exception of brain and nerve cells). Even as this material is being read, over fifty million new cells will be generated. With that much renewal, there needs to be a lot of death and destruction.

Under normal circumstances these processes are life sustaining and even life enhancing. They have, for instance, contributed to our movement up the evolutionary ladder. Cellular suicide is what allows the fingers of our hands to be separate digits rather than melded into a webbed paw. In the embryo, intervening cells between the nascent digits need to kill themselves off—victims of their own programmed destiny.[3]

Biological events can induce cellular death that works towards the overall destruction of the organism, rather than towards sustenance and growth. We call these destructive processes *diseases*, and they are myriad in their manifestations in both body and mind. The comparative evolutionary complexity of the human organism means that many more things can go wrong with us than with all other life forms. Error on any of the levels on which we operate—biochemical, neuronic, psychological, physiological—can mean drastic disequilibrium for the organism as a whole. Generally, these disease processes occur over time. Death often tortures us with its slowness.

The ability to use conscious awareness to convert a destructive, disease-producing process into a healthy, constructive end is uniquely human. It was through Freud's brilliant observations, over 100 years ago, of the inner workings of the minds of his patients that we began to learn how to use consciousness to master our inherent urge towards destruction.

Freud began a research experiment designed to study both the effect of words on the human system and the diseases of feelings. His theoretical understanding of the case of Anna O. marks the first scientific exploration of the power of words over a disease process. What Freud discovered was that as Anna O. talked, her symptoms of hysteria, paralysis, and the like remarkably abated. It was she who named the treatment the "talking cure."[4] Words can cure as well as kill.

Psychoanalysis evolved as a method of investigation of the mind and the mind's impact on the body. But it didn't begin there, and it seems worthwhile at the beginning of a book by a psychoanalyst about health and disease to remember that Freud's first scientific inquiry was as a research neurologist. He was interested in the brain as part of the body.

Freud's first great venture into new territory, a really new way of thinking about the essence of human nature, he called a "Project For a Scientific Psychology." If the project failed to conquer all it explored, as it surely did, it nevertheless established very broad boundaries for Freud's area of concern: it was not just mental health, nor human behavior, nor emotional life—nor all of these. And it wasn't just the brain or the psyche—it was the very nature of human life.

The human being was seen as one variety of organic life, distinguished by the specific nature of his mentality—which is to be understood as having its wellsprings in his biological existence. The human organism, with its complex physical and mental development, has organized and developed a very large variety of means of expression, manifested both by the body and the mind.

Psychoanalysis, then, is the system of thought that begins with the oneness of body and mind—which is where this book begins, too.

Freud never lost sight of that premise as his theories developed and ramified; he was always, as he has been called lately, the biologist of the mind.[5] He was certainly that when, late in his maturity, he arrived at the finished form of his theory of the instinctual drives. It seemed to him that none of what he had learned could be understood fully except by postulating two opposing drives, equal in primacy, existing on the deepest level of organic existence—below the level where a difference is seen between mind and body—contained, indeed, in every living cell.

The first of these that he had seen was eros, the life instinct, the creative drive. He had been working with some version of this from the first, having observed the dominance of sexuality in psychic life and behavior, and having followed that stream to its source. What completed his understanding of this foundation of his system of thought was the postulation of the opposing drive, the death instinct—the drive to death and destruction.[6]

Both of these biological strivings are expressed sometimes in emotional states, sometimes in behavior, sometimes in physical processes. How all this is accomplished, how these drives underlie and influence, and are incorporated and reflected in the life of the psyche has become the essence of psychoanalytic work.

It's not the most comfortable idea to live with—that death and destruction are at home within us, that each of us harbors a killer. And, this theory says, the killer is not to be killed—not by reason and not by rapture. No intellectual or emotional or spiritual enlightenment can—or should—eliminate this basic component of our nature. Efforts to smother the death instinct use up energy taken from the opposing creative drive, leaving less for the psyche to work with productively. The drives, both of them, must be harnessed and their energy directed, if life is to be as productive, and as fulfilling and fulfilled, as it can be.

But the news Freud brought with his formation of the death instinct was that mind and body share a compulsion toward destruction: cellular suicide will clearly have its psychic equivalent. The psyche will make choices that will give shape to the destructive drive: some version of suicide or homicide; aggression either turned inward against the self, or outward against another.

Freud's unified theory of mind and body, and of both external and internal causes of disease, can be seen as pivotal in the history of medicine. It recalls the earliest understandings of disease, and, at the same time, points to the future, toward the establishment of that practice of medicine we now call holistic—more technically, psychoneuroimmunology. We have come full circle.

The very earliest belief was that disease has its locus in the spirit or soul as well as in the body. Hippocrates, the father of the science of medicine, embraced that idea. It was Hippocrates who introduced the idea that a disease has a historical course, a story with a beginning and an end and all that lies in between.[7]

That insight, a powerful tool in treatment and in research, seems commonplace to us. Yet, it was lost sight of for much of medical history. The onset of almost any disease was thought to call for immediate intervention before its story could unfold. The intervention was often very aggressive—and often, as we discovered only a century and a half ago, far more destructive than the disease.

This discovery was made in the 1830's, when it occurred to medical scientists that, in some cases, it might be worthwhile to withhold treatment and to compare resulting death rates. It became over-whelmingly clear that patients' prospects for survival improved when the treatments then most relied on were withheld, and the disease was simply allowed to follow its natural course.[8] Thus came the rediscov-ery that a disease did indeed have a natural course—the end of which was sometimes, but not always, death. By this we were also led to think that the body might have resources of its own—defenses to protect itself, capabilities of regeneration—in short, the power to heal itself.

Finally the idea could find a home in our medical thought that it might be the whole *person*—both a biological and psychological enti-ty, host to both biological microbes and psychological anxiety, target of both toxins from the environment and murderous wishes from the psyche, assimilator of food for the body and feelings for the mind—that we should be working to understand.

Freud, in devising a therapy that was also an investigation, estab-lished the patient as an active partner in his treatment. A kind of interpersonal laboratory was created (It could hardly be avoided, once hopes and dreams, fears and desperation, love, hopelessness and vengeance were seen as important to the investigation.). The telling of one's tale of suffering—the taking of a case history—reached an apotheosis in the technique of Freud. Never before had the physician handed over so much power to the patient for his own cure.

Not that Freud's model immediately gained prevalence. On the contrary, until recently medicine and psychoanalysis diverged quite sharply: psychoanalysis concentrating on the inner forces that inhabit the mind—instinctual drives, feeling states, psychic conflicts—and medicine on external agents of disease—viruses and bacteria, carcino-gens, toxins, cholesterol-producing foods. But lately, medicine has come to acknowledge the influence on health of the inner world of the psyche, and the social sciences have become interested in studying the external forces of family and society on the personality. It may be that we are discovering a center.

Contemporary researchers have returned to the understandings of Hippocrates, and later of Freud, in using patients' self-reports as serious contributions to the understanding of their diseases. When they are asked, patients often reveal a great deal about the causes of their diseases. Patients have always wanted to tell the stories of their afflictions; the extent to which they have been successful has been in great part the extent to which we have been willing to hear. As we listen, we come closer to apprehending the patient in relation to his disease—to knowing, as Oliver Sachs has said, a "who" as well as a "what."[9]

My own work as a psychoanalyst has been conducted in good part with patients who have serious, often life-threatening, physical afflictions. Although they were not the original reason for my interest in medicine and physical health, my patients have been both a motive for my continuing studies and a crucial part of my education. They have privileged me in allowing me to know them. We have spent hours upon hours, and often these hours have added up to years, studying the nature of their illnesses. Every angle of observation has been tried, every possibility entertained—for both the cause and cure of their afflictions.

It is from them that I truly learned respect for the complexity of diseases—and of people. How we develop both physically and emotionally seems to involve a combination of factors from our inborn constitution to a wide variety of external influences that serve to move us in the direction of either health or disease. These forces have varying levels of potency, and an inclination in one direction may be either strengthened through a companion force or attenuated by an opposing force. There are no easy conceptualizations for disease or for health.

But a look at research tells us quickly that the forces that psychoanalysis has endeavored to study have to carry much more weight than medicine has thus far allotted. We now live longer, and by a lot of years, than ever before. To what can we attribute this fact?

Advances in medicine have almost certainly made some difference, though not nearly as much as is thought (as we shall see). Our physical environment has deteriorated—some think to the point of irreversibility—so it is obviously not this factor to which we can attribute our longevity. While the range of available foods has greatly increased, the quality of foods we consume has been, for the most part, seriously compromised, and we are as accustomed to eating nonfood foods as nutritional foods. Our longevity seems to be in spite of environmental conditions and dietary habits, rather than because of them. Finally, while late nineteenth century improvements in sanitation may have made some difference, and have certainly improved our living conditions, again the difference was probably not substantive.[10] It is true that the decline of the incidence of *mortality* from infectious diseases did coincide with these changes, but the incidence of *infection* did not drop during this time. As late as 1940, long after the peak of the tuberculosis scare, as many as 95 percent of Americans were still testing positive for the tuberculosis bacteria. Only a fraction of those got sick. Perhaps the same is true today of AIDS. Microorganisms have always lived around us and in us, most of the time harmlessly.

If we are not to attribute our increased life expectancy to improvements in the physical environment, what explanation can we find? Much more dramatic, consistent and long lasting, have been the changes in our psychological environment. Modernization has given us a whole new way of being together in the world. What we have today, unique to our time on earth, is an unparalleled sense of control. In spite of the nostalgia that we tend to feel about the peacefulness of primitive cultures, their lives were replete with stresses and strains of a quality that we hardly dare to even dream. To live without assurance of one's next meal, to live with continuous threat of death from one's neighboring enemies, to see most of one's children die in infancy, and to live totally at the mercy of environmental elements from which there is no reprieve—all this is the stress of premodern life. Today, control over these factors are taken for granted by most of us. We have protective services for fire, emergency medical care, disability insurance, and almost always, when we find our environment unresponsive to our needs, we have legal and regularity recourses. We are, for the most part, cushioned against physical and economic disasters.[11] Modern civilization has become the most successful test of the "pull yourself up by the boot straps" school of thought ever designed.

But some of us have failed to pass the test. Some of us don't, or can't, feel the heady sensation of being master of our own destinies. We are left with feelings of powerlessness and impotence. Considerable research shows that these feelings are more often associated with sickness and disease. Helplessness is not an uncommon feature in the psychological lives of primitive cultures, people raised in poverty, and, as we now know, physically and emotionally ill patients. How we can restore to these individuals this lost sense of personal mastery is the stuff of psychoanalysis, and the essence of what we will be looking at here.

My interest in health was first set into motion before I began my training as a psychoanalyst. Many years ago, my mother was diagnosed with breast cancer. As I remember, this wasn't terribly alarming to me. For a young girl like myself, knowing of a cancer death was unusual. I didn't expect anyone that I knew to die of cancer; I certainly didn't expect anyone in my own family to die of cancer. And, in any case, "they had gotten it all."

The fact that they hadn't really gotten it all became all too glaringly obvious long after my mother had gone down in the annals of medical history as a "cured" statistic. As we were to learn, medical definition of cancer cure is a five-year survival from the time of the original diagnosis. As it turns out, and as was the case with my mother, dead and dying breast cancer patients are often recorded statistically as cured. This is due to the particular nature of the breast cancer cell: it frequently takes longer than the stipulated five years for a breast cancer cell to migrate, implant itself in some other tissue or organ, and make its presence known.

My mother's own mothering was never what she needed or wanted. It took years, and possibly the safety of a family of her own, for her to come to know that she had always felt hated by her mother.

Her commitment to do better by her own family, to ensure that her own children felt a love, warmth, and security that she never did, was heroic. As I was growing up and basking in her love, I was sure there was no better mother in all the world.

Her generosity was paid back to her by her children when she needed it. When her cancer returned, and it became clear that her struggle now was going to be between life and death, we all rallied. Each of us committed ourselves fully to helping her to get well. My sister took over the tedious burden of managing her everyday life. My brother continued to work the family business, and funneled whatever money was necessary for her treatment costs and the expensive luxury of household help—at first simply to run the house, but later, as she got sicker, to care for her directly. I devoted myself to the task of discovering everything there was to know about the terrible disease that was threatening to take away the person I held most dear.

This book is an outgrowth of that commitment. Ultimately, my mother and I, together, came to understand both her own disease, and the disease process in general, in a way that was radically different from what we had both grown up believing. Not the least of the lessons was the essential meaninglessness of the concept "gotten it all." Cancer, like all the diseases I will discuss in this book, is a systemic process. Many things must go wrong for illness to take hold. Cure comes about not when the symptom manifestation of the disease (e.g., the cancer tumor) is eliminated, but when the underlying cause of the disorder is corrected.

Fairly early in my search, I acquainted myself with the idea that the biochemical disorders that contribute to the cause of disease can sometimes be corrected through improved nutrition. On my urging, my mother gave up meat and all refined and processed foods. Her program became much more than a life-style—it became a life force. It was, in her mind, what was literally keeping her alive. Indeed, it appeared to work. Time seemed to fall away from her; she felt better and looked better than she had in years.

Blissful years passed; we had, together, vanquished the great enemy of humanity. Her cancer was in the vanishing past.

When research on the so-called "cancer personality" began to be published, I was struck by a disturbing number of parallels with my mother's history and character. The point of the research was, of course, that on the level of the unconscious, there are no accidents, and that superficially unrelated events are interconnected within the hidden chambers of the psyche.

My mother's first cancer diagnosis had been made shortly after I (her youngest, her "baby" to the day she died) had gone off to college. Her second diagnosis came on the heels of my father's death. At that point, even the panacea of good, healthy food ceased to work its magic, and it became clear that there was a situation going on of much greater complexity than food alone could correct.

Even more, the food itself became a screen on which to project all of her concerns about her disease. It seemed as though her body was giving her a channel for expression of the psychic anxieties that had plagued her all her life. Her concerns about food became momentous;

she consumed each meal as though she expected that she might actually be able to fill the psychic hole that had remained deep inside her, and which had left her particularly vulnerable to separations and fear of loss of love. Each meal became an occasion for obsession. Ultimately, the food that had initially represented her freedom from disease became her imprisonment.

My mother was not, I think, so unusual in confusing food with feeling. Most of us do the same thing to some degree. And it's not only because one can come to symbolize the other that this inter-changeability between food and feeling, or body and mind, generally occurs. It is, too, that in some very fundamental ways, the workings of the body and of the mind are alike. Feelings bear the same relation to the mind that food does to the body. Each is sustenance; each must undergo a process of digestion to be used; what is not useful in both must be ultimately discharged in order not to become toxic. More than mere metaphor is at work here.

This interchangeability in thinking will be reflected in the language of this book, as well. I will, for instance, refer rather lengthily to psychological narcissism—that stage of early development first paid attention to by psychoanalysts. I am going to ask, as well, that you consider that the body has its own brand of narcissism. It may seem a little tricky, because I don't mean what most people have always meant by narcissism. Explanation is required here because this concept is central to this book; nothing will be clear if it isn't.

When psychoanalysts say narcissism, we don't mean vanity, or primping, or even self-love (actually self-hate is more likely to be found). We do mean self-involvement.

Psychoanalysts did not invent narcissism, exactly (the Greek myths were not, I sometimes remind myself, composed by Sigmund Freud). Still, Freud did define the word in its developmental sense, as a necessary step in the development of a personality and as a stage in that process where growth is, sometimes cripplingly, halted.

Freud did not learn as much about narcissism as he might have since he thought that the disorders associated with it were untreatable by his method. Later psychoanalysts have refined the concept considerably. We have had to. As the therapy has advanced through the underbrush of mental disturbances, we have found in our patient population a steady retreat from hysteria and other maladies of the so-called Oedipal crisis (which typically occurs within a year or so of age five), to disturbances arising in the very earliest stages of life, the "pre-Oedipal" and even preverbal stages (arising even in prenatal stages, many suppose.).

It is in this deep forest that narcissism has its lair—here that the mythological Narcissus became enraptured by his own image in a pool.

When psychoanalysts use the word, we are referring to that stage of development when the still rudimentary psyche—it can scarcely be called a personality yet—has not entertained the idea that anybody else exists. It may, in fact, only just have determined that *something* else—something "not-I"—exists, and thus that there is some identifiable "I" to consider.

A momentous discovery, that. A necessary step in that miraculous process: the development of a personality. It begins in the nascent nervous system with firings of synapses that are no different in kind from the reactions amoebas are capable of. Soon enough mental and neurological traces are left, which form patterns that gather into constellations: instincts, impulses, sensations, emotions, memory, ideas—until where there was just an organism, then an animal, now there is a person.

At some point in that process, after it's accepted that there is an "I" and a "not-I," there must dawn an idea of just how complicated that "I," oneself, must actually be; a very large concept to encompass. When we've achieved some grasp of that, then we finally have a conceptual means of considering that there might be others. So a close examination of the self is the first psychology. But whatever part of one's attention is fixed here—and some part of everyone's is—it never takes in anything else, and the personality remains stunted accordingly. Narcissism, then, refers to some aspect of this crippling self-involvement, some disability arising in this very early stage of personality development—a failure to distinguish between "I" and "not-I."

If the word brings the legendary young Greek to mind as, of course, it must, picture him with his gaze locked helplessly on his own image—unaware, of course, that it is himself. Pleasure is no necessary part of the picture; he may be so immersed in his reflection that the outer world and his relation to it has been obliterated, and he may well be starving to death.

And, as I have suggested, the psyche is not the only container for narcissism. The body has its own need to distinguish self from not-self. It, too, has its own mechanism for the recognition of all the "not-I" entities that surround it, invade it and even arise within it. We call this biological mechanism the immune system, and our physical health is altogether dependent on its proper functioning.

The process of differentiation between "I" and "not-I" can go awry for either the psyche or the soma. In its most extreme form, psychological narcissism leads to the psychotic state, marked by fusion between "I" and "not-I" entities, known as schizophrenia. The products of the mind ("I") are experienced as being a part of the external world ("not-I").[12] In its most extreme form in the body, biological narcissism will lead to cancer, wherein the immune system ("I") fails to recognize the difference between itself and the cancer cell ("not-I").[13] Indeed, at times the red carpet is practically rolled out to welcome this murderous guest. It is because of these artful deceits of mind and body—both on themselves and on each other—that disease is allowed to freely romp about. Normal defensive operations, protecting the "I" from damaging "not-I" entities, fail to occur, and we see what bears a closer resemblance to parody than to health. Defenses may go wildly out of control and a minor irritation becomes fiercely tumultuous; or, a desperate situation is responded to as though it were a passing vexation.

While there are striking, even startling, similarities between the disease of narcissism of the mind and narcissism of the body, as we shall see, there is one crucial difference. Narcissism of the mind will only torture us; narcissism of the body can kill us. They're not the kinds of alternatives that one would wish to choose between, yet there are times when we do position our conflicts in the body in order to avoid their placement in the mind. Such is the premise of psychosomatics. As the French psychoanalyst, Joyce McDougall, has said, "In the final analysis, it's better to be mad than dead."[14]

And so, if this book studies the body and those stimuli that impinge on it as much as it does the mind, it's not so much because I'm a psychosomaticist—which, of course, I am—as because of the variety of ways that mind and body converge, interact, reflect one another (or don't).

There are, of course, still those who reject the idea that the presumably ephemeral condition of the mind can have an effect on the solid matter of a body; but, in truth, there aren't many any more. And though it's tactless to say so in public debate and I rarely do, the truth is that I think of such people as very like flat-earthers.

Scarcely anyone doubts that there's a connection between mental states and ulcers, for example, and a physician who assumed *no* psychosomatic involvement in allergy symptoms and skin conditions would be thought radical. The majority is no great authority in these matters, of course—it hasn't been historically as we shall see—but it allows me not to bother much with the basic arguments. I simply assume (I don't know of a psychoanalyst who doesn't, to tell the truth) all the essential premises of psychosomatics. I don't, moreover, imagine that this book will have attracted readers who reject that way of thinking.

Psychosomatics is, though, an idea that doesn't want understanding too quickly. One of the ways that a little learning on this subject is a dangerous thing is in the temptation it presents us with to blame the victim—not always as crudely as to say, well it's all in her head, or, too bad he had to come to that, but it was just in his character (a formulation that, among the psychoanalytically-oriented at least, easily enough leads to blaming the mother, instead—which is equally idle and scarcely less cruel).

Another closely related temptation—and a seductive one whose allure I don't always resist myself—is to think that we can, or ought to be able to, make consistent connections between personality traits and particular physical afflictions (the Type A personality in relation to heart attacks, or the Type C personality for cancer, as two well-known examples).

Patterns are indeed discernible in statistics, and patients and therapists working on these problems often recognize such connections in their own cases. When it happens, it gives a gratifying sense of rightness-of-fit—and I don't doubt it can become a meaningful tool in diagnosis and treatment. But, as many cancer or heart disease patients will tell you, it's not a one-to-one correlation. Plenty of patients don't fit any such pattern, and for those plenty, a host of variables need to be considered.

We need not only a subtler understanding than we have so far developed of the mind/body dynamic itself, but also a more comprehensive way of factoring in all of the influences that bear on it— environmental, interpersonal, constitutional, and instinctual. Statistics are overwhelmingly convincing that certain environmental pollutants increase the risk of certain physical afflictions. What we mean by that is that they cause disease in some but not in others; in other words, having learned that, we've only just arrived at where the interesting questions are to be found. They are the questions this book means to address.

The lesson of Pearl Pizzamiglio is that feelings can kill. If the variety of ways we can fall ill and kill ourselves is to be transformed from a morass of chaos into intelligible meaning, feelings must be considered. Perhaps our new nosology of disease should be based on this variable of feelings. Feelings will lead us to hope and cooperation—and life—or to despair and rejection—and death. As one of my patients, Vera, said shortly before her death: "It's all getting the best of me. Either things are going to change, or I know I'm going to die."

In saying that "it" was getting the best of her, Vera was referring to a force seemingly out of her control and taking her over. Surely this was something like what Pearl Pizzamiglio felt that night in the police station, when her heart began its wild and out-of-control journey to her death. Both of these women experienced an internal process that seemed to be operating extraneously and independently of their conscious will. This force seemed to be propelling them in the direction of death and destruction. In spite of any attachment to health and life that they may have had, this "it" seemed to have gained ascendancy, and they seemed more bound by its laws than by any attempts that they may have wished to make to subdue it.

Freud's discovery that the enemy that is this "it" is only one's self—a fractionalized portion of one's inner self (and which he named "id," the German word for "it")—is hardly reassuring in light of their deaths. Yet, suppose it were possible that this force could be controlled—tamed as a rider learns to do with a wild horse. Could the biological destinies, the premature and pathological deaths of Vera and of Pearl Pizzamiglio have been averted?

Freud's solution was never to just get rid of feeling or the deeper origin of feeling, the instinctual drives themselves. It was, in fact, just such an attempt that usually got his patients into trouble. To the extent that we have leanings in the direction of destruction, such must be our confession. The killer in us can't be bound, but must be allowed expression. In the successfully integrated personality that will be done in ways which the ego will devise to keep the killing symbolic and not in the quotidian world destructive. This is a task of fearsome difficulty; most of us will fail at it much of the time. Insofar as this book is about disease, it is about some of the myriad ways there are to fail in that; insofar as it's about good health, it's about succeeding—for there are ways to succeed.

Finally, this is not a book arrived at through strictly intellectual pathways. Though it is, as the reader will discover, heavily weighted with ideas and theories, I hope that much more comes though. Each of the issues that I have chosen to discuss has been intensely personal for me. I have had not only to think through the issues, but to *feel* them through, as well.

It is, for instance, no mere abstract idea that a preoccupation with oneself can be murderous toward another, and that if murder is what the psyche knows how to do, then one may be forced to choose between the dismal alternatives of murdering another, of sacrificing one's self. This is a conflict not foreign to me; I have spent many a tearful night feeling my way through this in regard to my relationship with my mother. There is a sense in which I remain convinced that I helped to kill her. Of course not maliciously, not deliberately, not even directly. And, certainly not without her help in the matter. But, I knew her vulnerabilities—she had spent much of my childhood telling me of her fears and anxieties. I knew the heightened state of sensitivity she would be in at my father's death. I knew that for her to have reason to live, she would need to feel my presence in her life in a way that had been heaven for the young child that I once was, but burdensome for the adult I had become. These are no idle, vagrant feelings of guilt. They are rather, torturous concerns, not unlike those that my patients themselves feel—nor, I suspect, any feelingful person.

I suppose there is a sense in which my writing this book is presumptuous. I have worked with plenty of patients whose analyses rescued their psyches, but failed to save their bodies. As a treatment of disease, psychoanalysis was never meant to accomplish such a formidable task anyway. Yet, there are those who hold high hopes and strong beliefs in just this path to cure, and while therapy for the psyche does not predictably lead to reversal of somatic symptomatology, it does so in enough cases to command attention. Combined with a dietary regimen of food that is meant to sustain life (as opposed to merely pleasing the palate), a life-style that limits our exposure to biochemical poisons, and a program of psychological and physiological detoxification where feelings and food, once digested, can be released, we have acquired a tool of very broad power for prevention and for cure.

It hasn't taken so very long for psychoanalysts to realize that without a body there is no mind to heal. Psychoanalysts today will look for the subtle and not-so-subtle ways that patients neglect or abuse their bodies, and know that here, the death instinct prevails.

The cancer that stalked my mother for nearly twenty years finally caught up to her, some years ago now. But she left me with a legacy that seems invaluable to me: she gave me the sense that I could own myself.

Years ago, when my piano teacher would offer me a choice of pieces to learn next, I would hate to choose; I wanted them all: the Mozart sonata, the Beethoven, a Brahms. But choose I did, and over the next year, I would come to know every nook and cranny of that piece's architecture, until, at last, the music would be mine. I could love each of the pieces, but only some would be chosen to be lived in, and those I would own.

It was in this way, my mother showed me, that I could own my own self as well. Through intimacy—through my relationship with her, and the music that she encouraged me to play and to which she sat and listened from beginning (banging) to end (glorious harmony, at last)— I came to known the riches of ownership.

Too much of ourselves wants too strongly to remain in darkness. We are victimized by those processes that go forth in the dark, over which we can exercise no direction. We've learned from Freud that we can shed light, and gain control, over much more than we ever before imagined.

Most damage is done through ignorance. The violent stories are the uncommon ones. More usual by far are the hoards of patients seeking psychotherapy, not because their parents deliberately abused them, but because their parents did the best they could, and the best wasn't good enough.

It is through consciousness that we can come to own ourselves: by expanding and then filling consciousness, and by making all of ourselves, our bodies and our minds—all of our minds—at home in consciousness. This is how we can make choices for health and long life and fulfillment.

My hope is that I am enabled to pass on to others the same sense of ownership of body and mind that my mother gave to me. So that we can all do better.

Notes

1. Police Report, Montgomery County, Maryland, April 1984.
2. D. Monagan, "Sudden Death," *Discover* (January 1986): 52.
3. G. Montgomery, "The Case of the Suicidal Sex Cell," *Discover* (October 1987): 44.
4. L. Freeman, *The Story of Anna O.* (NY: Walker, 1972).
5. F. Sulloway, *Freud: Biologist of The Mind* (NY: Basic Books, 1979), 3.
6. S. Freud, "Beyond the Pleasure Principle," *The Standard Edition of The Complete Psychological Works of Sigmund Freud*, Vol. 18 (London: Hogarth Press, 1920). (S. E. in subsequent references denotes the *Standard Edition*, vols. 1–24, 1953–1974.)
7. Many books document the history of medicine. Perhaps the most enjoyable, replete with illustrations, is A. Lyons, and R. J. Petrucelli, *Medicine: An Illustrated History* (NY: Abradale Press, Harry N. Abrams Publishers, 1987).
8. L. Thomas, *N Y Review of Books*, 24 September 1987.
9. Sachs, O. *The Man Who Mistook His Wife For a Hat* (NY: Harper & Row, 1970), viii.
10. R. Dubos, *The Mirage of Health: Utopian Progress and Biological Change*, (NY: Anchor Books, 1959) was the first to address the myth of modernization (including modern medicine) on health. Ivan Illich's *Medical Nemesis* (NY: Bantam Books, 1977) and Rick Carlson's *The End of Medicine* (NY: Wiley Interscience, 1975) are other excellent references.
11. L. A. Sagan, *The Health of Nations* (NY: Basic Books, 1987) is an update of Dubos's, Illich's, and Carlson's works, with an abundance of supporting data.
12. T. Freeman, Cameron, J. L., McGhie, A. *Chronic Schizophrenia* (NY: International Universities Press, 1958).
13. G. F. Solomon, "Emotions, Stress, the Central Nervous System, and Immunity," *Annals of the New York Academy of Medicine* 164:2 (1969): 335–43.
14. Joyce McDougall, *Plea for a Measure of Abnormality* (NY: International Universities Press, 1980).

2

The "I" That Is "We"

> *Disease usually results from inconclusive*
> *negotiations for symbiosis, an overstepping*
> *of the line by one side or the other, a*
> *biological misinterpretation of border.*
> —Lewis Thomas

It is no accident that Freud chose the particular myths of Narcissus and Oedipus to illustrate neurotic patterns. His choices were well made; each story reflects a critical stage in psychological development, and how things can go awry when the normal process of psychic maturation does not occur.

Narcissus, alone with himself and oblivious to his external surroundings, reminds us of the newborn infant. Freud referred to this state, where self and not-self remain fused, as *oceanic*. Only gradually does the self wake to the idea that the world around him is populated with objects that are not part of him. As this process occurs, as consciousness of others is acquired and relationships are formed, the "I" is permitted to become a "we." At first, it is only a breast—part mother and bearer of the satisfaction of hunger—that the infant recognizes as other. Next, it is more of mother—a whole body, and a repository of feelings, as well. And then, relatively late in this process, comes awareness of family. This is the point at which we find Oedipus, struggling with his psyche to come to accept all of what family life can mean.

We live, from the very beginning, in a world of relationships. We are in and of relationships as fish are in and of the water: they are our emotional environment—the atmosphere we move through and

23

breathe, that warms us or chills us, holds us quiet and calm, or buffets us about.

The ways in which we influence one another, and the ways in which emotional states communicate themselves to another psyche, and sometimes even through that psyche to the body, have only begun to be understood. Experimental research convinces us that we have some mechanism for the intentional or unintentional influencing of biological and emotional states in one another. There is a large body of literature documenting the many ways that our blood chemistry is changed through our contact with others, and through the feelings we are exposed to. The menstrual cycles of college roommates and close friends, for instance, have been found to regulate themselves to fall together.[1] Similarly, the blood chemistries of three crewman working together on a B-52 flight reached similar elevated levels of 17-hydroxycorticosteroids (involved in stress reactions) at the same time of the day.[2] Female volunteers on a research ward showed changes in blood chemistry in a similar fashion during the working day.[3]

Feelings, too, seem to be passed, unwittingly, between individuals. Most of us have had the experience of "catching" a mood, and it appears that feelings, like a virus, are contagious. The most common response to a smile is a smile; the most common response to irritation is irritation. Our feeling states seem to be strongly related to the feelings we are surrounded by.

We now know a great deal about biological contagion. The meaning of the term is relatively simple, and refers to the transmission of disease through the spread of microorganisms. The contagion of feelings, however, is quite a different and difficult matter about which we know relatively little.

Psychoanalysts have borrowed the concept from biology, and have become interested in how we influence feeling states in another. The mother/infant dyad has been of particular interest, confirming the extreme susceptibility of one to the other.[4] Psychoanalysts have found similar levels of sensitivity in the emotional communication that takes place between patient and analyst. One experiment, where individuals received either positive or negative feelings from the experimenter, revealed that physiological changes could be experimentally induced. Heart rates of psychologists and patients were recorded as they interacted with one another. The psychologist was instructed, on sealed orders, either to praise or to criticize the patient, irrespective of what the patient had said. Most interestingly, it was not only the patient who had the adverse reaction. When the psychologist was critical, the tension level of both patient and psychologist was elevated, as measured by cardiac reactions.[5]

Even death from feeling can look as though it were contagious. The recent phenomenon of teenage suicide has the look of an infectious disease. Clusters of deaths are occurring. Apparently, once one occurs another is more likely, and yet another, until it begins to have the appearance of an epidemic.

Our ability to influence each other is surely based on our mutual dependencies. Dependency is a biological law of nature for all living organisms. Much of the time it works, and quite successfully at that. The orchid and the host tree upon whom it depends live happily symbiotically together. Social relations follow this biological law of nature. Much of the time our emotional needs for one another work to our mutual benefit. The research data on marriage, companionship, and social connectedness are overwhelmingly in favor of our being company to each other: simply, married people live longer and better (with less anxiety and less disease) than their nonmarried counterparts. Happiness, too, counts, but not as much as we might expect. Happily married women live longest of all; but for men, happily or unhappily married, it is mere togetherness that does the trick.

But, sometimes, in nature as in social relations, things can go wrong. Psychotherapists have now explored the idea that just as loved ones can mitigate disease and suffering, so too can they create tensions and exacerbate disease. Some years ago, clinicians began to notice that where families had members with physical illnesses, there were often patterns of disturbed psychological interactions within the family unit as a whole.[6] The physical diseases, such as asthma, diabetes, and arthritis were seen as mere symptomatic manifestations of a deeper disturbance involving the ways in which communication of feelings between family members takes place.[7]

How each of us is able to love—and be loved—is a skill learned largely in early infancy. The relationship between a child and his family, and the care he receives, will not only determine whether the child survives, but will influence the structure of his personality and his sense of well-being—how he manages feelings and impulses, his attitudes and values, his self-esteem, and the ways in which he interacts with others. The love he receives—or doesn't receive—is crucial to his development, and it is from exposure to these early feelings of his caretakers that lifelong patterns will be established.

Disturbances in patterns of loving are not new. In fact, it used to be a lot worse. Childhood was, until recently, quite a precarious affair. In preindustrial days, the chances of surviving childhood were not much better than the chance of not surviving.[8]

Modernization has included a radical change in fundamental views about children, their needs, and how we rear them in response to those needs. For most of western civilization, infants were objectified, and seen as a possession worth not much more than a newborn animal. In the Old Testament, for instance, we see that Job counts his children along with the number of his sheep, camels, oxen, and she-asses, as though they, too, were nothing more than livestock and property.[9] It was long taken for granted that parents had the right to use, or abuse, their offspring, and that the children, subject to the whims of their parents, had no rights at all. As late as the nineteenth century, Montaigne summed up the worth of children as being that they have "neither mental activities, nor recognizable bodily shape."[10]

Interest in and nurturance of childhood is a relatively recent phenomenon. In the era of the Enlightenment, childhood could be seen as something more than a mere prelude to adulthood, the important and real business of living.

Freud understood, perhaps better than anyone had up to that point, that this pattern of objectifying children was not without its consequences. He used the Greek tragedies to illustrate his theories, and in doing so, made clear his belief in the universality of conflict; the families of the Greek tragedies are not so different from our own.

The story Freud used that has become most commonly known is, of course, the Oedipus myth. Here Freud illustrates the principle of infantile sexuality: infants, like adults, have needs and drives that are tied to their instinctual sexual nature. The point also illustrated by the story, but often missed by readers of both Sophocles and Freud, is that the story is as much about aggression and murder and its relation to childrearing practices, as it is about incest.[11]

The part of the story that is often neglected is its beginning: Oedipus was the victim of attempted infanticide. The story begins with the prophecy that Laius, king of Greece, would be killed by the hand of his son, and this son would then go on to marry his own mother.[12] In a vain attempt to elude destiny, Laius ordered the death of his son. Since we are never told that Laius's wife objected to the decision, nor in any way tried to interfere with Laius's order being carried out, we can only surmise that she passively colluded with the murderous intent. The pity (or love) that a peasant shephard had for a seemingly homeless infant, abandoned by both mother and father, saved Oedipus's life, and enabled him to eventually fulfill the dreaded prophecy. When Oedipus, as an adult, met a stranger on the road, a brief altercation resulted in Oedipus's striking out and killing the man. This man, unbeknownst to Oedipus, was his father.

In his telling of the tale, Sophocles never makes explicit the reason for Oedipus's very dramatic response to Laius in their accidental meeting. Oedipus's striking out at Laius seems to have been an overreaction, unfitting to what should have been a mildly irritating situation, but surely not one where deadly force was either necessary or appropriate. The irrationality of the act suggests that some hidden force was at work, or, in Freud's terms, that Oedipus was the victim of his own unconscious.

In neglecting this part of the myth, readers miss making an important connection linking a child's preoccupation with incest, the concomitant wish for the death of the other parent, and the origins of these conflicts. By acting on his infanticidal impulses, Laius set into motion a chain of psychological events that were inexorable, and most importantly, linked to his initial act of murderous intent toward his son. Oedipus's ready availability to his own murderous aggression towards Laius can be seen, then, as a response (albeit unconscious) to Laius's own murderous intent towards Oedipus. The Oedipal complex might, itself, be a defensive reaction against the infanticidal impulse in the father, the last step of a process begun in the wish for the death of the child.

Lauis's decision to have Oedipus killed, shocking as the act may be to us today, was an appropriate solution for his day. Infanticide was commonly practiced for many years by the Phoenicians, Moabites, Ammonites, Greeks, Romans, and many other ancient peoples.[13] Infants were routinely chosen to either live or die. The newborn would be laid at the father's feet, and if he picked up the child, it was allowed to live. If he turned away, a slave was summoned to dispose of the infant, and popular methods for doing so were throwing babies into rivers, flinging them into dung heaps, or "potting" them in jars. As Euripides tells us, infants were exposed on every hill and roadside, "prey for birds, food for wild beasts to rend."[14]

Children were done away with for a variety of reasons in addition to propitiating the gods. It was the one sure method of population control. The killing of later children ensured that estates would not be divided, and in addition, left money for the education of the valued first son. Spartan children who would not make good Spartan soldiers were eliminated. In fact, any imperfection, in size or shape, in crying too little or too much—any variation from the ideal set forward in the classic text *How to Recognize the Newborn Who Is Worth Rearing*— was reason enough to do away with the child.[15]

Both Judaism and Christianity addressed the infanticidal impulse, and attempted to find a better solution. Abraham was fully prepared to sacrifice his son Isaac, and God's causing a ram to appear in Isaac's stead is the first recorded instance of animal sacrifice as a substitute for a human life.[16] The curbing of the acting out of the infanticidal impulse, at this juncture in history, marked a significant step forward for man's psychic and moral evolution. The impulse reemerges later, when we meet Job, whose children were killed by a pact between God and Satan. But Job's own infanticidal impulses are evident in that he shows no sense of loss or mourning over their deaths. And even later, Christ, as the son of God, was victim to the wish to kill the child. The impulse of infanticide is, in all likelihood, a universal drive.

The idea that there was anything wrong with infanticide must have occurred to the ancients only rarely, and as an individual parent's response to a threatened child. Infants were objectified, a possession worth not much more than a newborn animal.

The lessen of Sophocles is that acting on infanticidal impulses is not done without exacting a heavy toll of consequences. Exposure to murderous feelings can, and often does, lead to a like response. Analyses of contemporary murderers reveal that their early histories bear much similarity to that of Oedipus. They, too, were exposed to intense feelings of hatred that were acted on from one parent, while the other, typically, passively acquiesced. One study concluded that "Almost without exception, one finds in their early backgrounds not only economic want, but cruelties and miseries of every kind," and common features among the murderers were "the remorseless brutality at the hands of one parent in the face of compliant acquiescence of the other."[17]

The impulse to destroy, though, may be satisfied in any given personality by attacking either the self or another—depending on some factors that are quite identifiable, and others too subtle or complex to have yet been sorted out precisely. So it needn't be surprising that the personality profile and the early history most common to murderers has an unmistakable resemblance to that most typical of the psychosomatic personality.

The most dramatic similarity is that both of these patterns include exposure from earliest childhood to inadequately controlled infanticidal impulses. This may occur in a broad variety of ways, from overt physical brutality to much subtler, but still unmistakable, psychic murderousness. This seems to disable the personality's mechanisms for processing and expressing powerful emotions.

Both handle the arousal of strong feelings in later life in a similar way. Research describes the calm, unruffled surface appearance of the psychosomatic personality.[18] Murderers, too, are most commonly passive, overly controlled people, inhibited in both feeling and fantasy. They are typically meek and polite, and show little emotion. Their act of homicide was not "just one more aggressive offense in a person who had always displayed inadequate controls, but rather a completely uncharacteristic act in a person who had always displayed extraordinarily high levels of control"[19] (The response of a neighbor of a sudden killer—"Seemed like a nice enough guy, never bothered anybody"— has become a sort of black comedy cliché.)

But such rigid defensive structures tend to be brittle, and when inner pressures, never vented and building over a lifetime, become too much for such controls to contain, what results can be explosive. And when the developmental stage of such a personality has not surpassed narcissism, so that self and not-self are poorly distinguished and a genuine sense of the real existence of others has not been achieved, several really terrible outcomes are possible.

The story of Oedipus demonstrates another important principle in the psychic functioning of man. Later in the story, having learned of his horrible deeds in fulfilling the dreaded prophecy, Oedipus is filled with self-loathing, disgust and guilt. With the same fury that he lashed out at his father, he now turns this rage against himself, and inflicts irreparable damage to his body. We learn that unbridled aggression directed homicidally against another, with an easy twist of psychic directionality, can be transformed into suicidal destructiveness directed against the self.

Destruction may be directed either inward or outward. If inward, to suicide at the extreme, or to psychosomatic symptomotology at a lesser extreme. If outward, only social controls—fear of punishment, essentially—prevent murder. Other people are not real and have no emotional substance; they are seen only in terms of the self and its needs (as infants were once seen simply as satisfactory or unsatisfactory objects of ownership).

The psychological histories of murderers reveal a pattern of feelings of alienation and objectification of others. Murder is, in fact, often an incidental by-product of the striving to get what one wants, what one feels deprived of, and entitled to.[20] Human life may be nothing more than a mere impediment to this goal.

The Killing Mirror of Narcissism and Sacrifice of Self

The existence of the death instinct, the drive to destruction in all living matter—in all of us—means that murderous impulses will occur in all of us more or less regularly. People who pay attention to their feelings and impulses will find that wanting to hurt someone else, or of hating themselves for some perceived inadequacy or sin, is far from rare.

When these impulses occur in a fully developed personality at full strength, the structure of the ego is robust enough to allow them into consciousness and even to express them in nondestructive—even constructive—ways. The infanticidal impulses that can do such terrible damage are a not uncommon feature of normal family life. Babies, in their utter self-absorption, their insatiable demands, their obliviousness to others' needs, can be perfectly understood and forgiven only at a little distance, and theoretically. A baby's cries may be understood as simply the primitive organism's only means of expressing the tension of unmet needs, or as a request for help of some sort, but they can't help but be experienced by the parent responsible for meeting those needs as also a maddeningly persistent complaint, a criticism and an attack. As an extreme example, consider the words of Mary Beth Tinning, accused of killing eight young children—seven of her own and another she was caring for and planning to adopt—in describing the four month old daughter who she smothered with a pillow: "She was always crying and I couldn't do anything right."[21]

The parent who is in constant intimate contact with such a person— the person we all are and must be at that stage—will experience some rage, and the feelingful parent will allow herself transient wishes that the demanding baby would somehow just disappear. The integrity of that parent's ego, the part of the self that processes emotional and instinctual demands and devises means, symbolic or sublimated, to satisfy them constructively, protects the infant. These aggressive feelings can be experienced without producing destructive actions.

This parent will, even when she's in such a state of irritation, hold the baby comfortably, calmly and purposefully seek the cause of its discomfort, and correct the problem. A parent whose own inner needs were never adequately met, and whose ego as a result never achieved its full development, may instead act on her frustration and anger and her wish for the baby to stop irritating her: possibly just by closing the door so she can't hear the crying, possibly some more active, still more destructive aggressive behavior. Thus the emotional climate of this child's life becomes established. His own adaptation to frustrating, aggression-producing stimuli will have begun at this early age and will build on this experience of how his parents handled their aggressive impulses.

We know from analyses of children, who generally remain closer to their primitive fears than adults, that the fear of infanticide is quite common.[22] Fantasies of life and death emerge as a recurring theme in the mental life of a child. Most often the threat is transformed into the demonic creatures of imagination—forces unknown to the child. These exaggerated imaginings are, of course, the stuff of which childhood, dreams, and schizophrenia are made. Normally, though, the monsters of childhood and of dreams will become subsumed under the functioning of a healthy ego—encapsulating and containing the fear—and the exaggerated hallucinations of psychosis do not result. By the time we reach adulthood, most of us will have muted our fantasies. The demonic witches and monsters of childhood will have been laid to rest, or channeled into creative activity, with the ego vigilantly standing by as an ally.

But sometimes the protection of repression fails and the child is unable to make the symbolic transformation from parent as enemy to huge creature with red eyes and flaming breath as enemy. Acknowledgement of the original stimulus of the threat—the parent—emerges, and there develops in the child a deep conviction of his parent's intent to kill him. In the case of the abused child, this perception is, of course, an accurate sensitivity to the behavior of the parent. At other times, in spite of the child's unshakable conviction that his life is at stake, it is clear that he is not in any real, physical danger. Yet the threat of murder may still exist, though the danger is of psychological rather then physical annihilation. The fear of infanticide, here, is an accurate perception of the parent's feeling state towards the child.

Often, and particularly as one matures into adulthood, the witches and monsters of childhood are likely to be transformed into the culturally more acceptable fear of death and disease. The terror of death and disease can be as convincing of imminent destruction to the adult as the imaginary monsters were in his childhood. Yet, the demons of an impartial disease are merely thinly veiled disguises for a more deeply repressed concern: those individuals who are most depended upon, those who are, in a sense, lived for, are the real figures of death and disease.

In the case of psychosomaticism, these demons of the mind seem to be noticeably absent.[23] Rather than an abundance of figures—real and not-real, and human and not-human—populating the mind, there is an internal blankness, an empty space seemingly waiting to be filled. In the neuroses, such as hysteria, the very awareness of the presence of suffering gives the appearance of a psyche filled to the brim and spilling out beyond the boundaries of self, but here the inner core of the person seems hollow.

The psychosomatic, more often than not, has been exposed to more than his share of the threat of psychological annihilation. The parent, having not yet matured out of his own narcissism, experiences the child only as an extension of his own self-world. Rather than outright rejection of the child, as is observed more commonly in psychotic family situations; what is witnessed here is rejection of the child's urge to separate, his need to create his own self-world—to become not-self in regard to the parent. In interfering with these urges of the child, the parent may become too much the object of satisfaction. Avenues of expression and psychic investment unrelated to the parent are vitiated; psychic creativity is strangled.[24] Or, alternatively, it may be that the infant is too often left alone. The symbiotic union between parent and child—necessary for the child's emotional growth—doesn't occur; the calling to the outside world—an effect from these early relationships with parents—never happens. Cut off from any objects of the world, the mind is left with only its own reflection.

The end result, in the case of either too much or too little distance from the parent, is an internal life so deeply hidden in the unconscious that the symbolic monsters of the imagination are never allowed through to linguistic articulation, and, concomitantly, to conscious experience.[25] The individual who is prone to psychosomatic disorders has been robbed of the important experience of creating, struggling against, and mastering the fearful products of his mind.

The psychosomatic predicament, then, is that these stillborn monsters of the mind, denied any psychic existence, find representation in the body. The split-off portions of the mind and the afflicted body parts become, phenomenologically, outside the realm of self. The relegation of self parts to not-self status is often preparation for the next step of sacrifice. Turning an "I" into an "it," as the ancients did with their infants and as murderers do with their victims, makes it a relatively easy next step to a decision to get rid of that which is no longer of self. The symbolic act of sacrifice can then be performed.

The elevation of sacrifice to a spiritual endeavor in most world religions points to the important and universal psychological function of this impulse. Whatever is chosen as the object of sacrifice is the bargaining point, the tease to soothe the vengeful beast.

Sacrifice is a response, and an attempt at a solution, to a murderous impulse directed towards oneself. There is the hope that the wrathful and demanding monster can be appeased, and various bargainings will take place with the idea that a soft spot in the monster can be found, and the demon tamed. Bargaining is recognized as a stage in the process of dealing with a terminal illness ("I'll pray every day if I don't have cancer." "I'll never lose my temper again if I don't die from this heart attack."). In the psychosomatic situation, the sacrifice of both the internal life of the mind and the afflicted body parts represents this same kind of bargaining, a relinquishing of control of a part of one's self to a more powerful other in hopes of being spared the final outcome of death. In the unconscious, all objects to whom the sacrifice is made are experienced as the same, and these may be as varied as a god who promises salvation, a physician who promises cure, or a parent who promises love. We see in these patients an all-too-ready willingness to submit to any procedures involving surrendering of self, including a masochistic compliance, a sacrifice of the psychic self, or a silent and easy submission to surgical procedures, representing sacrifice of a part of the body self.

Exposure to a surfeit of infanticidal threats has the further effect of distorting the individual's ability to correctly perceive threats of danger. Repeated exposure to fearful situations can result in a chronic state of psychic anticipation of danger. It is the psychological equivalent of the body's being in a state of perpetual biological alarm. Errors in judgment are easy to make, and the individual can come to experience a mild threat as potentially annihilating.

Just as animals don't fight to the death physically, so primitive psyches, when they battle, never really mean to kill. They only mean to punish, or to create distance, or to create a sense of greater security within the self—some momentary psychic gain is all that's imaginable and all that's sought. And, as complex, multicellular organisms can survive massive injuries—even loss of tissue—so can our psyches sustain many injuries without irreversible damage. The infant can tolerate many outbursts of the parent's irritability without permanent damage. When the psyche is injured, the healthy ego can differentiate itself from the pain, and recovery from the injury is possible. Humans forgive even the grossest of sins when psychic recovery is achieved. But when the psyche fails to make the discrimination between injury and annihilation, any infliction of harm is experienced as life threatening. The psyche of the individual fails to make the important differentiation, and responds to a wide range of harmful stimuli as though they were annihilating. The child, for example, who cries out in the doctor's office as the needle approaches, or at the threat of some other relatively innocuous procedure, may have not learned to differentiate between pain as a result of injury and outright annihilation.[26]

A pattern of sacrifice, developed early in life from exposure to parenting unconcerned with the child's growth as a separate individual, is at the core of the psychosomatic personality. The parent has exhibited destructive impulses toward the child, and this behavior has been a form of psychological murder. The child, in turn, has had no capacity for adequate fight or defense, and his response is to sacrifice at least a part of his psychic functioning—psychological suicide. Essentially, then, what is being described is a powerful homicidal/ suicidal pact between parent and child that has been formed many years prior to the onset of any physical disease.

These individuals are usually able to confine any feeling about the relationship strictly to the unconscious, and remain unaware of both their psychic annihilation by the parent and their own self-sacrificing collusion. How it is that one chooses to respond to this process of mutual destruction varies, and depends on the individual's success in defending his narcissistic fragility. Some patients manifest a desperate clinging to one parent, a thirst for a closeness that seems unquenchable. Others attempt to maintain psychic distance, on the idea that psychic equilibrium is possible only through the creation of this distance.

Even seriously damaged children, however, can recover. Many individuals with traumatic early histories of this kind go on to develop successful intimate relationships in their adult lives. When an early parent/child dynamic remains unresolved, however, and the conflict continues through to adulthood, the choice of a marriage partner is likely to be made based on unconscious reasons replicating patterns familiar to the individual from his early history. The choice of a spouse will be an attempt to allow this new individual to fulfill the same function as the parent, and the original homicidal/suicidal pact will be recreated in the marriage.

It is as though, on the level of the psyche, time has stood still; the mind has become frozen and unchanging. The spouse has become the parent.

The research of Grossarth-Maticek has operationalized these concepts, and has given us extensive data on the relationship between patterns of interaction and physical diseases. Correlations with a variety of diseases have been discovered. In his classification of interactive styles, he distinguishes between individuals whose interactive pattern attempts to block others from feeling, and who would be experienced as psychologically homicidal, and those who permit themselves to be blocked from feeling, and in this way are psychologically suicidal. Cancer patients are found characteristically to allow themselves to be blocked, while cardiovascular, diabetic, and gastric ulcer patients show the opposite pattern in that they chronically attempt to block others from feeling.[27]

Although the many and myriad ways we have of affecting ourselves and one another destructively through our feelings have only begun to be documented, it is clear that the interactive partnering of individuals with complementary and meshing homicidal and suicidal impulses is a particularly dangerous combination. Feelings, used as a weapon against someone, can be as powerfully toxic as exposure to a deadly physical agent of destruction.

The Turkey and the Mycoplasma: Resolving Homicidal/Suicidal Marriages in Group Therapy

In the world of biology, it takes a lot of living together and a high degree of intimacy before a pathogen can cause illness in another organism. The turkey and the mycoplasma are a good illustration of this point just because of the high degree of specificity in their choice of who gets friendly with whom.[28] The mycoplasma is a form of life smaller than a virus, and structurally similar to a bacterium. Of all the creatures in the world, this mycoplasma has eyes only for the arterial wall of a turkey. We can take this tiny creature, and we can try to introduce it to a chicken, a mouse, a rat; we can give huge quantities of it to these animals. But no matter to whom or how much, the mycoplasma is adapted only to the walls of the arteries of a turkey, and it is only there that it will take up residence—only there that it will create disease. To the turkey, the parasite is lethal; to everyone else, it is innocuous.

Social relations sometimes look like the turkey and the mycoplasma. As analysts, we often see patients who are locked into similar fatal attractions. The need to be together, and to damage each other, looks to be as inevitable as the lethal symbiosis of the mycoplasma and its host, the turkey, upon whom it feeds.

A psychoanalytic cancer group that I have been running for several years illustrates the kind of homicidal/suicidal pacts that can be formed between spouses. Early in the group, much too soon for any benefit from the analysis to have accrued, several of the patients died. Tommy was the first to die. The group members did not yet feel discouraged or threatened by the death of one of their members. They resorted to a common defense, and blamed him for his death; they were quite clear and uniform in their impression that Tommy had been an active participant in his death process. The group had repeatedly warned Tommy, implored him, that if he didn't take better care of himself that he would get into trouble. His death seemed to be his own punishment, and a fit one, for not heeding the warnings.

Tommy's death became the rallying cry for any manifestation of self-destructive behavior. Ellie and George both revealed patterns similar to Tommy's, and both were warned that they were going to end up like Tommy. As George's condition deteriorated, he admitted his identification with Tommy. Both my own and the group's interventions pointed out the suicidal aspects of George's and Ellie's behavior, but to no avail. Both died.

Death permeated the air. Within just a few months we had lost three group members. Our glorious and optimistic expectations of saving lives was painfully punctured. We began to sense that we were all susceptible to a death from cancer.

I, too, never having had cancer, was not exempt from the emotional contagion of the fear that had been aroused by being surrounded by so much death. I became fairly obsessed with my own death. At the slightest sign of abnormality in the functioning of my body, I was convinced that I was entering the initial phase of a terminal cancer. I considered the immediate disbanding of the group. Death was too much in the air, and the immersion in it was too total for life inducing therapy to take place.

I discussed with the group the possibility that we were an antitherapeutic group. While they did not disavow the idea, it hardly mattered. This group was a married group, and they intended to stay together, no matter what, "til death do us part," if it came to that.

Their response to the idea of disbanding made me believe that we were forever locked together as a group. Living through the deaths together had given us too much of a common history. We had become a part of one another. Even if we formally disbanded as a therapy group in a desperate attempt to ward off the ever-encroaching menace of death, it was clear that a way would be found to maintain the group—in our psyches, if not in actual fact—and it was clear that attempting to escape from one another in order to escape from death was neither a solution, nor possible. Each of us—those dead and those alive—were imprinted on our minds. We were going to either get cured together, or die together.

Since disbanding was out of the question, I began to question the therapeutic efficacy of a cancer group. I asked my patients questions regarding this issue. Each expressed a growing concern for his own health. Disenchantment and disheartenment reigned. Clearly the hopeful optimism with which they had begun, the eager anticipation of discovering truths about themselves that would improve their chances of survival had altogether vanished.

The balm of death needed to be life. I wanted death to become encapsulated, contained so that it did not permeate every aspect of the group's functioning. I remembered living the last year of my mother's life with her, absorbed in every aspect of her cancer death. I had stayed in the house with her, had written about cancer, had thought about cancer. Her death had become my life. In the midst of this I was invited to visit friends. Their house was filled with light and space and air and children and everything that was associated with life. I hadn't realized how far into death I had moved until I saw the contrast of life.

I wanted to give to my patients, and to myself, a house filled with light and a world populated with people more attached to life than to death.

How does one go about transforming a death process into a life process?

Knowing something about how the cancer process develops may help our thinking. There is evidence suggesting that the cancer patient, as an infant, experiences serious disturbance in the primary nurturing relationship. The mother is experienced as "cold" and "distant."[29] Cancer patients whom I have treated have gone so far as to describe the feelings received from the mother as "murderous."

These dramatic claims by cancer patients need some clarification. Not all mothers of cancer patients are abusive. Rather, in cases where there is an emotional factor, the disturbance seems to be far more subtle and interactive. The mother's narcissism prevents her from having the kind of natural sensitivity to the infant that would stimulate her to behave in an emotionally maturing way to her infant, and the infant in turn seems to lack the ability to aid the mother in understanding his needs.

The next step in the process is that the child does not develop the ability to handle the aggression that would quite naturally be aroused by the frustration of this interactive pattern. Destructive methods of discharge of the aggressive feelings result.

These children grow into adults who have specific and well-entrenched character patterns that were learned in those early years. The lack of satisfaction of positive, intimate contact in the one-to-one mother/infant dyad has left a gaping maturational hole, and there develops a desperate need for closeness. But having been frustrated in the original search for closeness, and having developed the pattern of discharge of aggression against the self, they have come to feel that neediness is bad, and any exhibition of it may result in rejection or abandonment. Nevertheless, the need remains, on the unconscious level. And so, in an attempt to get the need satisfied while at the same time hiding the need, they erect a persona of independence, security, and satisfaction. It is a personality that is a false creation. The adult personality that is prone to the development of cancer, then, is one that is inordinarily pleasant, not prone to feelings of anger or aggression, and emphatically interested in pleasing the other.

One more step needs to take place before the actual development of a psychosomatic cancer. The defensive structure that the potential cancer patient has so carefully constructed needs to be broken down.[30] Without some assault upon its integrity, the defense system could possibly maintain a tenuous status quo for quite some time, and the cancer potential might never develop into fact.

The final, damaging assault may be physiological (e.g., exposure to carcinogens) or initially psychological, which, of course, ultimately becomes physiological as well. The psychological variable that has been shown to be the most powerful stimulant to the defensive structure's breakdown is what the patient experiences as a "traumatic loss."

The phenomenon of the multiple deaths in the group revealed a pattern that seemed to be a refinement of these research findings.

What was revealed was that the dead and apparently dying patients had recreated the original homicidal/suicidal interactive pattern of the mother/infant dyad in their marriages. All had chosen marriage partners who manifested either an insensitivity to their needs, or overt, destructive expression of hate feelings. All the dead and dying group members had continued their characterological defenses against aggression toward their objects—the turning of destructive impulses against themselves.

I began to conceptualize an isomorphism between the physiology and the psychology of the cancer process. The physiological representation of the process is the tumor manifestation. As we know, tumors are not, in and of themselves, dangerous. Rather, it is when the cells that comprise a tumor begin to encroach on neighboring tissue (metastasize) that the health of the organism is threatened. The difference is the distinction between a benign and malignant tumor. Fully contained and encapsulated, the tumor can lie unnoticed for years, or be carefully extracted (through surgery) in its entirety, without danger.

The tumor, in fact, appears to be a lifesaving mechanism. It is a collection of toxins and poisons that, if freely circulating throughout the body, would constitute a lethal dose of autointoxication. Its very encapsulation—the gathering together of dangerous components into one place—is the body's attempt, in the absence of being able to eject this material from the body, to wall off the poisons so that systemic damage is avoided. The usual success of this operation is evident in the fact that when autopsies are done randomly, a high percentage of people have been found to have cancerous tumors, though no clear diagnosis was made during the lifetime of the person, and death was from an altogether different and unrelated cause.

It is only when there is a disruption of the tumor, and its fragile walls are broken down so that its contents—both the toxic material and the cancer cells—spill over into the rest of the body that the systemic health of the organism is threatened. Disruption of the tumor can occur from both internal (arising from within the organism) or external assault.

Surgeons have noted the dire consequences of disrupting an encapsulated tumor through surgical assault. If the tumor cannot be removed as an encapsulated whole, splicing through it breaks down whatever protective barrier exists that separates cancer cells from normal cells. Cancer cells are free to roam unobstructed and invasively. A patient subjected to this unsuccessful surgical procedure is likely to die quickly.

It seemed to me that deeply embedded in the psyches of my cancer patients is something like a tumor—a psychological tumor, as it were. Their unresolved conflicts, begun in early childhood, had clustered together. They had contracted into a form whose contents remained unintegrated with the rest of the psychic apparatus. It was as though a big ball of poison had been swallowed whole, and could not be either eliminated or digested. Encapsulated in its protective barrier, it would lie in wait, but when the protective coating failed and the poison seeped out, it would take in its wake all that it touched.

It seemed to me that this lack of integration between the psychological tumor—that ball of thoughts and feelings that the person felt to be so malignant that he attempted to function as though those psychological contents were nonexistent, and instead erected a false creation of self that, in its detachment from the cauldron of activity, appeared to be quite normal—was precisely what the experiments on the psychosomatic aspects of cancer had been observing. Renneker refers to it as "the false self,"[31] and Greer noted that cancer patients revealed an inordinately pleasant personality.[32]

Reflecting on the psychic histories of the dead and dying patients, it was easy to pinpoint, in each case, what events could have acted disruptively on their psychological tumors; that is, how either shortly before or concurrent with the cancer beginning to assume control of the body, unresolved conflicts of childhood had been activated which sent the entire psychic functioning of the patient into dangerous disarray.

Tommy's marriage seemed to be the death knell for him. Tommy had known and courted Mona for eighteen years. She remained fully committed to him all that time, patiently waiting for a marriage proposal. It was only when Tommy was able to make a narcissistic identification with Mona that his resistance to marrying her was resolved. When asked how he finally came about deciding, he described a scene where she was going on an ocean liner. She had asked him to accompany her and he had refused, but as he stood at the dock, waving goodbye to her on the departing ship he saw, for the first time, her vulnerability and loneliness, and realized that he could not walk away from the relationship without hurting her. He felt moved by her attachment and dependence on him. It was the first real stirring of feeling he had had about her in all those many years. He proposed to her when she returned from the trip, and two weeks before the wedding received his cancer diagnosis.

Explorations within the group setting about a possible connection between the two proved futile. Tommy had no conscious awareness of a link. Mona could not consider the possibility, and experienced the idea as a narcissistic injury to herself.

One could hypothesize that Tommy had contentedly subsisted in an essentially nonfeeling state for most of his life. Whatever his childhood experiences had been, he had learned the lesson that to feel was dangerous. When the barriers to his feelings finally broke down he was flooded with feeling, and, indeed, the deluge was too much for his system to handle. Mona's own narcissism probably made her a reenactment for Tommy of a transference object, and he took seriously her objections to the exploration of the unconscious meanings of thoughts and feelings related to the marriage.

George's deterioration began when his past literally reentered his present. George had been married and living with his wife and four children in South America. He came to the States for a six-month internship. During this time, he formed a liaison with a young woman which resulted in a pregnancy. George felt obligated to marry this woman, and in doing so, abandoned his former family. The second marriage was shortlived, but George's guilt and shame prevented him from ever returning home to his previous family, or from maintaining any contact with them. George's cancer had been diagnosed years before his entrance into the group, but remained in check. Several events collided, resulting in what appeared to be an unmanageable assault on his status quo equilibrium. First, some twenty years after the abandonment of his original family, he attempted to trace them. They had virtually disappeared from the face of the earth. George's assumption was that they had all been killed in a political coup. Second, the daughter from the second marriage, after years of not being in contact with her father, suddenly reappeared. She was making demands on her father, and he felt, as he had twenty years earlier, obligated to acquiesce. She began living with her father in spite of the fact that her presence was a clear disruption of the relationship with the woman with whom he had been living for the previous seven years. The final assault was George's discovery that his girlfriend had been sexually unfaithful to him. This relationship was the first one that George had been able to maintain over an extended period of time. Since the initial marriage, he had moved recklessly from one marriage to another, and at the time of meeting his girlfriend, had married and divorced five women. His relationship with this girlfriend was the first one that he had been able to sustain, and the one to which he had become the most attached.

In Tommy's case the murderous component in the suicide/homicide pact appeared to be the narcissism of those around him; in George's case it was the combination of the effect of his daughter's presence and his sense of his girlfriend's betrayal. In Ellie's case, the murderous quality of her life was the most overtly evident of the three. She felt overwhelmed by the demands of her life, and her husband was threatening to leave her, and take the house and their small child for himself. His interaction with Ellie was, as had been the case with her mother earlier in her life, to force Ellie into submitting to his will, rather than helping her to accomplish what she herself wanted. The birth of Ellie's child had been the first time in her life when she felt hope and a positive attachment to life. Holding onto her child seemed to mean holding onto her life. Her husband's decision to send the child to the grandmother's house when Ellie was too ill to care for her was symbolic, for Ellie, of the destructiveness of her relationship with her husband—a relationship that bore remarkable similarity to her relationship with her mother.

In each of these three cases, physical deterioration occurred at a point where some stimulus served to convert the person from an essentially nonfeeling state to a feeling state: for Tommy, it was the allowing in of love feelings; for George, it was the activation of long-submerged guilt, his attachment to his girlfriend, and his feeling of betrayal by her; and for Ellie, it was her love for and attachment to her child. Each of them were rendered vulnerable through the process of transformation into feeling.

It appeared as though the cancer process in each of these patients began its lethal progression at a point where the stimulation of feeling was more than the psychic apparatus could comfortably handle. One is reminded of the analogous situation, on the physical level, with concentration camp survivors. Upon liberation, some survivors were so famished that they couldn't contain their impulses to gorge. The quantity of food overwhelmed their undernourished and underactive digestive systems, and some of these survivors died from eating, an act that is normally life sustaining.

If, as it seemed, the stirring up of the psychological tumors was a destructive process, then effective treatment would need to provide the patients with an environment that would help the tumors to remain encapsulated until discharge could be made slowly and without systemic damage. Feelings that would be overly stimulating would need to be neutralized.

I made two decisions that affected my interventions and the structure of the group. Death had been too much in the air; yet, it was an inevitable consequence of being in a cancer group. Freud was sensitive to the difficulties inherent to the endeavor of treating a patient with a life-threatening disease, and advised that it should not be undertaken. Cancer patients do die, and when put together in one group, the life of the group itself is threatened.

I declared that the group was no longer a cancer group. I told them that their diagnosis had been changed and they were now a couples group. I asked each of the cancer patients who had not done so to bring their spouses to meetings as regular group members.

Second, I had witnessed the suicidal character pattern of the patients who had died. Their psychic structures seemed so fragile that any tampering with their defenses and repetitions might prove to be dangerously over-stimulating. I had at times made interventions such as, "You are going to die if you don't. . . ." Such interventions frequently upset the patients and threw them into alarming states of anxiety.

It was clear that each of the cancer patients had formed relationships based on powerful unconscious negative patterns to the people in their lives. This is a fact which is, of course, true about most patients. Every patient enters analysis with preexisting difficulties. It is usually the presence of these difficulties in their relationships that motivates the patient to seek help. Under ordinary circumstances, preexisting attachments do not present a problem for the treatment. Gradually the patient makes the shift to a primary relationship with the analyst, and works through their interactive difficulties within the analytic situation.

What seemed a most obvious fact about my dead and dying cancer patients was that their unconscious negative attachments to the people in their lives were too powerful and too impenetrable. The strength of the interlocking homicidal/suicidal pact between them was far more powerful than the strength of the life-inducing relationship with me that I had hoped to achieve.

I decided that of primary and critical importance was the resolution of any remaining vestiges of this pattern in those patients who were alive. I became certain that where one partner harbored murderous feelings and the other partner, with cancer, struggled with suicidal impulses, a death was at hand.

With the change in group definition, the theme of murder came to dominate my interventions. Murder now replaced suicide as the agent of death.

Roger became the prime suspect of homicide. There were several reasons for my choosing to attempt the resolution of the homicide/suicide conflict by focusing on Roger. He was the patient whose ego defenses were strongest, who could best tolerate, and most needed, having his defensive structure battered against by the battering ram that I became. Chris, his wife, exhibited the most clear pattern of the cancer suicidal personality, and her cancer was the most life threatening. Chris was a pleaser, and without Roger's nod of approval, it seemed as though she would wither away. Roger was only too aware of his wife's regressive relationship with him, hated her for it, and took little pains to hide his intolerance and critical attitude towards her. He had married her believing the false front that she had exhibited, and as he had become increasingly disillusioned with who he found her to be, he never failed to fault her for her inadequacies.

Each week the group opened with some communication about what Roger had done that week to further inch his wife towards her grave.

He rebelled and disagreed violently. He insisted that he would not be held accountable for his wife's cancer and that he was most certainly not the bad person I was portraying him as being. I assured him that he was, and that even his very denial was an act of murder towards his wife. Chris made rather feeble attempts to defend her husband. I complimented her on her generosity of spirit, but informed her that she had one serious flaw in her character, and that was an inability to recognize a murderer.

Eventually the group rallied around Roger, and asked why I always blamed him. They pointed out Chris' suicidal inclinations and asked why, if she was destructive to herself because Roger didn't give her what she wanted, wasn't that her problem?

I responded by telling them that Chris was incapable of doing anything about it at this point. I reminded them of her childhood history, which was about as much of a horror story as one could ever imagine, and said that it was not her fault, that she had been extremely damaged as a child. Her problem was a longterm analytic problem that would take years to reverse, and that she would be dead of the cancer first. Roger was the one who had to change. He was the only one who could change in enough time to save Chris's life.

This intervention had a marked effect on Roger and the group. It became clear that the intent of my interventions toward Roger had not been to blame, but rather to enlist cooperation. It became clear that the proper response on his part (or theirs) would not be defense, but rather to elicit information on how he (or they) could cooperate.

This intervention permitted us to come one step closer to the edge of Roger's character, the resistance that prevented him from giving his wife the emotional communication that would give her the feelings of wanting to go on living for and with him. He admitted that he couldn't control himself. When she did things or said things that angered him he just automatically lashed out. It was what he had done with his anger all his life, and what his family before him had done.

Next, we approached his sadism. Roger admitted that he wasn't even sure that he wanted to control himself.

All this moved us toward the final admission that Roger was, as I had said all along, a murderer—a self-styled, and now self-admitted, murderer.

Verbalization of murderous impulses within the group setting proves to be, in most instances, helpful to the person talking. Talking is curative, but listening may not be, and so the skilled group analyst must monitor the pulse of the group and each of its members to make certain that what is being said doesn't have a destructive effect on those who, by virtue of group membership have been forced to hear it.

Thus, I needed to know the effect Roger's articulation of hate for his wife was having on Chris.

Chris brought in a problem which illustrates the process that was occurring in her. She and Roger had been fighting a legal battle to retain an apartment that they been using as a work studio. Chris had written a letter to the landlord explaining the urgency of her need. The landlord, in turn, had used information in the letter in the courtroom to validate his point that they were there illegally and should be evicted. The event threw Chris into one of her suicidal states. She couldn't accept or believe that someone to whom she had appealed for help would so utterly betray her.

The problem was an inability on Chris' part to recognize a potential (or actual) source of aggression directed toward her. In her naivete, she unrealistically assumed that the world was like cotton candy—sweet and good. Interestingly, the problem in cancer is precisely the same on the cellular level. The normal cells in the body don't recognize that an unwanted and potentially destructive intruder is in their midst. The alarm system that would ordinarily go off as a warning to stimulate the defenses does not go off, and instead of the intruding cancer being destroyed, it self-destroys. On both the psychic and cellular level, Chris was unable to make the distinction between those who were dangerous to her and those who were not.

Roger's designation as a murderer enabled Chris to understand that if she were to live, it would have to be without the help of Roger. Roger might be on good behavior one day, but it was not a certainty that she could count on. If she were to live, she would have to want to live with or without Roger's love, with or without Roger's approval of her and with or without Roger's cure.

The skewed attention that was being devoted to the resolution of Chris' and Roger's death dance with one another brought into the group setting yet another life-threatening resistance. Ursula, a relatively stable cancer patient, began to complain that I paid undue attention to Roger and Chris and not enough to her. The theme of my interventions changed, then, from murder to homicide to murder by neglect. I expressed great interest in the question of neglect, and asked her why I was neglecting her, how I was neglecting her, and how I could stop neglecting her. I avoided asking questions directed towards her ego that would have drawn us back to the suicide theme, such as "Why are you letting me neglect you?" or "Why are you neglecting yourself?"

By addressing this issue within the context of our relationship, Ursula became increasingly outspoken with her complaints, a mode of talking that she had never before allowed herself. She complained also about her husband, that he came home from work uninterested in helping her, assuming that her day with the baby had been a breeze. She hadn't felt justified in complaining because he wasn't doing anything bad; he just wasn't doing anything good. I reminded her of marasmus, and assured her that neglect was just as lethal a weapon as the overt abuse that Roger had been inflicting on Chris.

Eventually I was able to interpret to Ursula that she would rather complain than help to train me or her husband to treat her better.

As these urges toward death were moving toward resolution, I decided that changing a death process into a life process could be facilitated by the creation of new life. I decided to add new members to the group. While the group had been locked into the throes of the death agony, I had refrained from adding new members for fear of the effect on both new and old members. Too much exposure to death had already been destructive to the old members, and would likely have had that effect on incoming members as well. As with the concentration camp survivors, too much exposure to life might prove to be destructive to the old members.

I had thought before that if we were going to die, we would do it contained and intact as a group, and not spread our poison to unsuspecting, innocent victims. Now that it appeared as though we had a chance to live, I felt that it was safe to let in new life.

The task of finding appropriate new members needed to be approached with a great deal of caution. It was not as though the threat of cancer had disappeared; only the imminent threat of death had receded.

While it is true that we do not ordinarily think of death as contagious, most people do have unconscious associations to the idea of a contagious element in cancer. Whether one can catch it or not, cancer is a very powerful reminder of our mortality, and most of us would rather not be forced to confront it. Rare is the person who voluntarily seeks exposure to cancer and cancer patients.

Not many analytic patients would choose to enter a group that had formerly been a cancer group, and where half of its members still had cancer. Such a group would be contraindicated for most analytic patients.

The new couples I chose to enter the group were not indifferent to cancer. The woman in one couple had several years earlier nursed her mother who died of cancer, and she felt a need to talk to people who had had some exposure to cancer issues. The second couple contained a man who had considered himself to be cured of cancer several years before, and who had an interest in prophylactic treatment.

The group continues to function. Increasingly, issues unrelated to death and survival have become the material to be worked through. The tide of death seems to be receding.

Notes

1. M. McClinton, "Menstrual Synchrony and Suppression," *Nature* 229 (1971): 229–44.
2. J. Mason, "Psychological Influences on the Pituitary adrenal-Cortical System" *Recent Progress in Hormone Research* 15 (1959): 345.
3. Ibid.
4. S. Escalona, "Emotional Development in the First Year of Life," in M. Senn, *Problems of Infancy and Childhood (Transactions of the Sixth Conference)* (Ann Arbor, MI: Josiah Macy, Jr. Foundation, 1953.)
5. J. Lynch, *The Broken Heart* (NY: Basic Books, 1938), 100.
6. M. Kerr, "Cancer and the Family Emotional System," in J. Goldberg, ed., *Psychotherapeutic Treatment of Cancer Patients* (Free Press, 1981), 273–315.
7. M. Kerr, "Emotional Factors in Physical Illness: A Multigenerative Perspective," *The Family* 7 (1980): 59–66.
8. B. K. Greenleaf, *Children Through the Ages: A History of Childhood*, (NY: McGraw-Hill, 1978), 28.
9. D. Bakan, *Disease, Pain and Sacrifice* (Beacon Press, 1968), 109.
10. B. K. Greenleaf, *Children Through the Ages*, XIII.

11. D. Bloch, *So The Witch Won't Eat Me: Fantasy and the Child's Fear of Infanticide* (Boston: Houghton Mifflin, 1978), 8–9.
12. Sophocles, *Oedipus Rex*.
13. B. K. Greenleaf, *Children Through the Ages*, 17–21.
14. Ibid.
15. Ibid.
16. D. Bakan, *Disease, Pain and Sacrifice*, 117.
17. M. S. Guttmacher, *The Mind of the Murderer* (NY: Farrar, Straux and Cudahy, 1960), 13.
18. J. McDougall, *Plea for a Measure of Abnormality* (NY: International Universities Press, 1980).
19. E. J. Megargee, "Undercontrolled and Overcontrolled Personality Types in Extreme Antisocial Aggression," *Psychological Monographs* 80:3 (1966).
20. M. Guttmacher, *The Mind of the Murderer*.
21. N Y Times, 26 June 1987.
22. D. Bloch, *The Witch Won't Eat Me*, 6–7.
23. J. McDougall, *Measure of Abnormality*, 327–45.
24. Ibid.
25. Ibid.
26. D. Bakan, *Disease, Pain and Sacrifice*, 81.
27. R. Grossarth-Maticek, M. Jankovic, H. Vettor, "Changes in Psychosocial Context of Standard Risk Factors for Lung Cancer, Cardiac Infarct, Apoplexy, and Diabetes Mellitus," *Psychother. Psychosom.* 37 (1982).
28. J. Bernstein, "Interview with Lewis Thomas," *New Yorker* 2 January 1978, p. 41.
29. C. B. Bahnson, "Psychophysiological Complementarity in Malignancies: Best Work and Future Vistas," *Annals New York Academy of Science*, 319–334.
30. C. B. Bahnson and M. B. Bahnson, "Role of the Ego Defenses: Denial and Repression in the Etiology of Malignant Neoplasm," *Annals New York Academy of Science* 125 (1966): 277–86.
31. R. E. Renneker, "Cancer and Psychotherapy" in J. Goldberg (ed.), *Psychotherapeutic Treatment of Cancer Patients* (Free Press, 1981), 147.
32. S. Greer and T. Morris, "Psychological Attributes of Women Who Develop Breast Cancer," *Journal of Psychosomatic Research* 19 (1975): 147–53.

II

Psychoanalyzing Medicine

3

The "Out-There" Is "In-Here": The Evolution of the Concept of Defense

Whatever resistance to disease an organism may possess by virtue of species, race and the like, is profoundly influenced by its physiological state. In general, resistance is at its height when the organism is functioning normally in every respect and is reduced by a variety of factors which interfere with and alter the normal physiological state.
—Borrows, *Textbook of Microbiology*, 10th Ed.

Whether or not suffering can be alleviated and death postponed are questions that have interested mankind from time immemorial. Critical to these questions is a thorough understanding of the nature of the enemy. Freud made clear that, on the level of the psyche, the enemy to be beheld lies within. On the level of the body, the question of whether we suffer for reasons "out-there" or "in-here" is the central issue around which the history of medicine has evolved.[1]

In the beginning of the era to which we attribute the origins of modern medicine, before we had instruments with which to observe and measure the myriad of minute "out-there" particles, there was little choice but to see the causes of disease and death as arising from within the organism. For most of medical history, until roughly one hundred years ago, disease was considered to be due to inharmonious internal relations, reflecting systemic bodily imbalance.[2] Disharmony could arise from a variety of causes determined essentially by prevailing religious and philosophical beliefs. Chief among the disharmonies in prescientific medicine were those arising from behavior which was offensive to the gods. While the shaman, the culturally identified healer, often resorted to the practice of what we would today call magic, there was as well, a great deal of pragmatic thought in early medicine. The shamanic mind had respect for empirical observations, and as Oliver Wendall Holmes pointed out, appropriated "everything from every source that can be of the slightest use to anybody who is ailing in any way."[3]

Since health was connected to one's relationship with nature, or in religious terms, to the gods, illness was accepted as part of the natural order. Early Egyptians and Greeks used only the material creations of the gods, in the form of herbs, plants, and mineral substances in the effort toward restoration of health.

Hippocrates (460–377 B.C.) is usually credited with being the first physician.[4] He made the study of health a secular endeavor, as he was the first to characterize disease as a result of natural, not supernatural or divine, forces. His new theory of medicine had in common with the older, prescientific notion the idea that disease was based on a general disorder, and that the observable signs of the disease were the mere symptomatic manifestations of the disease process, rather than the disease itself.

Hippocrates's innovative contribution was in the development of a technique of diagnosis through objective observation and deduction which eliminated reference to philosophical or religious precepts. Ancient manuscripts tell us that he prescribed as treatment a special diet, as well as procedures to remove troublesome toxins lodged in the body. To get a sense of his theory of causation and cure of disease, we must understand that the Greek word *diata* means *mode of life*.[5] His treatment referred not only to nutrition, but also to abstinence from any stimulus that "might be deleterious to the mode of life in relation to the soul and spirit." Disease was an outcome of "bad living." Restoration of health depended on proper utilization of the natural substances of earth—fresh air, pure water, nutritious food, judicious exposure to sunlight, and the therapeutic application of the botanical medicines—special plants and herbs.

Hippocrates left a series of case histories documenting the successful treatment of diseases. In contrast to the powerful arsenal of drugs and other treatment modalities we wield today, these early methods would be considered primitive. Yet, the techniques developed by Hippocrates were convincing enough that his teachings remained the guiding principle in medicine for centuries.

Two thousand years later, the practice of medicine had not essentially changed. Parecelsus (Bambastus Theophrastus von Hohenheim, 1493–1541) agreed with Hippocrates that the causes of disease are "to be found in the soul and spirit as well as in the body." His treatments included the natural remedies, and he added, as well, an early form of psychotherapy.[6]

These understandings of the causes of disease led to a role for physicians quite different from the role they play today. The physician was not seen as a healer, since only nature (or the gods or God) retained that power. Physicians were merely one of several classes of agents who had weapons to promote healing, and of these, they were not always the most popular. Herbalists, barber-surgeons, and grocers far outnumbered the university-trained physician, who remained part of an elite class ministering only to the privileged in the community.

Further, the relationship that the physician developed with his patient was quite unlike what we are used to today. The number of patients that any physician worked with was quite limited, and as a result, the physician got to know the psyches of his patients as well as their bodies. It was the belief of physicians until well into the nineteenth century that diseases were intimately related to the psychological makeup of their victims. Hippocrates knew twenty-three centuries ago that asthmatic attacks could be brought on by violent emotions. During the seventeenth through the nineteenth centuries medical thought ascribed cancer to melancholy,[7] fright or violent grief,[8–10] "uneasy passions of the mind,"[11] "habitual gloominess of temper," depression,[12] and, according to the first statistical analysis of the relationship between cancer and personality—neurotic tendency.[13]

The diagnostic techniques of Hippocrates were followed by 2,000 years of increasing differentiation and distinction among diseases. Medical textbooks became elaborate in their descriptions of diseases. As a result we know a good deal about which diseases affected whom, when, and where. The main killer diseases of today—cancer and heart disease—are minor, mentioned almost in passing; discussions of smallpox and measles are extensive. Most of the illnesses that we have learned about from as far back as the first millennium until well into the nineteenth century, made their historical marks in epidemics: the plague, smallpox, cholera, typhoid fever, and leprosy.[14] Each of these infectious illnesses announced their presence through a resounding chorus of visible physiological activity. Primary among the symptoms was the presence of fever, suggesting an inflammatory condition. It was the breaking of the fever that gave the first indication that the crisis had passed, the inflammation had subsided, and the patient would live.

It is difficult for us today to grasp the extent to which the advent of laboratory science turned what had been a stable body of thought for well over 2,000 years into the topsy-turvy conundrum that characterized medicine in the nineteenth century. Darwin's use of the natural kingdom as his scientific laboratory led to the cataloguing and classifying of the relations among animals and the establishment once and for all of man as an animal. The transition from a divine being to the mere product of the process of natural selection among animals was resisted even by Darwin, who entitled the second edition of his work "The Origin of Species Out of God."[15]

It is understandable that Darwin, and the Victorians, clung to the notion of a divinity. While belief in a god did not prevent disease or death, it at least provided a conceptual frame within which to understand one's misfortunes. Up until that point in history, disease, suffering, and death had generally been understood as flowing from the gods.[16] The Egyptians understood illness as caused by an unnaturalness in one's life. The epidemics in medieval days were thought to be the "scourge of God" due to sinful ways. Without reference to a deity, illness became a matter of chance. Any of us might be susceptible, at any moment, for no intelligible reason at all. Perhaps even more profound, though, as a corollary to the belief in the strictly biological nature of man, was the confining of man's existence in time between birth and death. Immortality, partaking as it does of the idea of a spiritual existence, was dealt a severe blow. Religion and science, and with science its offspring of modern medicine, entered divergent paths.

As a result, disease was no longer seen as a natural and in one way or another appropriate product of how one lived or thought or felt; rather, it became an unnatural state—bad luck—forced upon its hapless, random victim. It became, as well, a state more feared than ever before, both because it seemed unnatural and because death, without the concept of an afterlife, had become more dreadful.

Without these fundamental philosophical changes, science might never have proceeded in quite the way it did. For science to become truly scientific, that is, objective, it needed to cast out any assumptions which could have predetermined the interpretation of data.

The year 1824 was a turning point in the burgeoning field of medical science. This was the year the achromatic microscope was invented, and this invention changed the face of research.[17] Although the microscope had been around since the end of the sixteenth century, it wasn't until Chevalier constructed his much more powerful instrument that access to the microstructure of the cell was gained. The component parts of the cell could now be discerned, and for the first time, normal cells could be distinguished from abnormal cells.[18]

Virchow's work in 1858 on cellular pathology established for about one hundred years what would be the mainstream of medical thought.[19] He demonstrated cellular involvement in the morbid processes associated with disease. Disease began to be conceptualized as a localized phenomenon whose origin and pathogenic involvement was to be understood on the cellular level. The older concept of disease as systemic disorder (imbalance, disharmony) faded into oblivion, and treatment and research became, instead, symptom-oriented. The symptom of the disease had become, in the minds of the experts, the disease.[20]

The young Louis Pasteur was a scientist fascinated by the seemingly limitless possibilities for understanding the world opened up by this new invention of untold power. Pasteur's isolation of the microbe complemented Virchow's work on cellular pathology, and the presence of the germ completed the equation for the modern medical theory of disease.[21] The germ gave ballast to the idea that there would be one causative agent of a disease, a concept known as the specific etiology theory. The host organism, wherein the germ comes to rest, was seen as being merely an innocent bystander, whose only mistake was to appear in the wrong place at the wrong time. The patient had become a victim.

Virchow, however, understood both the implications and the limitations of his work all along. He never abandoned his belief in disease as involving the entire organism, and hoped for research following his own that, instead of eclipsing the older idea, would incorporate his discoveries into what he considered to be basically sound preexisting notions of disease.[23]

Pasteur, too, came to understand the fallacy of ascribing to the germ the unilateral potency that he first assigned it. His colleague, Claude Bernard, never ceased debating with him, insisting that the germ was not what was important; rather, what should be studied was the *terrain*, the ground on which the microbe falls. Bernard argued that it was the state of the host organism that largely determined its own fate and that of the germ.[24] Germs—bacteria and viruses—do, after all, surround us all the time; yet, only some of us "catch" them, and only some of the time. So, Bernard maintained, it cannot be the entry of the germ into the system that produces disease. It must be the state of the ground on which it falls—the host organism—that determines whether the germ damages us, or we damage the germ, or we and the germ live in peaceful coexistence.

It was not until he was on his deathbed that Pasteur recognized that his lifelong preoccupation with the virus had been misdirected, and he uttered the following shocking valedictory to his own life's work:

Bernard avait raison. Le germ n'est rien, c'est le terrain qui est tout. [Bernard was right. The microbe is nothing; the soil is everything.][25]

The ease with which segmented and detailed entities could be discovered and studied with the newer and more refined methods of observation must have made for irresistible research. Whether the lens of the microscope was directed toward the outer world, following the lead of Pasteur, or toward the inner world of the human body, where Virchow had concentrated, the objects of study were isolated from their natural environment. The sense of the integrity of connections, the idea that disease had a logical connection to the disruption of a natural or divine order was eliminated. Disease became unnatural. The wisdom of the ages that the disturbances observed in the disease process were a result, or a mere manifestation, of a more profound disturbance seemed to be forever lost.

Simultaneous with the discoveries of the laboratory researchers, another group of scientists were attempting to study the pathology of the mind. These psychiatrists, like Virchow, were convinced that an abnormal mental construct would be reflected in tissue change. Brain functions were thought to roughly correspond with mental functions, and attempts were made to discover the pathological changes in brain tissue of the mentally disturbed. These attempts proved to be unsuccessful, and mental sufferers remained largely unhelped.

The hysterical patient was the most baffling and frustrating of all to the well-meaning physician. The symptoms were varied, and seemingly involved bodily dysfunctions, but didn't follow any known laws of anatomy or physiology. Physicians despaired of treating these patients. At times, their frustration turned into anger—or so it seems from this distance—and patients were either accused of being malingerers and not really sick, or were treated with harsh, unproductive, and perhaps even punitive methods.

It was in this environment that Freud began a task that paralleled the work being done in the biological laboratories. He, too, was interested in isolating a biological entity, but his object of interest was not the cell. It was the psyche. Scientific methodology was well entrenched by this time, and Freud's own thought, in keeping with his medical training, was systematic and rigorous, befitting a scientist. His method of investigation, as innovative as it was, was designed to meet the same standards. Scientific discipline demanded that the phenomenon in question be studied in its most elemental form, and apart from the influence of extraneous variables. Thus, the consulting room became Freud's laboratory, where his patients were to lie on the examining table and present the data of their minds raw. Dreams, hopes, fears, fantasies—all were laid before the analytic eye, to be resolved into their most elemental components.

Freud, like his contemporary Pasteur, first conceptualized the cause of dysfunction to be a contaminant, an *agent provocateur*. This contaminant he termed "trauma," and thus a name was given to the provocative stress in hysterical illness. Like the germ, it intruded into the body and continued to work its way toward destruction of the psyche (what Bernard would have called the terrain): "We must presume rather that the physical trauma—or more precisely the memory of the trauma—acts like a foreign body which long after its entry must continue to be regarded as an agent that is still at work."[26]

The isolation of the contaminant seeking to destroy the organism became as important to Freud as it was to Pasteur, and equally difficult to accomplish. Hour after hour of listening to his patients convinced him that psychic injury was the result of an actual trauma suffered at an early age. Many women patients described sexual seductions which confirmed Freud's belief in the significance of the traumatic event in the etiology of the neuroses.

Then Freud met with something unexpected, requiring reformulation of his entire theoretical construct. He was led by the evidence to the inescapable conclusion that the traumatic events his patients described were often imaginary. The stories his female patients told of sexual assaults by male relatives and friends sometimes existed only in the minds of his patients.

Material reported by patients as memory could not be separated out from the whole of their mental life. Memories, including those from which hysterics presumably suffered, need not be literal. The human mind was infinitely more complex than a mere collection of factual data; it consisted of wishes, fears, longings, expectations. Neurosis, then, could involve the maladaptive adjustment of any or all of these mental forces.

With the trauma theory now called into question, Freud changed his method of treatment. Freud had used hypnosis, and had been pleased by the ease with which reminiscences of the painful memory of the trauma could be evoked, experienced, and discharged. Yet, the rest of the personality remained unchanged. The newer method of free association, whereby the patient was instructed to say whatever came to his mind, was to uncover aspects of the psyche other than isolated memory fragments which, when left to emerge on their own, would reveal themselves with great clarity. What became clear was that it was not the external event that disturbed the mind; rather, it was the mind's own structure, its turning around on itself, that was causing the problem.

Freud's notions changed the face of medical science. While the scientific method of analysis of segmented and specialized mechanisms had led to fertile research in the physiological laboratories, it produced very little in the study of the mind, and these methods were soon abandoned. Freud's study of patients had convinced him that the personality reflected an intelligibly coordinated structure, whose parts were integrated, and seemed, as well, to somehow have an internal language that enabled the various parts to communicate with one another. In his quest to understand the totality of the mental life of his patients, rather than isolated traumatic events and their sequelae, Freud gave the first attention to the terrain of the human psyche.

Paramount among Freud's discoveries was the idea that the visible disability was only the symptom of an underlying disorder. This idea changed the very definition of neurosis. It is not something which randomly befalls one; rather neurosis is created, arranged, and assiduously protected. Freud's conceptualization of the communicative function of symptom was both a harking back to the earlier notions of disease, and a forerunner of the modern system of holistic healing.

With these changes in the concept of disease came a concomitant change in the roles of patient and physician. The patient had *cooperated* in the contraction of the disease, albeit in a peculiar sense of the word, since the nature of this cooperation was on the level of the unconscious. But, the cure, too, demanded involvement and efforts—conscious, intentional cooperation—on the part of the patient. On the part of the healer, never before had a physician spent so much time with a patient; never before had a physician participated so extensively in the cure.

Had medical science followed the lead of Freud, the history of the theory and treatment of disease would have evolved quite differently from the way it did. In spite of the fact that Freud's theories were firmly based in the hard sciences of the biology and neurology of his day, his treatment technique made no direct physical intervention. At this point in medical history, the physical, and what came to be known as the social sciences began a divergent path, the first emphasizing the mechanics of application of physical agents to treat disease, and the latter stressing the totality of the functioning of the human organism, body and mind alike, in the treatment of the patient in whom the disease resides.

Not that medical science was without its successes. Theories of disease have staying power only if they result in a method of treatment that has efficacy. Pasteur's isolation of the microbe and Virchow's work on cell pathology would not have been significant markers in medical history had they not led to resounding success. These discoveries led to work which resulted in the elimination of killer diseases which had yielded such destruction in their heyday as to have struck down one-fifth of the population of Europe.[27] By the turn of the twentieth century, a great number of specific viral and bacterial agents had been identified. This pioneering work in the elaboration of the art of diagnosis was seized as an opportunity to make parallel advances in the treatment of disease. Now that pathological entities could be clearly identified, it was an easy step to conceptualize eradication of the provoking agent.

Attempts were made from time to time to integrate the age-old lessons of the healing properties of natural substances into the findings of the newer sciences. The increasing sophistication in optics, for instance, reaffirmed the ancient idea of the healing properties of sunlight. French physicians in 1774 began to treat open ulcers of the leg with sunlight.[28] Soon after, there were frequent reports of cancer cures through the use of optic lenses which had the effect of augmenting the sun's power. Observations were made on sunlight's curative powers for ailments as diverse as muscle weakness, rickets, scurvy, rheumatism, tuberculosis, paralysis, and war wounds.

The year 1877 marked the first scientific confirmation of the sun's recuperative powers. Downes and Blunt established that sunlight had the ability to destroy bacteria.[29] For some years after this discovery, sunlight was studied as the only known effective treatment of bacterial infections. The tuberculosis bacillus and the contagious nature of the disease were discovered around the turn of the century, and Niels Finsen investigated the idea that light could cure tuberculosis. In 1903 he won the Nobel Prize for his successful treatment of skin tuberculosis with the ultraviolet portion of light.[30] Throughout Europe, and somewhat later in the United States, a proliferation of sanitariums was seen, and reports were released of 90 percent improvements and 78 percent outright cures of patients who had been considered hopeless by the medical world.[31]

Other technological advances transformed the art of administering medication into a science. In 1803 a German pharmacist isolated morphine from opium.[32] This event marked the first time that a pure, active ingredient had been teased out of the material in which it was embedded. Whole new vistas were opened up to physicians: they could now give exact doses, and in doing so, achieve a predictability of effect that had not been previously possible.

It was observed that the isolated drugs had reacted with the body much faster and more intensely than their raw botanical sources. Faster seemed to be better, and within a short period of time the hypodermic syringe was invented by Samuel Wood. With this instrument, medication could enter directly into the bloodstream.[33]

Even the administration of natural substances was subjected to scientific exactitude of dosage. Auguste Rollier, the French physician who is credited with the popularization in this century of sunlight as therapy, had carefully calculated programs of exposure to the sun. His schedule called for baring only the feet on the first day for only five minutes. The rest of the body was shielded from the sun. The next day, the feet were exposed for ten minutes while the upper legs received five minutes. Additional parts of the body were systematically added on successive days, until the entire body was exposed for a period of between one and three hours per day.[34]

The advent of drug therapy culminated in widespread use of exact dosages of refined and powerful substances which had been synthesized in the laboratory. The effect seemed astonishing. As quickly as antibiotics were developed, they were administered. This, in addition to mass immunizations, seemed to have the effect of suddenly and miraculously wiping infectious diseases off the face of the earth.

Of the synthetic substances produced, one of the most remarkable was an analgesic introduced in 1899 and marketed under the trade name Aspirin.[35] The high fevers that accompanied diseases brought great discomfort to the patient, and to the mind which had ceased to view illness and its multiple manifestations as having integrated meaning, fever seemed to be an unnecessary nuisance. Even a small amount of this potent new drug could provide the patient with hours of relief from his uncomfortable symptoms. The commercial availability of Aspirin changed the consciousness of the whole European continent, and opened the door for what was to become a seemingly endless proliferation of drugs and belief in their curative powers.

Some years following the introduction of Aspirin, Sir Alexander Fleming, in 1928, discovered the therapeutic use of penicillin, and with this drug, the era of mass deaths through infectious diseases seemed to come to a close. This discovery, however, had another momentous effect: it virtually ended mainstream medical interest in the curative powers of natural substances.[36] With the outbreak of World War II, scientists made a concerted effort to perfect Fleming's methods, and laboratory-produced antibiotics came into widespread use; research investigation and clinical use of sun, water, air, and food as therapeutic tools were completely eclipsed by the faster acting, seemingly more powerful drugs. Even more, belief in laboratory methods of synthesization had led researchers to experimentally replicate natural substances. Vitamin D, formerly a province of the sun, was produced artificially by irradiating a natural plant substance, ergosterol, with ultraviolet radiation from a light bulb.[37] The benefits of sunlight, it was thought, could be had—even improved upon through the increased ability to control dosage—from a light bulb or a pill. Research on the constituent parts of food, was also conducted at this time, and vitamins and minerals were extracted and made available independent of their original food source. Natural, whole food and pure sunlight, it seemed, were being declared obsolete as their more potent, artificial replicas gained in popularity.

The widespread use of drugs and synthetic replicas of natural products seemed to put us on the verge of a disease-free world. Rickets was cured by Vitamin D; various drugs had been discovered to be useful in the treatment of tuberculosis, and its presence had been reduced to a minimum; antibiotics took care of the remaining infectious diseases of cholera, dysentery, and typhoid, as well as infections from wounds. Historians still debate whether it was because of, in spite of, or independent of, the demise of infectious diseases, but it is at this point in medical history that the diseases that represent degenerative bodily processes—most notably cancer and heart disease—begin their ascent to prevalence.

The application of the germ theory to the treatment of the infectious diseases had made a great deal of sense; the leading diseases of the time were brought under control. Germs had been identified as present in the diseased conditions, the available drugs did effectively destroy the germ, and the patient did get better. So it seemed sensible to apply the same notions of causation and treatment to these newly prevalent degenerative disease entities. Cancer, in particular, seemed to involve the presence of viruses and came to be understood as a viral-induced disease, with this as its single cause. The cancer cell was seen as the pathological result of the introduction of the viral agent, and the tumor merely a collection of these abnormal cells.[38]

Unfortunately, this theory of the degenerative diseases is almost certainly dead wrong, and for several reasons. First, the inflammatory diseases reflect a different kind of bodily disturbance from those that produce the degenerative diseases.[39] The inflammation process reflects an acute disturbance; it comes on quickly, symptoms are overt and profoundly disturbing. If the patient doesn't die from the infection, recovery can be virtually complete. Even more, in certain infections the patient will develop an active resistance to the particular strain of virus or bacteria that precipitated the illness, and will become healthier as a result of the fight.

Degenerative diseases look, feel, and behave in a diametrically opposite fashion. They are silent, insidious, and largely unfelt until they have reached a relatively advanced state. Fever, as a sign of a disease process, is notably absent.[40]

But beyond that, the premise on which this theory of disease is based—the attribution to modern medicine of the eradication of infectious diseases—is largely a myth. The incidence of infectious diseases had already been on the wane before the introduction of antibiotics and immunizations.[41] Pasteur had not only identified the microbe; he documented the method of transmission, as well. The concept of spontaneous generation, the idea that germs are created out of the void, was dealt its final death blow as Pasteur demonstrated the organisms could be transmitted by air.

Principles of cleanliness, combined with aesthetic concerns, motivated the humanitarian efforts of social reformers in the middle of the nineteenth century.[42] These led to improvement in sanitation and living conditions, and a drastic reduction in the prevalence and virulence of germs. In spite of the neglect of the medicinal value of fresh air, clean water, and sunlight, architectural and life-style changes confirmed their value. Inhabitants of cities were largely deprived of these essential substances. Multistoried structures, narrow streets, inadequate sewage, limited outdoor recreational space—all contributed to the conditions of cities as havens of disease. Until 1851, residents of London were subjected to a window tax, and the poor were forced to choose between sunlight and food. In short, the late nineteenth century introduction of inexpensive, easily laundered cotton undergarments, and of affordable transparent glass that brought light into the most humble of dwellings, contributed more to the control of infection than did all of the available drugs and medical practices.[43]

Applying the naive formulation of infectious disease to the newly prevalent degenerative diseases made the treatment of these diseases appear to be, at least conceptually, a relatively easy matter. All that was needed was a treatment procedure that would make possible the elimination of the offending organ or tissue—the cancer cell or collection of cells comprising the tumor in the case of cancer; the damaged part of the artery or heart in the heart diseases.

Science cooperated, again with the help of Pasteur. Following Pasteur's work on the air transmission of microbes, Joseph Lister introduced the procedure of sterilization into the field of surgery. Problems of pain, infection, and bleeding remained, but technology quickly caught up with medical knowledge.[44] Commercial firms were founded to manufacture large numbers of surgical instruments. Techniques of surgery advanced rapidly, and surgery seemed to be, for a broad spectrum of diseases, what immunizations had seemed to be for infectious diseases—immediate and virtual elimination of the disease. From one hour to the next, the disease could be gotten rid of, and the body "made as fit as it had been originally."[45]

The science of diagnosis received an important boost when, in 1896, Roentgen read his classic paper announcing his discovery of x-rays.[46] It was soon realized that x-rays could be used in the treatment of diseases, as well as in their detection. Within a decade the inhibitory effect of radiation on any growing tissue had been observed, and by 1910 radiotherapy had become a formalized method of treatment for malignant diseases. With technological advancement of machinery and refinement of the technique for administering x-rays in accurate dosages and in precise locations, radiation had obvious advantages over surgery. The rays could penetrate deep into tissue, to places where it was difficult or impossible for a surgeon's knife to reach. On this front it seemed that cancer would soon cease to be a terrible threat. Few would have predicted that it would become the scourge of the earth that it was destined to be.

The advent of chemotherapy in the 1940's promised results where even the powerful treatments of surgery and radiation had failed.[47] The idea of applying poisons was not new; for centuries physicians had treated patients with concoctions meant to destroy the infecting agent while leaving the patient unharmed.[48] Currently a number of poisons which have specific effects on the body are in use: chemotherapy to suppress cellular division, digitalis to stimulate the heart, cocaine and its analogues (Novocaine) to block nerve transmission.

Surgery, as a treatment for disease, is now over one hundred years old, radiation over eighty, and chemotherapy over forty years. The initial euphoria concerning each of these treatment techniques has waned. We have increasingly become experts in the efficient removal of diseased tissue, through the alternative methods of cutting them out, burning them out, or chemically dissolving them. Yet, the degenerative diseases seem to be outsmarting us all, and their victims are increasing rather than diminishing in number. The limitations of each of these treatment approaches have become all too apparent.[49]

As a case in point, the statistics of cancer have just been upgraded. This is a disease from which one out of three Americans will suffer. Cancer is an insidious disease. In two-thirds of all cases, by the time a cancer diagnosis is rendered the original cancer will already have produced secondary tumors, and have infiltrated other parts of the body.[50] Surgical approaches have sometimes degenerated into a desperate hacking away at the body, cutting away parts in an effort to catch up with the growth of the cancer. It has become the practice to remove more and more of the surrounding tissue in an effort to ensure containment. The cancer grows invisibly, though, and such attempts usually prove futile. In an attempt to outsmart the cancer some surgeons try to anticipate the next targeted organ for the prowling cancer cells, and remove as yet unaffected body parts.

Radiation, too, is effective only as a localized weapon. Where cancerous tissue is embedded deep within the body, the ionizing rays penetrate and affect equally all tissue that they pass through—healthy tissue as well as diseased. In addition, intensive radiotherapy damages the mesenchyme, the body's soft connective tissue, thus interfering with the body's natural resistance. Consequently, secondary cancers are now being observed as a result of initial radiation therapy.

The agents in chemotherapy, too, are not selective. As with radiation, the interference with all growing tissue and the resultant immunodepression are serious disadvantages to the chemotherapeutic approach. The difficulty was summed up in a World Heath Organization report in 1962, where an expert committee described the colossal task of tumor chemotherapy. The treatment must "first learn how to destroy all of the cells of each of an enormous number of varieties of tumors, and, at the same time, avoid irreparable damage to any of the essential normal tissues, from which tumor tissues differ, in the main, only quantitatively."[51] Some twenty-five years later, the state of the art remains the same.

It is now clear that the pursuit of the single etiology theory—the idea that disease is caused by one inducing agent—has led to a series of mainstream medical treatment modalities which have been disappointing in their failure to reverse the course of the disease process. Viruses are still being sought in many of our most debilitating diseases.[52]

For the most part, the strongest connection science can make between cancer and viruses is that there is a relation:[53] The nature of the relation remains obscure.

There is still no medical method for reversing neoplastic disease.[54] The apparent rise in cure rate is more an artifact of medical terminology than a reflection of change in treatment efficacy.[55] Cure in cancer, is defined as five years of survival from time of diagnosis. Improvement in medical technology and widespread deliverance of health services has led to much earlier detection of cancers; diagnosis is now often made at an earlier point in the disease's inexorable progress. But the definition of cure remains unchanged: five years. As a result, more patients are falling into the cured category without living a day longer than they would have a generation ago.[56] Breast cancer, for instance, normally takes longer than the five risky years to metastasize. A breast cancer patient who, nine years after her initial diagnosis, falls victim to a metastasized brain cancer and dies, has been, nevertheless, a cured statistic in the medical annals.

While the childhood leukemias, Hodgkins' Disease, and skin cancers have shown genuine statistical improvement, the reason is more related to the nature of the host organism than to the efficacy of the treatment. Hodgkins' and the childhood leukemias are found primarily in young people. The regenerative power of cells is still high in this stage of life, and this quality of rapid renewal means that the permanent damage incurred from the medical treatments to healthy cells is less.[57] Skin cancers are rarely invasive, and surgery, the least offensive available medical treatment, is usually sufficient to remove all traces of the cancer cells.

Where viruses have been found, in most cases medical remedies have little therapeutic effect. Only one viral disease—smallpox—has been eliminated.[58] The common cold and the array of other respiratory viral infections, including influenza, remain essentially untreatable. The best that is accomplished is symptom relief, and many of the methods employed to facilitate recovery—bed rest, liquids, and tender loving care—remain unchanged and unimproved since the days of our grandmothers, or indeed, since the days of Hippocrates.

In diseases where there is no thought of an infectious agent, we don't fare much better. Virtually the same treatment approaches are utilized—drugs and surgery. Even in cardiovascular diseases, where technically dazzling surgical innovations have possibly prolonged some lives with bypasses and transplants, we are still on the level of symptom removal rather than understanding and finding ways to reverse disease processes.

However, fortunately for the advancement of science, different laboratories generate different hypotheses to test different theories. While the mainstream of medical research has been directed toward the isolation of the microbe, and treatment techniques designed to eradicate the offending organism or cell, a few researchers have followed Bernard's idea and made investigation into the conditions of the human body that would permit a noxious agent to enter and render its destruction.

For Bernard, on the physiological level, organisms were exposed to the same germs—some succumbed to the destructive properties of the germs and some did not; for Freud, on the psychological level, the fantasies and fears of his patients were remarkably similar—some patients were profoundly sick and others functioned reasonably appropriately. Equally puzzling was the fact that some patients who did suffer from the noxious effect of the germ, or trauma, ultimately got well, while others did not. To what could the differences be attributed?

Bernard was able to give a comprehensive answer to this question on the biological level. He began by observing that the internal and external milieux of the human organism are distinct from one another, separated by the skin and mucous membranes. This notion once stated may strike us as banal, but its implications are profound. In distinguishing precisely between what is human and what remains outside of being human, Bernard discovered a new line of research into the process by which the nonhuman is allowed to intrude into the human. He discovered that the body had a defensive strategy that normally enabled it to successfully ward off dangerous intruding agents.[59]

Two conditions needed to coincide for disease to become manifest. First, there needed to be the disease-carrying agent—the germ that Pasteur had identified. But, equally important, there needed to be some change in the internal milieu of the body. The healthy organism had an ability to regulate itself so that unwanted biological freight could be eliminated. It was when this homeostatic ability was impaired that the internal milieu became hospitable to agents that would, under healthier circumstances, be either ejected or destroyed.

Bernard's formulation led to a line of research—and treatment—that forked off from the mainstream, single etiology germ theories. The year 1891 marked a dramatic turning point in the history of this new line of research. A German physician, E. A. von Behring, treated a young girl dying from diphtheria with a serum taken from a sheep. Research a year earlier had shown that the serum appeared in the bloodstream of animals after infections, and that the serum was capable of neutralizing poisons. Through the effect of the serum in stimulating her own defensive mechanisms, the girl revived; von Behring won a Nobel Prize in Medicine.[60]

Also in 1891, an American surgeon, William Coley, observed that certain infections seemed to have a beneficial effect on cancer patients.[61] He acted on this insight by injecting patients with bacterial toxins in order to induce immune responses that could change the course of malignancies. In total, Coley treated nearly five hundred cancer patients, each of whom showed clear clinical improvement. A later assessment of his work revealed that two hundred eighty-three of those patients survived for a period ranging from five to seventy-two years longer than their medical prognoses had predicted. In spite of his successes, Coley's work went unrecognized.

In experimental laboratories, Bernard's ideas produced investigation into the precise functioning of the immune system, the body's mechanism for warding off the dangerous, invasive microbe. Understanding the functioning of the immune system was bolstered when Sir Frank Macfarland Burnet asked an essential question: what is the precise mechanism in the immune system that permits a discrimination between self and not-self? How is it that the body tolerates its own worn-out and unnecessary constituents without effecting an immune response while, on the other hand, matter from the external milieu stimulates the immune reaction?[62]

The question led him to the discovery of the agent of defense—the lymphocytes, comprised of cells labelled "T" and "B". The cells of the immune system patrol the body, searching out foreign invaders. Recognition of invasion comes from clues, in the form of antigens, that these intruders leave. These antigens are a particular variety of molecule which serves as a kind of signature, a mark of the presence of an alien entity. Once these antigens are recognized, the immune system leaps into action, manufacturing a substance that has the specific task of binding with and neutralizing the invading entity. This antidote is called an antibody, and there is always an exact chemical linkage between the particular antigen and its corresponding antibody.[63]

While these advances were being made in the medical and physiological laboratories, social scientists were making their parallel discoveries in the laboratories of the psychoanalytic consulting rooms. Freud, whose training was in the physiological and neurological sciences, conceptualized the psyche as a biological system. Just as the body wards off destructive agents to ensure its survival, so too does the psyche. But what was the psychic counterpart to the immune system? Freud's answer changed as his clinical experience broadened.

Freud's early work reflects Darwin's influence.[64] Instincts were the deepest drives, those permanent somatic demands which lie at the bottom of all human activity. Loyal to the Darwinian perception of the individual as a member of the species, the young Freud distinguished between what he then termed the self-preservative ego instincts, and the pleasure-seeking sexual instincts. It was these internal drives that threatened psychic equilibrium.

As early as 1896, Freud postulated that it was the efforts of the ego to defend itself that could be regarded as the nucleus of many neuroses.[65] In 1920 Freud was forced to revise his instinct theory, when he looked *Beyond the Pleasure Principle* (in the title of his great essay on these issues) and found the repetition compulsion, and behind it, the death instinct.[66]

He found the compulsion to repeat all-pervasive, underlying every neurosis and clearly more powerful than the pleasure principle, since it produced behavior and feelings which could not be understood as pleasurable to the psyche on any terms whatever—direct, indirect, or perverse.

Freud described the repetition compulsion as giving "the appearance of some extraneous force at work."[67] It is without the conscious will of the individual that he is, seemingly forced to think, feel, and behave in particular ways. These responses are often in conflict with the conscious intent of the individual and, at times, are even to his detriment.

It is precisely the compulsive aspect of the response, the fact that it occurs as an automatic response, independent of the conscious ego, that signifies the presence of a neurosis.[68] Freud came to identify this compulsion as yet another instinct. Instincts, though, are biological, and the compulsion to repeat is a manifestation in organic life of the conservative nature of all matter; it wants not to progress but to return to an earlier state. A return to the past for any living thing means a return to the inanimate state—the death instinct. Every living thing dies for internal reasons, and in death becomes inorganic once again.

But living matter is enlivened by an opposing instinct, as basic and as powerful: what Freud had long since called eros. As a result of this creative opposition, the function of the life instinct was not only to make connections and to create new life, but also, "to ward off any possible ways of returning to inorganic existence other than those which are imminent in the organism itself."[69]

Freud was beginning at the same time to understand that external psychic threats could be as destructive as those arising from within the organism. In *Beyond the Pleasure Principle*, he also conceptualized the living organism as a tiny vesicle suspended in the midst of an external world against which it needs a protective barrier. This shield has the function of insulating the personality against the stimuli that would work toward its destruction. Here again, it is the response of the organism itself to outside agents—the relative strength of the life and death instincts—that determines whether disease or health prevails.

The analogy to the germ and the immune system is complete now. Just as only some organisms succumb to the destructive power of either physiological disharmony or of germs, so do only some succumb to the destructive powers of the id and external agents that threaten the survival of the ego.

What mechanisms, then, protect our psyches from the ravages of forces threatening destruction? The answer for Freud was the same on the psychological level as Bernard and his followers had discovered on the physical level—the defense, or the psychological representation of the biological immune system.[70]

It was through his working out of the nature of anxiety that Freud came to understand the protective function of defense.[71] It is the ego's job in the face of danger to evaluate the situation and devise the best response. But when the dangerous situation is the product of intense instinctual demands, arising from below consciousness, regardless of the existence of a real external threat, an excessive burden may be placed on the ego. Under pressure, the ego may lose its ability to distinguish between real, remembered, or even anticipated dangers.

The danger presented—the source of anxiety—may be a psychic representation of one experienced earlier in life, such as in infancy, but the differentiation between present and past—never a distinction of much interest to the unconscious—has disappeared in the ego. Defensive stratagems then may be inappropriate to current life, counterproductive, disease producing—by definition: neurotic.

The defense mechanisms offer opposition to both the emergence of dangerous impulses, and the danger of external threatening forces. Anna Freud's systemization and codification of the defenses identified each of these mechanisms: regression, repression, reaction-formation, isolation, undoing, projection, introjection, turning against the self, denial, and identification with the aggressor.[72] Defenses are seen, then, as devices used for the maintenance of psychic and systemic equilibrium.

It is through the working out of the problem of defense that scientists have come to more fully understand the susceptibility of living organisms to disease. Specific disciplines for the study of the mind and body together have been created—the fields of psychosomatic medicine and psychoneuroimmunology—to study how it is that we ward off both internal and external dangers. As a result of these studies, we have been led full circle, back to the early days of medicine. We now have convincing evidence of the integrated functioning of the human organism. Those aspects of human functioning so long neglected—the soul and spirit of Hippocrates and Parecelsus, the basic elements of good food, air, water, and sunlight—have been reassigned to their rightful place in our understanding of the successful functioning of the human being.

Notes

1. The controversy between "germ theory" and "host-resistance" is increasingly heated. For a good, succinct exploration of the history of medicine from this vantage point see: J. Issels, *Cancer: Second Opinion* (London: Hodder and Stoughton, 1975), 32–47; or J. Goldberg, *Psychotherapeutic Treatment of Cancer Patients* (NY: Free Press, 1981), xix–xxvi.
2. Lyons & Petrucelli. *Medicine: An Illustrated History.*
3. Ibid.
4. J. Issels, *Cancer: A Second Opinion*, 24.
5. Ibid.
6. Ibid. 25–6.
7. R. Wiseman, *Severall Chirurgicall Inestises* (London: 1676).
8. D. Gendon, *Enquiries into the Nature, Knowledge and Care of Cancer* (London: 1701).
9. J. Z. Amussat, *Quelgues Reflexions sur la Curabilite du Cancer* (Paris: 1854).
10. J. Burrows, *A New Practical Essay on Cancer* (London: 1783).
11. W. H. Walshe, *Nature and Treatment of Cancer* (London: 1846).
12. Sir J. Paget, *Surgical Pathology* 3rd ed. (London: 1870).
13. H. Snow, *Cancer and the Cancer Process* (London: Churchill, 1893).
14. L. F. C. Mees, *Blessed by Illness* (Spring Valley, NY: Anthroposophic Press, 1983), 64.
15. Ibid. 77.
16. Ibid. 65.
17. J. Issels, *Cancer: A Second Opinion*, 32–3.
18. Ibid.
19. Ibid. 33–5.
20. Ibid. 35.
21. J. Goldberg, *Psychotherapeutic Treatment*, xix.
22. J. H. Knowles, "The Responsibility of the Individual," in *Doing Better and Feeling Worse*, J. H. Knowles ed. (NY: W. W. Norton, 1977), 58.

23. J. Issels, *Cancer: A Second Opinion*, 35.
24. H. Selye, *The Stress of Life* (NY: McGraw-Hill, 1956), 205.
25. Ibid.
26. S. Freud, Breuer, J., "Studies on Hysteria," *S. E.* (1893–1895): 6.
27. L. F. C. Mees, *Blessed by Illness*, 64.
28. M. Lillyquist, *Sunlight and Health* (NY: Dodd, Mead & Co., 1985), 16.
29. A. Downes and T. P. Blunt, "Researches on the Effect of Light Upon Bacteria and Other Organisms," *Proc. Roy. Soc. Med.* 26 (1877): 488.
30. M. Lillyquist, *Sunlight and Health*, 17–8 and Z. Kime, *Sunlight* (NY: World Health Publications, 1980), 162–4.
31. M. Lillyquist, *Sunlight and Health*, 23.
32. Andrew Weil, *Health & Healing* (Boston: Houghton Mifflin, 1985), 98.
33. Ibid., 100.
34. M. Lillyquist, *Sunlight and Health*, 22–3.
35. I. Illich, *Medical Nemesis*, 69.
36. M. Lillyquist, *Sunlight and Health*, 34.
37. Ibid., 35.
38. J. Issels, *Cancer: A Second Opinion*, 35.
39. L. F. C. Mees, *Blessed by Illness*, 132–6.
40. Several researchers have noted the inverse relationship between cancer and inflammation. E. von Rindfleisch made note of it at the end of the last century in *Die Elemente der Pathologie*, 3rd ed. (1896). Lambotte noted the striking rarity of a common inflammatory disorder in the history of cancer patients in *Eng. Ges. Med.* 19 (1896). R. Schmidt wrote that childhood infections were less common in cancer patients in *Med. Klin.* 6 (1910). G. von Bergman has done the greatest amount of research in this area, see *Funktionelle Pathologie* 173 (1932).
41. J. C. Norton, *Introduction to Medical Psychology* (NY: Free Press, 1982), 6.
42. L. Sagan, *The Health of Nations*, 32–5.
43. R. DuBos, *Mirage of Health*, (Anchon, NY: Doubleday, 1959), 220.
44. S. Reisor, "Therapeutic Choice and Moral Doubt," in J. H. Knowles, ed., *Doing Better & Feeling Worse*, 52.
45. K. H. Bauer, *Das Krebsproblem* (Berlin: Springer, 1963).
46. J. Issels, *Cancer: A Second Opinion*, 39.
47. Ibid., 41.
48. Ibid.
49. J. Powles, "On the Limitations of Modern Medicine," in R. L. Kane, ed., *The Challenges of Community Medicine* (NY: Springer, 1974).
50. J. Issels, *Cancer: A Second Opinion*, 37.
51. Ibid., 43.
52. E. Potts and M. Morra, *Understanding Your Immune System* (New York: Avon Books, 1986).
53. Ibid.
54. *Cancer Forum* 7: ½, 6.

55. Statistical techniques boosting cancer survival was reported by both a study to Congress from the General Accounting office (1987), and a study by A. Feinstein, reported in *The New England Journal of Medicine*.

56. A report prepared for the National Cancer Institute concluded that there had been no improvement in cancer-survived statistics for the last twenty-five years. Each of the cancers is broken down statistically in the Sixth National Cancer Conference Proceedings (Lippincott, July 1970).

57. L. Roy, personal communication.

58. *NY Times Magazine*, 1987.

59. C. Bernard, *Introduction a Letude de la Medicine Experimentale*, (Paris: Editions Flammarim, 1945).

60. J. Issels, *Cancer: A Second Opinion*, 93–4.

61. W. B. Coley, *Ann. Surg.* (1891) and *Am. J. Med. Sci.* (1893).

62. F. M. Burnet, *Immunological Surveillance* (Oxford: Pergamon Press, 1970).

63. E. Potts and M. Morra, *Understanding Your Immune System*.

64. The best integration of Darwin, Freud and Selye is in D. Bakan's *Disease, Pain & Sacrifice*, (Boston: Beacon Press, 1971), 19–30.

65. S. Freud, *S.E.* 1, 155–82.

66. S. Freud, "Beyond the Pleasure Principle," trans. J. Strachey (London: Liveright, 1950), 59.

67. Ibid., 45.

68. Ibid.

69. Ibid.

70. S. Freud, "Inhibitions, symptoms and anxiety," *S.E.* 20:77–175.

71. Ibid.

72. A. Freud. *The Ego and the Mechanisms of Defense*, (London: Hogarth Press, 1948).

4

Diseases of Defenses:
Too Much and Too Little

The history of cures for the diseases of the mind is not unlike the evolution of ideas of how to cure the body. Mental illness had been regarded as the intrusion of an outside force—like the germ on the biological level—variously understood to be a punishment of God, or an evil spirit, or even the devil himself. Freud's formulations, however, placed the enemy squarely within the psyche; his work paralleled the line of pursuit in the biological laboratory that focused on the terrain, the afflicted organism, rather than the invading germ.

In proposing the idea of psychological defense, Freud showed how defensive operations, supposedly erected to protect the organism, instead make up the nucleus of the disease. The work of psychoanalysis, then, is in good part an inquiry into why it is that the person is injured, rather than truly defended, by the defense mechanism.

In 1926, the same year in which Freud published *Inhibitions, Symptoms, and Anxiety* (where he first set forth the nature of the psychological defenses), two other researchers asked the parallel question on the level of the body. As a second year medical student, Hans Selye noticed that individuals suffering from a wide range of physical disorders all seemed to have a constellation of common symptoms: loss of appetite, decreased muscular strength, elevated blood pressure, and loss of ambition to accomplish anything. In puzzling over why these symptoms appeared, regardless of the nature of the somatic disorder, Selye labeled this condition the "syndrome of just being sick."[1]

Simultaneously, Walter Cannon first wrote about a phenomenon he termed *homeostasis*.[2] The concept had been studied earlier by Bernard, whose identification of the internal milieu—the biological representation of self—had led him to study the commerce between self and not-self on the biological level. Bernard had postulated a notion of biological stability, pointing out that the body tended to maintain constancy in its internal milieu, counteracting impinging external events. Cannon renamed the phenomenon, and continued Bernard's investigations. He emphasized the idea that in all open biological systems, there is a bilateral exchange between the organism and the environment, and that the organism wants always to return to the steady state that it is comfortable with. This biological desire becomes translated into real biochemical changes in response to the adaptational efforts of the body. Each of the body's regulatory and compensatory mechanisms are efforts to maintain the basic level of functioning of homeostasis.

Cannon was particularly interested in one particular aspect of this homeostatic phenomenon. He noticed that when the part of the body that we call the autonomic nervous system is activated, there is a typical response. He termed this response ''fight or flight'' and saw it as a primitive mechanism which involves the mobilization of the body to prepare for muscular activity in response to a perceived threat. This mechanism, then, permits the organism to either fight against or flee from the perceived threat.

Selye, in his early research, began looking for the hormone which was secreted during this autonomic nervous system response of fight or flight, the hormone which would trigger the reactivity of the body. He found a hormone which, when injected into the body, set up the chain of physiological responses that Cannon had observed in the fight/flight phenomenon. He termed this reaction a stress reaction—borrowing the term from physics and giving it the same meaning: a strain or pressure or force applied to a system. The stress reaction Selye found consisted of a stress ulcer. Through this discovery, Selye thought he had identified the hormone. Subsequent research, however, revealed that the application of a host of stimuli would cause this same stress ulcer—noise, x-rays, excess activity. Indeed, any stimulus which provoked the organism into its emergency fight/flight response was discovered to be a stressor.

Selye applied these findings to the notion of disease, and concluded that most diseases of organs and systems of organs of the body are diseases of adaptation. He points to various mechanisms that the organism resorts to in its effort to more successfully adapt itself, that is, return to homeostasis, and essentially arrives at Freud's understanding of the psyche's tendency to defend itself. In diseases of adaptation, as in the disease of neurosis, it is the defense itself which causes the disease. He explains:

> Many diseases . . . result from the body's own response to some unusual situation. . . . We have seen, for instance, that if a dirty splinter of wood gets under your skin, the tissues around it swell up and become inflamed. You develop a boil or an abcess. This is a useful, healthy response, because the tissues forming the wall of the boil represent a barricade which prevents any further spread throughout the body of microbes or poisons that may have been introduced with the splinter. But sometimes the body's reactions are excessive and quite out of proportion to the fundamentally innocuous irritation to which it was exposed. Here, an excessive response, say, in the shape of an inflammation, may actually be the main cause of what we experience as disease. . . . Could, for instance, the excessive production of a proinflammatory hormone, in response to some mild local irritation, result in the production of a disproportionately intensive inflammation, which hurts more than it helps? Could such an adaptive endocrine response become so intense that the resulting hormone-excess would damage organs in distant parts of the body, far from the original site of injury, in parts which could not have been affected by any direct action of the external disease-producing agent?[3]

Selye's observations clearly position him on the side of Bernard and Freud; it is mechanisms within the organism itself that lead to destruction. It is the *automaticity* of response for both Freud and Selye that defines the state of disease. For Freud, it is the way in which events take place automatically, without conscious direction, that gives the meaning of neurosis.[4] Similarly, Selye's description of the adaptational efforts of the body refers to an automatic physiological response that leads to injury of the organism. For both the mind and the body, the organism is damaged by the defensive mechanism itself when this response is uncontrolled and inappropriate to the stimulus.[5]

Selye's work converges with Freud's in yet another way, too. By studying the nature of the stressing agents, he was led to the idea that the particular character of the physiological changes resulting from stress was dependent on the dual variables of the duration of time and the intensity that the stress-provoking agent was applied. Freud's interest in this same question took the form of his reversal of the concept of trauma. The trauma, like the germ, was the application of one severe assault on the organism. Psychoanalytic treatment of patients revealed, however, that mental disorder could rarely be fit into so neat a package; rather, injuries to the psychic structure of the patient were usually chronic, subtle, and insidious. Furthermore, injury could only take place when the defensive apparatus was sufficiently weak so as to permit the damage. Selye observed, similarly, that in healthy persons even very severe stress presents no danger. If injury results, a healthy organism retains the ability to rally from the insult and limit the duration of this condition. While there may be an immediate outpouring of stress hormones in reaction to the stressing agent, causing a transformation of the nervous and chemical functioning of the entire organism, a healthy organism can quickly recover and return to its normal level of functioning once the stress agent is removed.

It is, then, in the imbalance between the potency of defense and the demands on it that the determination of disease is made. If the factors inhibiting disease formation, that is, the inherent powers of resistance that hold in check stressing agents, remain stronger than the power of the stressor, then health reigns. Conversely, if the stressing stimuli or predisposing factors dominate, disease ensues.

Diseases, then, can be categorized according to the ratio between the intensity and duration of the elicited defense mechanisms, and the intensity and duration of the stimulating agent. A stimulus becomes a stressor either because it has inherent properties which are absolutely destructive to all sensory and metabolic systems (as with caffeine, nicotine, amphetamines), or, because the individual assigns a cognitive interpretation of destructivity to it. Psychosocial variables, including our interactions with others, chiefly fall into the second category, and of course, these interpretations will vary widely from individual to individual. What may be a perfectly acceptable way of speaking to one person can be experienced by another as insulting, damaging, or critical. One man's pleasure is another man's poison.

Freud proved that it is not true that nature always knows best, and thus we should not always trust our instinctual and biological responses to situations. Both our bodies and our minds make mistakes; our bodies often react to stimuli as though they were dangerous when objectively there is no danger. Conversely, our immune system sometimes fails to take into account the presence of an intruder which in fact represents a life-threatening situation. So, too, on the level of the mind. We can cognitively perceive danger when there is none; we can assume safety when the situation is perilous.

There are few universal factors in the creation of disease. It is within the interplay of the opposing forces of stressor and defense against the stressor that disease and resistance to disease can be defined. There is only each individual organism's ability to withstand the vicissitudes of injury, those acquired both from ordinary living and from exposure to pathological stimuli arising from within and without.

Further elucidation of the nature of somatic disease came when the biological equivalent of Freud's repetition compulsion was discovered. Freud had noticed that his patients reacted to the present as though it were the past. It seemed as though the individual typically came to organize his cognitive experience of the world in some way that would then be repeated over and over again, even when the situation was objectively quite different and demanded quite a different interpretation. Thoughts and feelings, were often echoes of past experience rather than spontaneous responses to an ever-changing present.

Similarly, continuing Selye's line of research, Sternbach identified what he termed *response stereotypy,* in which the individual tends to exhibit a characteristic pattern of psychophysiological reactivity to a variety of stressful stimuli. Again, the nature of the particular stressor is unimportant; the reactivity seems to be a "predisposed response set."[6]

As researchers studied various organisms' coping capabilities, they noticed that the body's adaptability is finite. Exposure to stressing agents can be withstood only for so long. Eventually, if the stressor is applied with sufficient intensity or duration, the demand on the body exceeds its coping potential and exhaustion ensues.

The particular organ or system that most overtly manifests abnormality will determine the particular disease diagnosis. Arthritis, for instance, attacks the joints; muscular dystrophy settles in the muscles; arterial heart diseases reside within the arterial system; cancer is reflected most obviously in cellular dysfunction. Further specificity of disease can be determined by the stage the defense is in—the alarm phase, as in any inflammatory condition where there is overreactivity, or the exhastion phase, where there is underreactivity.

Diseases, reflect a condition of too much response, or not enough. Diseases are the organism's being out of touch with reality; the reaction to the stimulus reflects an incorrect evaluation of the danger or innocuousness of the stimulus. This psychotic process holds true whether the disease is of the body or the mind.

Selye's example of the inflammatory process gives us a clear picture of what happens when the body responds energetically to a stimulating agent. His observations follow a line of thinking originally formulated by Hippocrates. Hippocrates's understanding of how the body deals with foreign entities follows the model of how the body handles the foreign material of food. The disease material is cooked through the accompanying heat of the inflammatory process, and then subjected to pepsis, or digestion. At this point, the foreign material can either be overcome and assimilated (corresponding to breaking down and reabsorption in the digestive tract), or else there is a crisis and subsequent discharge to the outside (paralleling excretory elimination).

The research of Selye and others has confirmed the profound rightness of Hippocrates's observations. Inflammation, indeed, occurs whenever a foreign body or foreign process manifests itself in the organism. The foreign presence may be accidental (as in Selye's splinter), a physical invader from the outside (germs, viruses, and bacteria), or a disturbing psychosocial stimulus (as in the interaction between Michael Stewart and Pearl Pizzamiglio). Much more important, it occurs as a result of an internal dysfunction or disequilibrium. Sensing the foreign presence, the biological alarm system is set into motion. Recognition of not-self entities stimulates the production of antibodies; the number of lymphocytes rises; there is capillary activity and cell activation. In short, the state of the organism has become highly energetic. Inflammation is a healing reaction aimed at eliminating foreign or pathogenic substances or processes.

Inflammation can occur almost anywhere in the body, and as a reaction to almost any kind of stimulus, with a range of diversity as wide as from a particle of dust to an atomic explosion. It begins as a local reaction to injury. Its early description by Aurelius Cornelius Celsus in the Third Book of Treatise on Medicine, written a few years before the birth of Christ, is probably the most quoted sentence in medical writing: "Indeed, the signs of inflammation are four, redness, swelling, with heat and pain."[7] The reddening and heat are caused by a dilation of the blood vessels. Swelling is caused by both a leakage of fluids and cells from the dilated blood vessels and an intense proliferation of fibrous connective tissue, whose cells multiply rapidly in response to irritation. The pain is due to an irritation of the nerve endings which are involved in and invaded by the inflammatory process.

The location of the inflammation determines the disease: a particle of dust can get under the eyelid and cause an inflammation of the outer eye membrane called conjunctivitis; sore throat can produce a proliferation of certain microbes in the tonsils and cause inflammation of the tonsils called tonsillitis; inflammation of the appendix is appendicitis; of the peritoneum, peritonitis; of the liver, hepatitis; of the kidney, nephritis; of the joints, arthritis; of the nerves, neuritis; of certain portions of the central nervous system, poliomyelitis; of the inner surface of the heart, endocarditis; of the stomach, gastritis; of the skin, dermatitis; of the nasal mucosa, hay fever.[8]

The presence of a fever is a clear indication that the inflammatory process has generalized within the body. Fever evolved at least three hundred million years ago in cold-blooded vertebrates as a means of fighting invading organisms. It has developed into a response to any internal imbalance, whether the origin of the stimulus be internal or external. It is a good example of the supremely well-designed biochemical regulatory engineering of the human body.[9]

When the body becomes overly acidic or alkaline, the thyroid responds by increasing the metabolic rate and raising the body's temperature. Similarly, when an infection is detected by the body's immune system, activation of white blood cells occurs, and fever results. These activated white blood cells stimulate the release of a hormone called endogenous pyrogen, which travels through the bloodstream to the brain. Here, in the brain, the hormone acts on the hypothalamus, and the process of a thermostatic regulation between brain and body begins. Upon receiving the hormone's message the hypothalamus sets a new temperature for the body; the body responds with chills which forces it to raise its temperature to the new setting. Heat is produced through the constriction of blood vessels, through the breaking down of body tissue such as fat, and through rapid muscle contractions known as shivers.[10]

Fever, then, burns out the presence of the pathogenic material—that is, it changes the internal climate in a way that makes the body inhospitable to the infecting agent.[11] Fever is the body's natural chemotherapy. This regulatory aspect of the inflammation process can be disturbed in two ways. Either it can be cut short, as it commonly is through the outside agency of medication (aspirin), so this natural corrective process is curtailed before it has accomplished its restorative task; or, it can go on too long, and cause exhaustion from which it can be difficult to rally.

The newly acquired commercial availability of aspirin compounds in the 1800s abruptly changed medical opinion on fever and the inflammatory process. The two thousand year old notion that fever was usually a beneficial aspect of the inflammatory process was discarded, and the treatment of diseases through a controlled cultivation of that process was abandoned.[12] For the next one hundred years the focus was on bringing down fevers and inhibiting the inflammatory process through the use of medications.[13]

Aspirin was, of course, only the beginning. Antibiotics also have the effect of curtailing the healing power of inflammation. Antibiotics kill some microorganisms, too; but even this power is vastly overestimated.[14] Since the germ is involved in the disease only as agent and not as cause, it is probably ill-advised to concentrate our attack so entirely on it.

Indeed, recent research shows the pitfalls of such practices. Animals infected with bacteria have a higher death rate when treated with aspirin than when untreated. It turns out that aspirin interferes with the body's natural fight against viruses and bacteria for the same reason that it brings fever down. Aspirin blocks the output of prostaglandins, the chemicals which have the dual function of raising the temperature and allowing the body's natural antiviral substances, interferon and lysozymes, to act chemically on the infecting agent.[15]

In the case of antibiotics, most often when an inflammatory process is interfered with, it will return. We see this demonstrated in the fact that many patients must take repeated rounds of the drugs, in ever more desperate attempts to rid themselves of their disease. Treatment frequently drags on for much longer than had originally been planned, and so does the disease. Even more serious, however, is the fact that the body's natural defensive response to dangerous foreign entities can become permanently hampered to the point that it will no longer retain its capacity for reactivity. In weakening the development of its inflammatory reaction, the organism is made susceptible to even relatively weak pathogenic entities. Without the organism's capacity to defend itself, even a mild situation becomes much more serious, and develops ultimately to a life-threatening point.

As the overuse of antibiotics has weakened our own resistance, it has simultaneously strengthened that of the germ. Bacterial strains, in struggling for their own survival, have adapted easily to our usual arsenal of antibiotic armatorium and develops new, much more highly resistant versions of themselves. In Mexico, where antibiotics are acquired with great ease as over-the-counter drugs, laboratories have observed that one-fifth of *salmonella* strains are nonreactive to eight or more antibiotics. Central America has reported strains of resistant dysentery, and South Vietnam and Thailand have resistant typhoid fever strains.[16] Whatever efficacy judicious use of antibiotics may have had, it has now been, probably permanently, undermined.

Notes

1. Most of Hans Selye's research is represented in three works; beginning with his initial 1926 work, *The Stress of Life*, NY: (McGraw Hill, 1956). *Stress Without Distress* (Philadelphia: Lippincott, 1974) brings a more human element to his theories, through the application of his concepts to the interactions between people and to a philosophy of ethics. *Stress in Health and Disease* (Reading, Mass.: Butterworth, 1976) applies his notions to specific diseases.
2. Most of Cannon's research is represented in three works: W. B. Cannon, "The Emergency Function of the Adrenal Medula in Pain and in the Major Emotions," *American Journal of Physiology* 33 (1914): 356–72; *Bodily Changes in Pain, Hunger, Fear & Rage* (Boston: C. T. Bronford, 1953); and with D. Paz, "Emotional Stimulation of Adrenal Secretion," *American Journal of Physiology* 28 (1911): 64–70.
3. Selye, *The Stress of Life*, 128–29.
4. Sigmund, Freud. *Beyond the Pleasure Principle*, Trans. J. Strachey (NY: Liveright, 1950), 45.
5. Bakan, D., *Diseases, Pain, Sacrifice*, p. 22–31.
6. Sternbach first documented the response stereotypy: (R. Sternbach, *Principles of Psychophysiology* [NY: Academic, 1966]). Since his discovery, others have documented the phenomenon in both patient and normal populations. See, J. Lacey, & B. Lacey, "Verification and Extension of the Principle of Autonomic Response-Stereotypy," *American Journal of Psychology* 71 (1958): 50–73; R. Malmo, & C. Shagass. "Physiologic Study of Symptom Mechanisms in Psychiatric Patients Under Stress," *Psychosomatic Medicine* 11 (1949): 25–9; R. Moos, & B. J. Engel, "Psychophysiological Reactions in Hypertensive and Arthritic Patients," *Journal of Psychosomatic Research* 6 (1962): 227–41; M. M. Schnore, "Individual Patterns of Physiological Activity as a Function of Task Differences and Degree of Arousal," *Journal of Experimental Psychology* 58 (1959); 117–28.
7. F. Husemann, *The Anthroposophical Approach to Medicine*, revised by Otto Wolff, (Spring Valley, NY: *The Anthroposophic Press*, 1982), 163.
8. H. Selye, *The Stress of Life*, 163.
9. Ibid.

10. L. Jacobs, "Childhood Fevers," *East—West Journal* (April 1983): 15.
11. Ibid.
12. Ibid.
13. "Fever for Healing," *Cancer Forum* 3(718):7.
14. J. H. Alston, *A New Look at Infectious Disease* (London: Pitman, 1967).
15. L. Jacobs, "Childhood Fevers", 15.
16. Bernard, Dixon. "Overdosing on Wonder Drugs," *Science 86* 7:4 (May), 40.

5

The Psychological Impact of the Diagnosis

In the mid-1800's, at the Vienna General Hospital, there occurred an episode in the history of medicine that has become legendary. Ignez Semmelweis noticed that there were more frequent maternal deaths in the ward where physicians were delivering babies than in the one where midwives were being used. A chance event gave him the clue as to why this was occurring. Following an accidental cut from a scalpel that had been used in an autopsy, a colleague developed precisely the same illness that was killing many of the delivering mothers. Semmelweis reasoned that the illness was related to the autopsy, and assumed that some of the material from the cadaver had entered the bloodstream of his colleague through the open cut, infecting him with the fatal illness. Semmelweis concluded that the physicians were causing the diseases of the mothers by carrying the cadaveric matter on their skin from the autopsy room to the delivery room. Accordingly, Semmelweis required the procedure of hand-washing in a solution of chlorinated lime before delivering babies. The rate of maternal death on the physicians' ward immediately dropped to that of the midwives, who had not performed autopsies.[1]

As our medicines and medical procedures have become increasingly potent, the physician's ability to damage his patient has risen concomitantly. Studies on clinical iatrogenesis, the current name for this phenomenon, have found that patients suffer from drugs that are wrong, contaminated, or in dangerous combinations; surgical procedures that are unnecessary, and at times, create their own set of infirmities.[2] Radiation is a powerful carcinogen; chemotherapy is poisonous by definition. In fact, standard medical treatments for many disorders are either poisonous or potentially life threatening in some other way.[3] The trick to successful treatment seems to be to make sure that the damage of the treatment doesn't just replace the damage from the disease.

With the powerful weapons of drugs, surgery, and x-rays, it would seem that the power of the words of the physician pale in comparison. Moreover, the words of today's physician to patient tend to be quite sparse. The time that patients spend face to face with their physicians has been dramatically reduced as medical technology has burgeoned; in one study, the average visit was 1.7 minutes.[4]

The role of the physician is one that has become increasingly active. Since physicians first tasted the heady flavor of success in the use of chemicals to seemingly eradicate diseases, they have become ever more aggressive in their approaches. The physician will prescribe tests, order treatment interventions, monitor effects, change treatment, until he achieves efficacy—and this process is continued until the patient is dead, cured, or gives up the pursuit. Psychoanalysts spend more time with their patients than any other type of physician. They also do less since their only treatment intervention is the use of words. The role of the psychoanalyst, on the other hand, *is* to listen and talk. Yet, even a child knows that words have tremendous power to harm. We know very well that *sticks and stones may break my bones, but names will never hurt me* is the cry of one who has in fact been hurt by names.

Psychoanalysts have long been aware that some patients, when talked to in particular ways, get worse instead of better.[5] The mere act of explaining to patients the nature and causes of their illnesses— that is, the standard intervention in classical psychoanalysis, the interpretation—could be illness producing.[6] No matter how sympathetically or patiently one talked to these patients, they would experience the words as assaultive and would react as though they had been accused of wrongdoing and were damaged by the accusation.

Physicians treating patients for physical ailments have long noted the same phenomenon. Some patients, when forthrightly given their diagnosis and prognosis, flourish with the information; they see their disease as a challenge to master, take an active role in their treatment, and work cooperatively with their physicians. Others seem to crumble under the weight of the information, and many physicians witnessing this phenomenon became convinced that these adverse psychological reactions, at times, directly precipitated physical deterioration.[7]

Giving Name to Disease

Giving name to a disease, one of the initial tasks of the physician, can be the most significant communication the physician makes to his patient. The potential that this act carries with it for damaging the patient was made pointedly by Karl Menninger when he noted that the very word *cancer* is said to kill some patients who would not have succumbed (as rapidly) to the malignancy from which they suffer.

The ability to give patients detailed information about precisely what ails them is a modern convenience. While there were broad diagnostic categories in ancient medicine, criteria for specific diseases remained quite primitive. Galen had taught that the composition of urine bore a direct relationship to the composition of blood, and the taste, smell, and weight of urine was the only form of measurement available. By the sixteenth century, when specific gravity could be measured with precision, dozens of meanings had come to be attributed to the multitude of differences detected in the specific gravity of urine. This early emphasis on measurement, and the attribution of meaning to the nature of disease, set the stage for the shift in thought that culminated in giving diagnostic and curative meaning to any new measurement that was able to be performed.[8]

The use of measurements had an important role in the transition of thought that declared disease to be everpresent in the environment, simply waiting to invade and infect its victims. The first statistical study was done in the United States in 1721, published in London in 1722, and provided compelling evidence that the state of Massachusetts was being threatened by smallpox. Presumably, only those who had been innoculated would be protected.

At the point in history at which naming a disease seemed to bring confidence that such an act would lend power over it, physicians became more seriously interested in finding names consistent with their hopes for cure. Bleuler, a psychiatrist in the late nineteenth century and a teacher of Freud's, recognized the potential power of conceptualizing diagnoses in this manner. He objected to the term *dementia praecox* generally used to describe seriously disturbed mental patients, and sought a new label with more linguistic flexibility. *Schizophrenia* fit the bill; now the patient suffering from *schizophrenia* could be a *schizophrenic*. With this linguistic twist, the mentally ill became transported into a world of nonpersonhood.[9] Rather than being a person suffering from a disease, the term suggested that the individual had become identical with his disorder. The quantifier in *in remission* does nothing to restore to the individual his original identity. The term *schizophrenic in remission* leaves the patient forever tied to his disease, and though there may be no signs of symptomology, one anxiously and knowingly awaits their eventual return.

Bleuler's idea was not without precedent. From the beginning of history, man has had an intuitive understanding that there is great power embodied in the act of naming. Names have been thought to influence the nature of the person or the thing named. In one ancient system the verb *to be* and *to name* are the same word.[10]

The situation is scarcely different today. In modern times, the person who is assigned to find the correct name is the physician. The name looked for is the diagnosis of the disease, and once found, has all the power to assign its recipient a new identity. The accuracy of the name is essential, for both psychological and physiological reasons.

When the name given is that of a degenerative or recurrent disease, the psychological effect on the recipient is dramatic.[11] The person is transformed, in both his own mind and in the minds of others. From a state of relative health, he has joined the ranks of the sick and dying. Once touched with the name of a life threatening disease, he can never regain the state of innocence that he embodied before the diagnosis. Even if declared cured, there lingers the constant threat of the name once again, someday, being invoked to describe his state of being.

These issues become most poignant when the particular name given is cancer. It is for good reason that cancer has remained to considerable extent the unnamed disease. Until recently a cancer diagnosis was shrouded in mystery and secrecy. It was rarely communicated to the patient, and often the family, too, was excluded from the horrific news. The recent interest in humanizing the physician, and in improving their psychological relationships with patients, has led some to reexamine the ways they communicate to patients.[12] Most have concluded that it is best to be honest and forthright, and patients now receive frank information about their disease, the available treatments, and their chances for recovery.

Even so, the word itself is often not used. Other terms such as "tumor," "neoplastic disease," or the particular appellation given to the type of cancer (e.g., "lymphoma," "carcinoma," "Hodgkins")

are substituted. Similarly, newspaper obituaries have traditionally referred to death by cancer as a "prolonged illness." Those working in
the field typically avoid the direct use of the term, and instead, refer to
the abbreviated term, "CA."

By avoiding direct articulation of the name, we suggest that we
think that the act of conferring a name on the disease makes the disease
more real. A "tumor" feels to be a more manageable entity—
something more localized, less threatening. The term "cancer"
evokes a fundamental fear of death by torture, a slow, painful, eating
away of ourselves.

In spite of the fact that heart disease kills more people than cancer,
the disease does not evoke the same primitive terror. When hypertension patients are asked what causes their disease, most will reply
confidently that it is their nerves and diet; heart attack patients will
freely admit their lack of exercise as contributory. These patients
generally have a sense of their own contribution, through bad living
habits (diata), to the disease. They willingly confess that they themselves are the main cause of their disease. Further, the determination of
whether the disease will kill them is felt to be a matter of their own
making. They feel that it is within their power to reverse the course of
the disease. If they decide to continue to smoke, not exercise, and not
change their diet, they tend to accept that they've made a choice, and
that the disease is the inevitable, deserved consequence of this decision. In heart disease there is no cursing the gods.

The correctness of the name is crucial to the treatment of the
disease, as well.[13] Researchers have identified numerous separate disease entities, each with its own laws governing its growth, potential for
destruction, and most importantly, its susceptibility to medicines. We
have at our disposal abundant data as to which diseases respond in
what ways to the various treatment procedures, and it is through ever
closer approximation to successful good matches between the two that
researchers hope to improve medical treatment. In the case of cancer,
for example, some breast cancers are hormonally sensitive, while
others are not. One need not subject cancer patients to unnecessary and
perhaps ineffectual or damaging treatment in order to determine this
fact; cultures grown in the laboratory will confirm whether or not
hormonal treatment is the appropriate one. Because most cancer treatments are destructive to the patient, subjecting the patient to the wrong
treatment can kill rather than cure. In the case of heart disease,

diagnostic procedures can accurately pinpoint the precise location of the dysfunction. As in cancer, the success of these surgical interventions relies to a great extent on accuracy of the diagnosis. The treatment itself is life threatening, given the preexisting debilitated state of a patient who would require the dangerous risk of heart surgery.

Incorrect naming of the disease entity is no less a serious and punishable offense in our own culture than it was in ancient times.[14] The life of the patient may be dependent upon accurate diagnosis, and the healing practitioner is required to use all the skills available to his discipline in order to determine the correct name and the correct treatment. Choosing the wrong name, offering a misdiagnosis, can lead to the namegiver paying for his error, at best, through financial remuneration to the patient (or survivors), or loss of reputation, and at worst, revocation of permission for him to continue to practice his discipline.[15]

Especially troublesome for naming as a step in the treatment is the fact that the person who is assigned to find the name is the same person whose responsibility it is to tell the name.[16] The physician is both the diagnostician and the messenger of the news of the illness. Irrational though it surely is, it is impossible not to experience the bearer of bad news—if only for a moment, or only with a small part of ourselves—as an enemy, and the news as an assault. So the transmission of the finding demands particular talents and skills in addition to those required in making an accurate determination of the disease.

It is the physician who carries with him most of the available information about the patient's condition, and it is the physician who, as well, must decide how much of this information to communicate to the patient and in what manner. This issue is one that has not been scientifically explored, and thus, physicians are left on their own to wrestle with it each time anew.[17] Research three decades ago found that most physicians did not tell their patients that they had cancer, with one study showing this practice to be as high as 90 percent.[18] With the recent emphasis both on death and dying and on patient's rights and responsibilities, the direction has shifted, and more physicians are giving their patients a frank account of their diagnoses.

Physicians generally say that they treat each case on its own merit, and come to determinations based on their understanding of the individual case.[19] Factors physicians claim to consider in weighing the decision of how much to tell are judgments of the patient's likely reaction and coping mechanisms for dealing with the disease, the age of the patient, the prognosis, the physician's perception of the patient's awareness of his condition, and the socioeconomic status of the patient. However, determination of these factors is usually made on the basis of very limited contact. Most serious diseases are diagnosed not by the family physician but by a specialist who may scarcely know the patient. It is probably true that the determination of what to tell and whom to tell is usually made by subjective criteria on the part of the physician, rather than an objective study of the patient.[20]

Some physicians say that they impart information as it is requested, on the assumption that patients will ask to hear what they're interested in finding out about.[21] The assumption presupposes sufficient conscious awareness on the part of patients to be cognizant of what they want to know, in addition to the ability to translate this curiosity accurately into words.

Yet, in spite of physicians' avowed policy of evaluating each case separately, there's a good deal of evidence that in actual fact the policy followed is quite different. In the case of cancer, studies have shown that most physicians either tell their patients or don't tell their patients of a cancer diagnosis, and the practice seems to be based on some general principle of the physician's rather than an understanding of individual cases[22] (The obvious symptoms of heart disease make it mostly unnecessary for the physician to wrestle with this question, as most of his patients will correctly surmise the nature of their problem.)

Although differences among physicians in the practice of communicating or withholding information has been documented, relatively little research has gone into the question of why some are free with information and others more reticent. The research that has been conducted clearly indicates that medical training per se has little or nothing to do with determining how physicians handle telling cancer patients their diagnoses.[23]

Research and reason alike suggest that the emotional makeup of the physician is an important contributing variable. For instance, Medical researchers have reported the great sense of relief they felt upon the decision to abandon a project investigating the psychological reactions of cancer patients. They characterized the difficulty of tolerating the feelings stimulated as ''very nearly intolerable,'' and came to understand the psychological necessity for many of the defensive mechanisms physicians employ to prevent themselves from being contaminated by the distress of their patients.[24]

Psychoanalysts working with severely regressed neurotic and psychotic patients experience this same phenomenon of arousal of intense, often uncomfortable, feelings.[25] It seems to be the case that the more serious the disorder of the patient, the greater the potential for impinging destructively on the treating analyst. Psychoanalysts who have studied the phenomenon conclude that it is precisely on the management of these intense feeling states that the success or failure of the treatment rests.

Yet, in spite of the inherent difficulties of the physician's position, he must render his services as best he can. It is the unfortunate fact of the contemporary practice of medicine that physicians are not trained to know and be sensitive to the psyches of their patients, as well as to their bodies.

The Patient's Perspective

Patients, too, fall into different categories around the issue of knowing. Some want to know everything, some want to know nothing, and some want to know some things but not everything.

There are generally a limited number of questions which the patient is, at least initially, interested in having the answers to. These questions are in an order of interest to the patient, the answer to each question determining the next. The first question is, "Am I sick?" If the answer is affirmative, the next question follows: "Is it treatable?" If it is not, the next question becomes the final one in the series: "How long do I have?" An affirmative answer to the question of treatability leads to a whole new series of questions on the nature and duration of the treatment, and it is only when mutual understanding has been arrived at that the series of questions reaches its logical endpoint.

Patients complain about the interactive aspects of the doctor/patient relationship around these issues of diagnosis and prognosis. This complaint is most frequent when the prognosis is not a good one. When the news that must be conveyed is bad, there is little doubt that this is the most difficult aspect of the job for the physician, as well as for the patient. The difficulty arises, in part, from the intensity of the feelings that are aroused in both patient and physician. Defenses that had previously allowed each to successfully fulfill his respective role functions without intense emotional regression may now be broken through. The physician can no longer feel secure in his healing stance of administering treatments; the patient can no longer feel assured that his health and wellbeing are indefinitely extended into the future.

To add to the complication, even when the physician has both the emotional and philosophical understanding required to discuss sensitivity with the patient the patient's concerns, he may rely on cues from the patient in order to read how much the patient wants to know. But the behavior of the patient is not necessarily a good clue to the real intent of the patient. Some patients will follow the stepwise process of questioning, yet will stop assimilating the answers at some point in the sequence. The physician may take at face value the overt behavior of the patient, and be tricked into revealing information which is psychically unwanted.

A good example of this process is given by Lucien Israel. He reports on a patient who appeared to be stable and sensible. Responding to her rational behavior, he informed her in detail of her condition and the treatment that it called for. When that treatment failed, he found himself regretting his initial frankness because he knew that in now informing her of the necessity of changing the course of treatment he was, in effect, communicating to her a dire ultimate prognosis. But her cheerful response startled the physician by revealing a massive defense of denial: "I don't care about all that, Doctor, and I'll do whatever you want. Ever since you explained to me that I don't have cancer, I am ready for anything."[26]

It is helpful to consider that the patient who asks whether or not he has a disease is not precisely interested in the factual answer to that question. The intent behind the question is, rather, to learn whether the disease will pose a problem that will impinge upon the consciousness, becoming a matter of relevance and concern to the patient. If the physician is looking for nonverbal cues from the patient, on the assumption that a literal reading of the patient's stated concerns may be a subterfuge, then it is useful for him to attend to the manner in which the questions are asked.

Submission to the diagnostic procedure is usually the initial act of asking. Patients, however, agree to diagnostic tests for a variety of reasons, ranging from benign indifference to pathological preoccupation. Whether it is puzzling or worrisome symptoms, a routinely scheduled examination, or a life threatening crisis that has led to the procedure of diagnosis, the patient is behaving in a way that allows concern for his bodily condition. Too obsessive a concern may reflect Freud's principle that a fear is an unconscious wish, and death may be an unconsciously longed-for solution to intolerable suffering. Benign indifference may lead to a behavioral compliance in submitting to the procedure, perhaps to please a worried physician or spouse. Between these two attitudes lies a vast field of variability, including a healthy, attentive concern for one's well-being. The extent of authentic involvement with the diagnostic procedure is often a clue as to the true wish of the patient to know the nature of his disease.

Statistical research suggests that patients generally do want to be told of their disease, and that this desire holds true whether the disease is curable or incurable.[27] Statistical techniques for gathering data, however, may not be sensitive to unconscious conflicts, and again, we must consider that what the patient says may not be what, on another psychic level, he means. The frequency with which cancer patients have ambiguity about their diagnoses and prognoses suggests that this set of data is sensitive only to conscious desires on the part of the patient.

Physicians who respond to unconscious cues that the patient does not want to know, or who are constrained by their own emotional difficulty in revealing unhappy information, may decide to tell family members instead of the patient. The responsibility has, thus been shifted to those who the physician feels are in a better position to determine the strengths and weaknesses of the patient's coping mechanisms. Family members may or may not follow through on conveying information, depending on their own psychological coping capacities, and their real abilities to appraise the patient. Even when the physician makes a conscious choice to tell all, he may unwittingly communicate the information in a sufficiently ambiguous way that the patient is left confused, and without a clear understanding of the implications of his disease. And finally, even when information is communicated directly and unambiguously, the emotional defenses of the patient may be such that the information can simply not be psychologically processed.

In each of these cases, there is generally arousal of feeling between those who have been given diagnostic and prognostic information, and those who haven't. Often the feeling aroused is aggressive, and may remain unconscious. Those who are placed in the position of having the information will frequently have a wish that the patient know the information without their having to take the uncomfortable role of telling. The physician or the family member wants the patient to be psychic, and will, in fact, often treat the patient as though he were psychic, and did know without having to be told. It is not an uncommon topic of conversation among those who know to assess how much the patient has figured out. It can even become a badge of merit for the patient when the speculation concludes that "he really does know." If the patient insists on being "stupid" however, and not knowing, those who know may experience the patient as being uncooperative or burdensome.

But in fact the word "know" is of questionable utility here. Patients, by persisting in asking questions on diagnosis and prognosis, and physicians, with consequent persistence in answering these questions, both behave as though there were actual definitive answers that are capable of being known. But the problem of how much, and how, to tell is rendered even more complex by the inherent ambiguity of the cancer situation and the effects of the treatment. In spite of the patient's wish to have his questions answered, and in spite of the physician's wish to be able to answer these questions, the questions are often inherently unanswerable in any meaningful way. The best that can be given is a close approximation of expectations based on statistical probability. The experience and intuition of the physician may add to the probable chance of a successful evaluation and predictive capacity, but we must never forget that this is the practice of an imperfect art, not of precise science.

When the patient asks whether or not he has a disease, he uses the diagnostic label as though it were a defined and discrete entity. In the practice of diagnosing and treating an illness, there is a great advantage that is given in the act of conferring a name. The diagnosis yields an organizing principle to otherwise chaotic data.

However, diseases are not, as a diagnostic label can lead us to believe, fixed conditions. They are processes in a living, everchanging organism. Disease conditions can come and go, with or without treatment, with or without our ever knowing that they are there. If the disease stays around long enough to produce noticeable and disquieting effects, the determination of a diagnosis does not always lead to advantage. Diagnoses are notoriously unreliable entities. Many a cancer patient has been given a clean bill of health immediately preceding a subsequent diagnosis of a lethal and rapidly growing cancer. The pervasive inaccuracy of laboratory reports is telling evidence of the potential meaninglessness of a diagnosis. Laboratory reports, upon which treatment depends, have been shown to have significant error rates, for both cancer and heart disease.[28]

Further, many diseases initially look alike, as Selye astutely pointed out. It is only very late in the game, when differential deterioration has set in, that symptoms become specific enough to attribute labels to the process. The fact that experts frequently disagree on diagnoses has led to the now routine practice of seeking second opinions. When given the same set of x-rays on different occasions, specialists changed their minds on their readings in 20 percent of the cases.[29] One quarter of simple hospital tests, when performed from the same sample but by different labs, have shown seriously divergent results.[30]

Machines do not improve the situation. Pathologists evaluating diagnoses made by both machines and physicians found both to be correct together in only twenty-two of eighty-three instances; the physicians correctly rejected the computer's diagnosis in eleven cases and the computer correctly rejected the physician's diagnoses in thirty-seven instances; both were in error in ten instances.[31]

The fact that diagnoses are often inaccurate becomes anguishingly important when the diagnostic procedures themselves cause disease. Mammography, for instance, can lead to cancer, and the uncovering of this fact has led physicians to reformulate their recommendations for this test that was performed routinely on so-called high-risk women for many years of medical practice. The widespread administration of this cancer-inducing treatment has produced a pool of data from which it's no longer possible to tease out true high-risk patients from those whose cancers may be effects from the diagnostic tests.

Even where cancer is correctly diagnosed, the evaluation of danger to the patient remains difficult to assess. The diagnosis of cancer is arrived at through the identification of the entity of the cancer cell—full-fledged cancer cells do have characteristics that distinguish them from other cells. We generally think that we either have cancer or we don't—a cell is either a cancer cell or it is not, and if it is, then we worry about the implications. This distinction, however, is not always as clear-cut as we would like to believe.

In point of fact, the determination of a cancer condition is an ambiguous affair. There are a host of variables that add to the ambiguity. First, there is some question about whether or not a cancer cell is a fixed entity. Cancer cells are living organisms, and like all other living organisms, they exist in a state of flux. Cells move organically from one state to another, and reflect varying degrees of "cancerness," from not cancerous at all, to precancerous, to a full-fledged cancer cell with all of the typical attributes of a cancer cell.

Accurate determination of the presence of cancer cells is not necessarily cause for great alarm. There is no evidence that the changes in cells from noncancer to cancer is unidirectional. The frequency of remissions certainly suggests otherwise; cancer cells can either revert back to normal cells, or at least, be effectively neutralized so as not to cause damage to the host organism. The presence of cancer cells may or may not lead to a more advanced stage of cellular disturbance. Even when cancer cells have reached the advanced stage of diagnostic detection, the natural strength and resiliency of the whole organism can cause a return of cancer cells to a normal state.

Treatments, like diagnostic procedures, can be damaging. Most chemical and radioactive treatments of cancer lead to secondary cancers. The never-ending search for the omnipotent drug has led to a situation where patients have become human guinea pigs, testing each laboratory's new arsenal of drug therapy. It is not unusual to see a patient taking a plethora of drugs, one to combat the toxic effect of another. Hypertension patients have been converted into cancer patients through their ingestion of medicines.

The question of whether most of the diseases that we suffer from are treatable at all is by no means a simple one. More people than ever are dying of heart disease. The official word about cancer is that great inroads have been made in its treatment. The truth is that only the skin cancers and childhood leukemias have improved their status. Advances in diagnostic procedures, as we have seen, have led to earlier detection, and there is now a much larger pool of patients to be included in the data. Cancer cure is medically defined as a five-year survival rate from the time of diagnosis, and earlier detection makes it easier to fit into this protocol of cure.

There is no certain way of predicting what effect any given treatment will have on a biological system. Patients do, of course, want and ask their physicians to be soothsayers, and to predict their futures to them. Each biological organism has inherent strengths and weaknesses that will determine how it responds to any intervention. Medical science has come a long way toward being able to determine the genetic and constitutional makeup of individuals that reveal its biological destiny. But we have not yet reached the point where we can say with any assurance the effect of either physical or psychological treatments on a disease condition. The best we have, on the physical level, is statistics; on the psychological level, we barely have even that.

The Physician's Feelings

While there has been no experimental research to guide physicians on the effect of the patient having been told diagnosis and prognosis, we do have psychoanalytic data on patients suffering from both physical and psychological diseases. The clinical literature provides a wealth of information about patients' emotional and cognitive grappling with the implications of their diseases. These in-depth analyses of patients' conscious and unconscious concerns and conflicts give us a valuable research tool for understanding the effect of information on the mind. They have also given us a therapeutic tool to aid the patient in removing barriers in coming to terms with the full awareness and meaning of his disease and suffering. As a result of these studies, we have come to a clearer understanding of when, how, and with whom, information should be shared.

One of the founding insights of the school of therapy called modern psychoanalysis was Hyman Spotnitz's recognition that the interpretive work of classical psychoanalysis—telling disturbed patients the ways in which they were sick and why—was often far more damaging than helpful.[32] Through this, he was led to a careful study of the defenses. Freud had, of course, understood the necessary function of defenses in the development of disease. Though he had some glimmering of the idea that he himself could be a toxic stimulus (he did contraindicate psychoanalysis for the treatment of certain classes of regressed patients and warned that the treatment might exacerbate the disturbance), he had more than enough to accomplish in one life's work in consolidating and clarifying the vast advances he had made; this idea among others he perforce left to future generations to develop.

Spotnitz hypothesized that the defenses, erected to ward off toxic stimuli in infancy, were just as necessary in adult life, and especially in such highly charged relationships as those involving the patient's own sense of self-definition and well-being; for example, that between analytic patient and therapist, and undoubtedly, that between patient and physician. The highly narcissistic patient, in a state of self/not-self fusion and hardly able to distinguish between people at all, would be highly infused with aggressive impulses. And wouldn't his narcissism lead him to attribute these same aggressive inclinations to the analyst, as well?

Perhaps the most enlightening of the findings of the modern psychoanalytic school is that consciously and unconsciously communicated attitudes and feelings could prove more powerful than any specific informational content of an interpretation. The implications of this finding were extraordinary, for it meant that physicians were not able to hide comfortably behind their masks of professionalism. Sensitive patients were picking up feelings from their physicians and often, these nonverbal modes of communication were more powerfully felt by the patient than the words themselves.

It had long been known that the expectations and attitudes of the physician could influence physical states in patients. This phenomenon, known as the placebo effect, is one of the most documented in all medical and psychological literature.[33] It was by observing phenomena of this kind that analysts were led to study the ways in which their own feelings were being subtly, and at times unwittingly, communicated to their patients. The phenomenon of countertransference—the feelings of the analyst to his patient—was thoroughly reformulated as a result, and resolved into subjective and objective countertransference. It was true that some of the analyst's feelings were the result of his own unresolved conflicts, and these could get in the way of the treatment. There were others though, and these tended to be the more intense feelings, that were stimulated directly by the patient and related to the patient's character, not the analyst's. These were *objective countertransference*, and proper understanding of these feeling states, induced by the patient, could be utilized as valuable allies in the treatment.

Spotnitz was led, then, to the concept of *right* feelings. The patient needed the communication of very specific feelings from the analyst in order to get well. Which particular set of feelings were curative was determined by the history of the patient, and varied from patient to patient. Interestingly, the feelings necessary for cure were not always positive; in the cases of the most regressed patients especially, it seemed that the communication of negative feelings was often a more effective therapeutic tool.

This idea revolutionized the practice of psychoanalysis. If the success of the treatment depended on the analyst having a certain set of feelings, and the nature of the required feelings changed from patient to patient (depending on the emotional needs of the individual patient), then the analyst had become a patient of sorts. The analyst's task would be, first, to remove any barriers that he might have to the experiencing of all feelings, then to sort through those induced in him for the ones that would be curative, and to express those appropriately while tolerating the others without expression. Given the power of emotions to evoke responses—often so subtly it feels like ESP, though it needn't be—this task may never be perfectly done. Yet the balance can be kept heavily on the therapeutic side, and much can be accomplished by proper preparation and supervision.

The feelings of the physician, as well as creating a placebo effect on the patient, can produce a "nocebo" effect.[34] Physicians damage as well as heal, and not only with their medicines; their words and their feelings, both spoken and unspoken, can be equally injurious.

Spotnitz has argued for a rigorous study of the toxic, as well as the constructive, effect that the verbal communications of a physician may have on the patient:

> Consistently constructive emotional interchange with our patients and the elimination of errors that are grossly contrindicated would be facilitated by the development of a science of *toxipsychology,* which would perform a service similar to that of toxicology in clinical medicine. I anticipate that toxipsychology will eventually come into being and provide vital information will eventually come into being and provide vital information about the toxic effects of certain psychological communications and attitudes, in contradistinction to therapeutic psychology and psychotherapy. As this knowledge of therapeutic versus toxic psychology and psychotherapy accumulates, it is reasonable to assume that psychotherapy in the many areas of psychological and psychosomatic illness will become more efficient.[35]

The Mysterious Case of an Ichabod Crane
(Whose Defense of Denial Probably Saved His Life)

Ichabod Crane is the unsophisticated non-hero of the *Legend of Sleepy Hollow.* Compared with his enemy he is under-horsed, physically inferior, and hardly clever in battle. Until his final race he does not even believe that his enemy is real. He does, however, have the nerve to keep going, whether this is born of naivete or fear. It seems a miracle that he makes it across the covered bridge, although in the end, there is no certainty about his fate or, indeed, about the reality of the Headless Horseman himself.

This is a case history of a certain commonplace man, Carl, who developed a malignant tumor of the pancreatic islet cells during his late fifties. The case is of particular interest because it is the story of a man whose cancer surely should have killed him, but somehow did not.

Carl's unconscious self has made use of denial as a mainstay defense mechanism throughout life. It was not surprising, therefore, that he initially denied the cancer and settled for an "obstruction" as a diagnosis. What was surprising, however, was the extensiveness and the depth of his failure to know so much of what was going on, and also his persistence in that unknowing through time.

Health care professionals are taught that a person with cancer who is using denial, for example, is denying (unconsciously) the fact of the cancer. Analytic theory seems to say that an appropriate therapeutic intervention would be to help him work through this unconscious stance toward the illness. If one believes that denial is harmful in some way and that denial in the hospitalized cancer (or cardiac or orthopedic) patient is stimulated by the cognitive awareness of himself as a diseased person, altering the denial might be a logical therapeutic approach to reinstating a reality-oriented integrity. That is to say, one might treat the patient as if his psychological reaction was an undesirable response to his disease state because it prevents him from coming to grips with reality.

From another point of view, one could hypothesize the whole, immediate life situation, rather than the diagnosis and its meaning for the future, as the stimulus or unconscious defense mechanism. In the case of a hospitalized patient, this stimulus would include the hospital and the treatment, as well as the disease. One could also view the evoked defense as beneficial or perhaps, necessary in the presence of a noxious stimulus.

From this alternative perspective, one could argue that when a person is in the hospital, he might need to begin denying what was happening to his human dignity as a healthy way of remaining integrated. From the first implications of eating in bed, to sharing living space with a stranger during a time of stress, to finding out that the flu is really cancer, it seems that denial might as easily block out all awarenesses, as well as only one or two. Once denial is operating it behaves like the unsophisticated chemotherapy agent, which effects nearly every cell in one way or another. Making this kind of paradigm shift, one might then see the therapeutic task of changing the environment and leaving the patient's defenses against it undisturbed.

There are fascinating studies of what happens to people in intensive care units which support this alternative viewpoint. For example, postoperative psychoses as well as other noticeable personality changes of a less severe nature have been observed in patients who have had open-heart surgery. At one time it was thought that some type of oxygen deficit during surgery, some other chemical problem attributable to the surgery, or the heart-lung machine was responsible. New work, however, suggests that it is the intensive care unit itself combined with the stress of surgery that is causing the changes. Documented effects of the intensive care unit on patients are illusions, auditory and visual hallucinations, and paranoid delusions of a transient nature. While being hospitalized on a medical unit does not comprise a threat of the same intensity as being hospitalized on an intensive care unit, it too is a powerful psychological event that is finally coming under serious scrutiny in nursing research.

Kubler-Ross's psychological stages of denial, aggression, depression, and acceptance may be useful or nonuseful responses to a life threatening situation such as a fatal illness. Regardless of the usefulness of the response in relation to the diagnosis, it may not be emotionally possible for the person to stop denying the nature of the disease if turning off that denial also means turning off his unawareness of his current life circumstances in the institution. To put it another way, the person who admits to himself that he is dying of cancer may also have to admit to himself that he is an unfree person in a potentially unsafe situation, dependent upon strangers who regard him as a work object. Acknowledging his illness, he may also begin to see and acknowledge the incompetence of the staff, the callousness in the system, and the misery of the patients around him. Denial is not a particularly selective force. It is very hard to stop denying some things and maintain the unknowing about others. Perhaps it is better in some circumstances to stay dumb all around.

Carl maintained his unknowing across the board. He never felt that there were problems with his medical care or with the hospital regime. Although he was told explicitly that he had cancer he did not attend to or perceive the word for about two months. Maybe that was just as it should have been. Through the most desperate period of his illness the only thing that kept him going was his belief that what he had was a terrible case of pneumonia, and he knew of many (including an infant son) who has survived that. One wonders whether he could have kept eating, turning, getting up for inhalation treatments, and so forth if he also knew that he had a futile, fatal disease. It is possible that his denial saved his life. The same denial has also caused serious interpersonal problems for him. One would not recommend it as a panacea.

During this time he not only denied the fact of cancer, he also failed to see meaning in what was happening to his body before his very eyes. In December, he was critically ill, losing weight at a frightening rate and requiring a transfer to the state medical center, but he was asking for a chainsaw for Christmas. In January when he was cachexic and barely able to feed himself, he began planning a fruit orchard which he intended to plant that spring. The impact of changing from a durable backpacker to a person who fell over trying to put on slippers and then couldn't get up did not impress itself. The situation was cooled of its existential meaning and was dealt with as an engineering problem.

I fell down twice while I was in the Medical Center. The first time, I had gotten out of bed to sit in the chair looking out of the window. I was putting on my robe and turning around at the same time, missed the chair, and went down. No harm done except that a nurse heard the commotion and came flying in. The next time I was sitting on the side of the bed feeling around with my toes for my slippers. One had gone partly under the bed and reaching for it I went off on the floor. No one heard this except my roommate. I figured I'd get up before anyone came in and grabbed the wheel of the bed to pull myself up. But the wheel turned. There was a brake lever. I pulled that to lock the wheel, but this time the wheel swiveled. Meanwhile my roomie was pushing his call button hard enough to dim the lights in the operating room and in came a nurse and a big Negro orderly. He scooped me up in his arms an popped me back in bed with the comment, "We're trying to put you back together, not break you apart!"

From the point of view of the outsider, denial was at work in every conscious fact of his life. From his point of view, however, life at that time was a series of mountainous problems which could not be denied or ignored. From his perspective, the realities of life were these:

1. Eat! (Even though I can't open the milk carton much less cut the chicken from the bone.) Eat more than I want because there is no snack between now and dinner. Eat even though the tray is going to sit here stinking for an hour after I'm done.
2. Keep track of the aide I saw trying to steal my watch.
3. Keep track of time by remembering the meals (now that my watch is at home). Try to figure out what happened yesterday when dinner came after breakfast, missing lunch entirely.
4. Keep track of the old man in the next bed who talks about suicide after his sons leave.
5. Keep your wife and kids from causing trouble with the doctor.
6. Remember to tell the aide not to fill the water jug so full and not to put it out of reach.
7. Figure out how many days of sick leave and how much insurance money are left.
8. Before turning over remember to think for a bit about which arm to move first so I don't get stuck like yesterday unable to move or get the call button.

Looking at the world from this personal perspective, Carl was not denying much at all. Philosophical considerations of life and death take a back seat when simply turning from one side to the other requires at least five minutes of sustained mental and physical effort, causes pain everywhere, and demands a conscious memory for the correct placement and sequence of hands and knees. Denial from one point of view may be irrelevance from another.

In the case of Carl, his strong mental set of not knowing brought many problems with it, both for himself and for others in the family. For him there was a tense, almost fierce (if one can be fierce and debilitated at the same time) determination about him. There was, of course, a need for constant effort just to keep going. The fact that the tension came partly from the denial is clear from the periods of relaxation and sleep that followed the infrequent breaks in unknowing. The few months when he openly asked for help or prayer or experienced relief for having made it past a certain milestone were moments of deep feeling. In these moments he was in touch with the truth of the situation as others knew it to be. His experience of closeness to death was awesome for those at hand.

His ability to not know, in other words, was pervasive but not universal. His dreams particularly revealed an unconscious awareness of the seriousness of the life threat and of the overwhelming proposi- tions of trying to struggle against it. There was an evolution in his dream toward a clearer definition of reality. The changes in his dreams coincided with an increasingly conscious awareness of his uncertain circumstances and, paradoxically, with an improvement in his physical condition. The following dream occurred so often that at one point he dreaded going to sleep for fear of having to go through it again.

He dreamed that he had to do something and that he was struggling very hard to do it. In some dreams he didn't know what it was he had to do, while in others there was a specific task. Always, however, something would come in the way of doing what had to be done. The thing that came in the way was horrible but had no specific shape or identity. He had no image of the thing but was aware of the feeling of horror and dread that it stirred up. In another version of this dream he was trying to do a task that involved walking past a certain pole that looked harmless, but was really an antimatter pole. In this dream the pole was absolutely horrible in feeling and there was no way to complete the utterly compelling task without walking past it. The dream was so frightening and frustrating that it often woke him up (These dreams continued for several months during which time he was taking Percodan. Percodan is an addictive pain medication, but he used it only at night believing that it was a sleeping pill.).

He told the dreams as if they were a curiosity and saw no meaning in them himself. They are dreams in his own symbolic currency of work and effort, containing perhaps to those who read this, powerful sym- bols which describe the stance of his conscious life in relation to cancer. On an unconscious level he knew that he was going about his business in the very face of antimatter.

Another dream that came later in the summer is more explicit and full of detail. At this point he was getting around by himself and was recovered from the more urgent effects of the hospitalization, but he was certainly not getting better in the sense of progressing past mini- mal independence. He was receiving minimal chemotherapy without side effect or benefit, and he seemed to be at a skeletal standstill. He dreamed that he and his young son-in-law (who, in fact, resembles Carl in several ways) were trying to put a heavy box on a high shelf in the basement work room. Carl was lifting the box alone. It became too heavy for him and began to fall down on top of him. When he turned to George to ask for help he saw that George had turned into a werewolf. The dream was terribly frightening.

This dream also involves the sense of going about one's business as usual, doing one's work. But there comes the recognition that not only is one's body inadequate to do the job, but (in the dream-form of George's body) is transformed into a monster and adversary. The life-threatening element is no longer an abstract, harmless-looking rod whose killing powers are perceived only from an intellectual knowledge of it. The life-threatening element in the form of a werewolf was just as deadly, but it also reveals itself in the way it appears, in the way it changes from friend to foe. In the first dreams he had only to avoid a pole to stay safe, even though it engendered fear and frustration by standing in the way of completing necessary work. In the last dream he was caught between the heavy box crushing him and the werewolf eating him alive. The sense of being trapped and of disappearing alternatives is apparent in the progression of the dreams.

As the sequence of the dreams suggests on an unconscious level, Carl consciously began to acknowledge the reality of his situation over a period of time. Six months after the surgery, when he was past the crisis point, he began to acknowledge in conversation that his life might be in danger, statistically, since his own father had died of cancer. He did not feel, however, that dying of cancer was a realistic possibility for him. Three years later he speaks with awe about the closeness of his brush with death. The denial, it seems, worked when it had to, by protecting him from giving up, and receded when there was mental space to cope with reality. As he became healthier, he could grapple with the possibilities of dying. It seems uncertain that therapeutic intervention to help him overcome the denial would have been of any service to him. He was aware at brief, discrete intervals of how near the edge he was. Bringing this awareness into conscious interpersonal communication, however, would seem to have weakened what grip he had left for hanging on.

The other side of belief, namely disbelief, was important to the preservation of his faith in his ability to recover. Of course disbelief should not be confused with denial even though, in this situation, they did coincide regarding Carl's outlook on cancer.

While Carl did not believe in cancer as a fatal illness for him, he did (and still does) believe in heart attacks. If he had become equally as sick from a heart attack, his family believes he would have died of it.

Carl has been an employee of a large American conglomerate corporation for more than twenty-five years. This company has pioneered some of the practices in employee health care which are now standard in this country. Beginning in 1955, when he was thirty-nine years old, Carl was asked by his company to participate in a longitudinal study of diseases affecting executives. This invitation coincided with a promotion and a transfer to division headquarters in Chicago. He was among the young or potential "executives," that is to say "victims." An extensive physical exam was done each year for a period of ten years or so. Among other tests, an EKG was done during each two-day exam.

Being part of the "heart attack study," as the employees called it, made an impression on him and on the entire family. His own fears about ill health tended to be expressed in terms of a heart attack, rather than any other type of illness. Both his own father, and his father-, and brother-in-law had died of cancer. These experiences, however, were not as personally impressive in terms of his own health as the repeated two-day medical examinations for the "heart attack study." Furthermore, he had been keenly impressed by Eisenhower's heart attack. For him, Eisenhower was a giant figure and the power of a heart attack to strike this man even as he held the highest office made it a sure embodiment of death. In terms of the illogic of the unconscious, one might escape the diseases of mortals like one's aging father but one could not escape a disease that could strike at the gods. To put it another way, cancer might have been able to "get" him physically, but it couldn't "get" him psychologically because he did not believe in it, unconsciously, as a reality. He believed in something else (and still does): namely, heart attacks. The sense of his resemblance to Ichabod Crane lies partly in this disbelief in his pursuer.

Among professionals, lay friends, and family members alike, there is a consistent belief that Carl is alive today because of his unrelenting drive for physical activity. His desire and struggle for physical activity are related in some ways to the denial, since many of the things he worked so hard to do while he was sick would have made no sense if he had believed he was dying. He had a number of long range projects underway at home at the time of the first surgery and he automatically assumed that he would go back to work on them as soon as he got home. Actually, he continued the mental work, in terms of planning and decision making while he was still in the medical center. His conversations were reminders of a story about an American war prisoner who stayed sane by planning every detail of his dream house during his brainwashing imprisonment. Although Carl began at one point to become disoriented regarding the time of day and the day of the week, he could talk lucidly about the fruit orchard he intended to plant. While his conversations about long range physical labor-intensive projects were ludicrous and maddening to the family members, and labeled by them as straight-out denial or brain metastases, these conversations could also be seen as a healthy means of remaining psychologically integrated.

Carl's professional work involves repairing and designing modifications for enormous heavy industry machinery. While he does some desk work each day, he also does a great deal of walking about the factory.(Other workers in his kind of position ride golf carts or bicycles from one point in the plant to another.) At home, he spends most of his waking hours in his workshop on intricate and demanding projects. For example, he has an old car which he has been restoring himself for fifteen years, and is designing and building a four cylinder steam engine by hand. While he was still ill, he began digging and laying a system of clay drains around the farm house, and building a guest house on top of the garage. There are a half-dozen smaller projects, as well as the restoration of the bicentennial farmhouse, which requires every repair that there is. As one might guess, his physical activity is closely linked with the maintenance of a familiar body image. Since he knows himself so much through his work, the planning and doing of physical work during illness was a way of staying psychologically whole as well as of discharging frustrations, of experiencing his powers, and therefore of fighting the depression that he felt about being so sick, weak, and thin.

It remains to be learned whether physical activity in itself does anything to stimulate the body to fight cancer. If nothing else, it indirectly promoted physical health, perhaps allowing the body to then fight the cancer in some unrelated way.

While he was in the Medical Center, he forced himself to turn and move about in bed even though he was painfully frail. Besides avoiding a stasis pneumonia, his ability to push himself kept him alive by keeping him fed. By the time he was discharged from the medical center it took him about thirty seconds of effort to spear a piece of lettuce on a fork, and that was after he got the fork up to the plate. He did not have the strength to open the milk carton by himself, and the coordination required to spoon soup was out of the question (The soup was out of the question anyway because it came with a tight foil lid that took two hands and strong nails to open. The soup inside stayed hot, though.). He could have gotten someone to feed him, but since it took a long time for him to chew and he had to rest between bites, it would have meant less food in the long run. An aide would not be able to spend an hour with a "feeder." He would have been patiently rushed through a few bites of each thing and the tray taken as she left.

Besides keeping him fed, his ability to push himself helped him regain muscle strength. Once he got home he decided, within two or three weeks, to start going down to the basement work room. The family was decidedly against it. Falling in the bedroom was one thing. But falling down the basement stairs was something else. Nevertheless he began the month-long attack on the stairs by going down three steps with his wife holding onto him, resting against the wall for a few minutes, going down the next three steps and sitting on the landing for ten minutes, and so forth to the bottom. At that point he walked a few steps to the playroom couch and slept the rest of the afternoon. Going back up was much slower. At the end of about a month of building up to it he was able to go downstairs unassisted, poke around in the shop for ten minutes, and sleep on the couch for an hour to recuperate. Then he would come back up with his wife steadying his balance from behind. Whatever being busy in the shop meant for him, it must have been impressive to warrant that kind of strain.

Although it would have been much easier physically on both him and his wife, he absolutely refused to have a hospital bed, wheelchair, or even an overbed table at home. The implication of these items—that he was physically unable—was just too obnoxious. He also wanted to establish a clear break with the hospital, regardless of the pain and effort involved in getting into and out of a flat bed. Perhaps a very strong need for physical activity involves a diminished sense of the awfulness of physical discomfort.

Once he was able to leave the house by himself, he began driving out to the farm. Once he got there, it took him six months of daily effort to complete what he could have done in two weekends the year before. It was painful to watch him. There was no joy in the exertion, only grimness. He had to set up a long beach chair out there to rest on since the drive of twenty minutes over dirt roads was exhausting in itself.

On the one hand he seemed to be a lunatic. He certainly looked like a lunatic, emaciated and in work clothes leaning on a shovel. The effort he expended was out of all responsible proportion to the results he obtained. On the other hand, he did get stronger, the projects did get done (eventually) and he never turned into an invalid. His surgeon wrote at one point:

> One thing I can tell you about him; he is a very determined, cooperative man that has good will power and wants to get well. He loves physical activity and even in those darker days he was looking forward to seeing his farm and doing some work. Maybe that might have something to do with his unusual recovery.

> Why he should get well after being signed out as a terminal carcinoma of the pancreas is a mystery to me. Medications that I used on him could be counted on one hand. I was sure that some tumor was left behind at the time of the operation. I suspect that his immunity took over, but I certainly cannot explain the dramatic result.

By the summer of 1978, Carl had been working fulltime for a year. He went on a victory hike in Yosemite and Kings Canyon, crossing several high passes. He hiked for five days at altitudes over 6,000 feet carrying a forty pound pack. The pace was slow but comfortable, with grandchildren along.

He remained healthy until the summer of 1980 when another obstruction developed just beyond the pylnas. Surgery and cell studies revealed a large metastasis of undifferentiated tumor contained primarily behind the bowel. Once again, after grim forecasts and an uneventful recovery, he is gaining weight, working fulltime and receiving the same minimal chemotherapy at weekly intervals. He is beginning to become interested in nutrition in the hopes of avoiding repeated surgery.

And this is the conclusion of the mysterious case of Ichabod Crane, a middle-aged engineer turned farmer who somehow made it through the covered bridge with his head and life intact. The unreal, illogical quality of his recovery lends the feeling at times that, like Ichabod, he made it because of terrific effort, luck, and a certain lack of belief in the power of the enemy. One hopes that writing about these events does not tempt fate or break the spell for him, but only serves to benefit others living now in Sleepy Hollow.

Notes

1. G. Gortvay, and I. Zoltan. *Semmelweis, His Life and Work* (Budapest, Akademiai Kiado: 1968). Or, for a novelistic treatment of Semmelweis: M. Thompson, *The Cry and the Covenant*. NY: New American Library, 1973.

2. R. H. Moser, *The Disease and Medical Progress: A Study of Iatrogenic Disease,* 3rd ed. (Springfield, IL.: Charles Thomas, 1969).

3. D. M. Spain, *The Complications of Modern Medical Practices* NY: Grune and Stratton, 1963), 3–16.

4. H. G. Overrath, and W. and U. Thure, "Organisations Problem der Arztlechen Krankenversorgung: Dargestellt am Beispiel Einer Medizinischen Universitatskli Nik," *Deutsches Arzteblatt - Arztliche Mitteilungen* 71 (1974): 3421–6.

5. The toxicity of the psychoanalyst has been an active area of interest for modern psychoanalysts. For a specific elucidation of the problem see S. Hayden, "The Toxic Response in Modern Psychoanalysis," *Modern Psychoanalysis* VIII:1 (1983).

6. H. Spotnitz, *Modern Psychoanalysis of a Schizophrenic Patient* (NY: Human Sciences, 1985), 166–8.

7. F. Rosner, "Emotional Care of Cancer Patient: To Tell or Not To Tell," *NY State Journal of Medicine* (July 1974): 1467–9.

8. For the history of measurements: H. Woolf, ed, *Quantification: A History of the Meaning of Measurement in the Natural and Social Sciences* (Indianapolis: Bobbs-Merrill, 1961) and D. Lerner, *Quantity and Quality: The Hayden Colloquium on Scientific Method and Concept* (NY: Free Press, 1961).

9. For a detailed description of Bleuler's change in naming "schizophrenia," and for other implications of the diagnostic process, see P. W. Pruyser, and K. Menninger, "Language Pitfalls in Diagnostic Thought and Work," in P., Pruyser, *Diagnosis and the Difference it Makes* (NY: Jason Aronson, 1976), 209–15.

10. For a wonderful and original discourse on the importance and implications of naming in premodern cosmologies, see M. Mayer, *The Mystery of Personal Identity* (San Diego, CA: ACS Publications, 1984), 4.

11. H. Shands, "The Informational Impact of Cancer on the Structure of the Human Personality," *Annals NY Academy of Science.*

12. L. Leigner, "Humanizing the Physician," *Modern Psychoanalysis* 2:2 (Winter 1977–1978).

13. J. C. Norton, *Introduction to Medical Psychology* (NY: Free Press, 1982), 11–12.

14. In ancient Rome, a physician who bungled was condemned to deportation, or if of low fortune or rank, was put to death. Montesquieu, *De L' Esprit des Lois,* bk. 29, chapt. 14 Paris: Plieiade, 1951), 6.

15. T. J. Scheff, "Decision Rules, Types of Error, and Their Consequences in Medical Diagnosis," *Behavioral Science* 8 (1963): 97–107.

16. For a thorough review of the literature on whether to tell a cancer patient the diagnosis: J. McIntosh, "Processes of Communication Information Seeking and Control Associated With Cancer," *Social Science and Medicine* 8: 167–87.

17. E. Freidson, *Professional Dominance: The Social Structure of Medical Care,* (NY: Atherton, 1970).

18. D. Oken, "What To Tell Cancer Patients," *Journal of the American Medical Association* 175:86 (1961).
19. B. Glaser, and A. Strauss. "Temporal Aspects of Dying as a Non-scheduled Status Passage," *American Journal of Sociology* 71:51 (1965).
20. Ibid.
21. H. C. Shands, et al., (1951): "Psychological Mechanisms in Patients with Cancer," *Cancer* 4 1159.
22. W. T. Fitts, and I. S. Ravdin. "What Philadelphia Physicians tell Patients With Cancer," *Journal of American Medical Association* 153:901 (1953).
23. D. Oken, "What To Tell Cancer Patients".
24. H. Shands, "Psychological Mechanisms".
25. H. Spotnitz, Modern Psychoanalysis, 218–48.
26. L. Israel, *Conquering Cancer* (NY: Vintage, 1979), 211–2.
27. V. A. Gilbertson, and O. H. Wangenstein, "Should the Doctor Tell the Patient That the Disease is Cancer?" *Cancer* 12:82 (1962).
28. Wall Street Journal, 2 February 1987 and 3 February 1987.
29. L. H. Garland, "Studies On the Accuracy of Diagnostic Procedures," *American Journal of Roentgenology, Radium Therapy and Nuclear Medicine* 82 (July 1959): 25–38.
30. Ibid.
31. O. Peterson, E. M. Barsamian, and M. Eden. "A Study of Diagnostic Performance: A Preliminary Report," *Journal of Medical Education* 41 (August 1966); 797–803.
32. The body of Spotnitz's work is found in 3 books: *Modern Psychoanalysis of the Schizophrenic Patient* (NY: Human Sciences Press, 1985); *Psychotherapy of Preoedipal Conditions* (NY: Jason Aronson, 1976); and *Treatment of the Narcissistic Neurosis* (with P. Meadow) (NY: The Manhattan Center for Advanced Psychoanalytic Studies, 1976). Concepts for the remainder of this chapter are represented in those writings.
33. The word *placebo* first appeared in the title of a medical journal in 1945. Since then research has been voluminous. Benson and Shapiro have been the most ardently interested. See A. K. Shapiro, "Placebo-induced Side Effects," *Journal of Operational Psychiatry* 6:1 (1974): 43–6; H. Benson, and M. Epstein, "The Placebo Effect: A Neglected Asset In the Care of Patients," *Journal of the American Medical Association* 232:12 (1975): 1225–7; and D. Sobel, "Placebo Studies are Not Just 'All In Your Mind'," *NY Times,* 6 January 1980, sec. 4, 9.
34. R. L. Pogge, "The Toxic Placebo," *Medical Times* 91 (August 1963): 778–81.
35. H. Spotnitz, *Psychotherapy of Preoedipal Conditions,* 20.

III

A New Nosology

6

The Unfelt Diseases (of the Body)

> *Give me the power to create a fever and I can cure anything.*
> —Hippocrates

Physical Diseases of Too Little

Cancer

The disease that will kill at least one-third of us is the disease which manages to disarm its host's inflammatory reaction. That is cancer, and it is precisely this inhibition of the body's chief defense mechanism that gives cancer its life-threatening aspect.

It is not surprising that, of all diseases, cancer, while not the most prevalent, is the most feared. All of us have heard stories of someone who, in the prime of life and an apparent picture of health, was suddenly transported from the domain of the living to that of the sick and dying by a cancer diagnosis. It seems to be an entirely democratic disease; it has the appearance of being able to strike anybody at any time. We feel like innocent spectators to our own hovering destruction, hostage to the whims of an utterly mysterious process. Those of us who have not yet been touched await, anxiously wondering whether it will be our turn next.

Yet, the whimsical nature of cancer is its greatest myth. Cancer is not demonic; it is a somatic disease. It is one, as I have said, where activation of the organism's defenses never occurs, and destructive and pathogenic entities are allowed to take hold. Overtaxed to a state of utter exhaustion, the immune system no longer has the capability to fulfill its function.[1] The rise of childhood cancers suggests that immunological insufficiency is now being passed on in utero, as well as being acquired through bad living habits (diata).

Seyle's idea about the particular disease of cancer was that the stress experienced by the organism was of a kind that distinguished it from those that result in other diseases. Cancer, he found, was the result of the stressing agent being administered in chronic, small doses. The wearing away of the defensive structure of the organism in cancer appears to be a process that occurs repetitively, over time—a slow eroding away of whatever inherent powers of resistance the organism may have had.

Because most of the stressing agents that we are routinely exposed to are of relatively weak potency and administered over a long period of time, the cancer process is both slow to develop, and insidious in its effects. This silent though persistent encroaching of the cancer cell into the rest of the organism gives cancer the apt description of being the unfelt disease.

Unfelt, it establishes itself within us; when the cancer diagnosis comes it shocks us with a feeling of suddenness and of the unexpected. There have been few, if any, telltale signs that this situation of lethal proportions has been developing within our midst. So instead of any subjective sense we might have of our own condition, it is the physician's giving name to the state of our bodies that convinces us of the deadly danger.

The cancer condition is one where insidious morphological changes have occurred over a period of time, most often over many years. The fact of cellular change is undisputed, and remains the leading determinant of accurate clinical diagnosis. Yet, in spite of the profound changes taking place within the organism, there are generally no signs or symptoms, either subjective or clinical, that are suggestive until quite late in the development of the disease. Cancer remains one of the most difficult diseases to detect in its initial phase, and the attempt to do so leads to a degree of inaccuracy that may range as high as 30 percent.[2] In addition, the medical history of the person is rarely suggestive; there are usually no prior manifestations of serious illness that would lead to suspicions about the state of health.[3] And indeed, it often seems as though quite the opposite phenomenon has occurred: cancer patients are commonly heard to proclaim their former state of good health, and will voice the sentiment that they are perfectly healthy, except for the cancer.

Even after creation of the tumor, a cancer condition can remain undetected for quite some time. It is usually not until complications associated with the tumor arise, such as damage to neighboring tissue or nerves through either pressure or infiltration, that a diagnosis is rendered.[4] When a tumor infiltrates into other tissue, blood vessels open up and bleeding occurs. Uterine bleeding can indicate cancer of the uterus; blood in the stool is suggestive of cancer of the colon; traces of blood in urine can mean tumors of the urinary tract. Obstruction of normal processes can also occur: tumors in the esophagus will make swallowing difficult; tumors of the stomach can interfere with normal emptying of this organ; cancer of the intestinal tract can cause partial or complete retention of stool.[5]

On the psychological level, as well, there is often found a parallel veneer of normality.[6] Cancer patients do not, at first blush, appear to be particularly distinctive from noncancer patients in their psychic makeup. The disease seems to be strictly somatic, and without psychological involvement in either its contraction or its progression. Here, too, cancer patients are often doggedly insistent on their good health, and less frequently avail themselves of psychological methods of treatment than do noncancer patients.[7] Given the extreme psychic stress that a cancer diagnosis confers on the patient, this finding seems puzzling.

Yet, as the subjective sense of good physical health is an illusion for the cancer patient, so too is the sense of psychological well-being. Research on the psychological makeup of cancer patients reveals a distinct cancer personality, referred to as type C. Attributes of this pattern have been delineated, and show a tendency for particular ways of thinking, feeling, and behaving. These attributes have been related not only to whether or not one is susceptible to cancer, but also how fast the cancer grows, and whether one lives with or is killed by the disease.[8]

Cancer patients, when they permit themselves introspection, reveal that, contrary to their surface appearance of normality, they are subject to intense fears, worries, and anxieties. Their psychological histories reveal that they experienced their childhoods as particularly difficult. Early relationships with their mothers are described as unfulfilling and distant. Fear of separation and loss—and this can pertain to a relationship and involve a death or divorce, or can relate to something inanimate such as a job—is perpetually present, and its actual arrival is experienced as overwhelmingly traumatic. The cancer diagnosis is typically made within a few years of this kind of trauma for these patients.

The general picture is one of resignation. This affective state has been variously described as despair, depression, giving up, grief, hopelessness, and helplessness. The physiological state, too, reflects a condition of giving-up; the functioning of the biological systems is depressed and underactive. There is some evidence that this process of underreactivity begins in the brain.[9] The portion of the brain that acts as the neural alarm system is the locus coeruleus. This small structure's location at the base of the brain provides it with an unusually extensive network of connections to other parts of the brain, giving it a major role in mental life.

The locus coeruleus is the brain's center for the feeling of fear and anxiety. The degree to which this portion of the brain is activated governs the extent to which these feelings are experienced. A highly activated locus coeruleus produces panic; moderate activity evokes a vigilant attentiveness, while very little activity brings a dulled or nonexistent awareness of danger.

The middle-age years, when the locus coeruleus begins its process of deterioration, have long been identified as a phase of life where there is less anxiety. New psychosocial studies have demonstrated that as anxiety decreases in these years, depression rises. The risk of depression increases significantly after the age of forty, and explanatory theories include documented physiological evidence showing too little norepinephrine, a substance highly concentrated in the locus coeruleus.

When we look at the features of the victim of an underactive locus coeruleus, we find characteristics strikingly similar to those of the cancer patient. Both share a blunted sensitivity to feelings of anxiety and fear, and both share an increased incidence of depression. The highest cancer incidence is coincident with the time period of greatest and most rapid deterioration of the locus coeruleus—after the age of 40.

Organisms in a state of health have normally adequate responses to injury. On the biological level, the three basic responses of regeneration, isolation, and inflammation will, in most cases, protect the organism from what would, in an undefended state, be a life-threatening situation.[10] The particular response chosen will vary according to innate limitations which are determined by the organism's innate capacities, by the nature and strength of the demand, and by the amount of strain the demand places on the organism.

Cancer is a response more prevalent in the more highly evolved animals. As one descends the phylogenetic scale, the incidence of cancer gets increasingly rare.[11] As we make this trip down the evolutionary ladder, we also find an increasing ability to regenerate—that is, grow anew—tissue, organs, or even parts of the body. Certain lizards can grow a new tail; salamanders can regenerate a new leg; the starfish is able to grow a new appendage. These evolutionary phenomena teach us that the primitive cellular response to loss, injury, or irritation is purposeful new growth or regeneration.[12] Mammals, including human beings, retain some capacity for regeneration but, on only a limited scale. Every cell in the body has the potential ability to duplicate itself, thus making it theoretically possible for every human being to have its own clone. We don't know yet how to force this potential into actuality, and so we are dependent on our own natural, and severely limited, ability to regenerate tissue.

The ability to regenerate is related to dedifferentiation. The more specialized the cell is, the less its capacity to regenerate tissue. Skin has great regenerative capacity, and a wound which punctures the skin can heal quickly and entirely. Corneal cells in the eye still retain regenerative ability, and within a day of injury, old, damaged cells will be sloughed off, and a new layer of cells will have grown. Heart muscle is more specialized. When a muscle cell is irreversibly damaged, it will die and be replaced by scar tissue rather than new muscle. Of all the cells in the body, nerve cells in the brain are the most specialized of all, and these have the least regenerative capacity.

Where regeneration occurs, the cell loses its specialized function, and regresses to its embryonic state. Here, the cell has returned to the state where it is primarily still potential and embodies the ability to turn into any of a wide range of tissues, including bone, cartilage, and all the other components of, for instance, a new tail or leg.

The inverse relationship between cancer and regeneration is not just a phylogenetic phenomenon; it is documented in experiments, as well. When chemicals known to be human carcinogens are injected into the limb of a lizard, malignancy does not occur.[13] Instead, the animal grows an accessory limb. Similarly, when carcinogenic substances are injected into the lens of the eye of this animal, cancer does not result, but instead a new lens is regenerated.[14] It would seem, then, that the identical stimulus induces either regeneration or malignancy, depending upon the organism's stage of evolution.

This same relationship is apparent in the human body: the nervous system, which is highly structured and differentiated, only rarely gives rise to cancer. On the other hand, the digestive and reproductive organs, where regenerative capability is relatively strong, account for 75 percent of all cancers.

These facts are suggestive of a phylogenetic origin of cancer. New growth is stimulated in an injured organism. The new growth—the neoplastic proliferation—in the cancer situation may be an attempt by the body to return to this once useful adaptive response to injury. But, as Selye and Freud pointed out, defenses pertinent to the past are not always adaptive in the present. Like many of man's present adaptive responses, cancer, as a modern replica of this regenerative trait, has become harmful and dangerous.

The example of the "born-again spleen" is convincing evidence to this point. It has been observed that in cases where the spleen has been surgically removed, there can be a regenerative growth of the organ. Remnants of functioning splenic tissue were found many years after the removal of the organ. Thus, spontaneous regeneration of an organ in the human body was demonstrated. In addition, anatomists have occasionally observed that accessory spleens occur; in rare cases, several hundred have been present, representing a return to a more primitive condition where the organ tissue is not contained within the normal and self-limited boundaries of the organ.

What makes these occasional observations remarkable is that the spleen, in addition to being the only organ that has spontaneously regenerated itself, has the other distinction of being the only organ in the human body that is not susceptible to cancer.[15]

It is evident, then, that regeneration is a natural and normally successful healing response on the part of early phylogenetic species. In addition, some species have the defensive maneuver of isolation, or encystment. The organism can erect a partition between a damaged area and the rest of the body to protect itself from infiltration by the diseased tissue. Oysters do precisely this when foreign particles have become irritating presences, and as a result of this mechanism a pearl is formed. Certain tissue in the human being has this ability to form protective barriers. Tuberculosis is an example of an infection that is contained within the lungs. The healing capacity of the body may not be sufficient to rid the body entirely of the infection, but at least the diseased area can be isolated. A fibrous wall surrounds the infected tissue and successfully separates the damaged area from normal lung tissue.

It is likely that the cancer tumor also represents this form of defensive functioning. We know that tumors consist of all kinds of bodily debris. They seem to function as garbage pails, collecting and accumulating toxic and unwanted waste matter.[16] The depositing of all this "junk" into one place, cordoned off by thick membrane walls, is a lifesaving attempt. The circulation of this toxic material throughout the body would cause immediate systemic poisoning and death to the organism.

But mammals depend less on regression and isolation than do animals lower on the evolutionary scale. Regeneration remains possible in relatively few tissues in the human; isolation occurs, but not with great frequency. The much more common healing reaction in the human body is that of inflammation. Inflammation is a biologically mature reaction to an injury or irritation. Redness, warmth, swelling, and tenderness around the injured tissue are the overt manifestations of an inflammation.[17] These changes occur because of the influx of white blood cells rushing to the injured tissue. Their job is to remove foreign matter and defend against infection. Inflammation as a defensive reaction is the price paid by metazoan organisms such as ourselves for having grown increasingly differentiated, and for the ability of living substance to be irritable. To the extent that inflammation does not occur in a state of tissue injury or damage, a natural healing response has been lost.

The fact that the healthy human being normally reacts to cancer with the inflammatory response was first demonstrated in 1777 by James Nooth, surgeon to the Duke of Kent.[18] He inserted cancerous material into a small incision in his arm, and later reported:

> Two hours afterwards I felt the part uneasy, with a strong pulsation. On the following day, it was more uneasy, and much more inflammation appeared than generally attends so small a wound inflicted by a sharp instrument; on the third day, it remained nearly in the same state; on the fourth day the wound became easier, and the inflammation and pulsation began to subside. A few days afterwards a large dry scab was formed, which I removed and found the sore perfectly healed.[19]

Nooth repeated the experiment on several occasions, each time with the same result.

In 1908, shortly after Nooth's experiments, J. L. Alibert, a prominent Paris surgeon, took cancerous material from a woman's breast tumor, broke it into small particles, and injected himself and three of his students with it. In each, a severe inflammation appeared and lasted a few days; no other reaction occurred. Several days later, Alibert repeated the experiment on himself and a colleague with the same results.[20]

In this century, Nicholas Senn and Gerhard Demagk (a Nobel Prize winner for his discovery of sulfa drugs) replicated the finding in 1901 and 1949, respectively.[21] It wasn't until more recently, however, that a scientist demonstrated that even the state of an initially healthy organism can be compromised if sufficient demands are placed on it through repeated exposure to carcinogenic material. In 1954, Thomas Brittingham noticed that patients who had received multiple blood transfusions had a high ratio of white cell antibodies. He theorized that the white blood cells of the donor were being recognized as foreign, and the recipient's body was producing antibodies to these invading cells, thus inhibiting the production of the white cells. Brittingham put this information together with the fact that leukemia patients produce an excessive number of white cells, and hypothesized that if the blood of an individual who had already produced these antibodies were to be injected into a leukemic patient, the increased white blood count in leukemia might be neutralized.[22]

From 1954 through the 1960's, Brittingham used himself as a subject, repeatedly injecting himself with blood from leukemia patients. Most of the injections were followed by innocuous inflammatory reactions. One time, however, after he had given himself a particularly powerful dosage, the inflammatory reaction became quite severe. It was only an injection of hydrocortisone, an antiinflammatory drug, that enabled him to recover. That Brittingham never contracted leukemia seems persuasive evidence of the noncommunicability of that affliction. His death (in 1986) of cancer of the kidney is supportive of the notion that excessive inflammation will ultimately exhaust the body's ability to respond.

Laboratory research has confirmed these researchers' empirical findings. Both animal and human cancer tissue have been shown to be unable to survive in fluid where an active inflammatory process is present.[23] Inflamed tissue has high oxidation power (aerobic), while cancer tissue has low utilization and exchange of oxygen (anerobic). Further, the composition of inflammatory exudate is such that the cancer cell cannot find enough sugar to sustain the process of glycosis.[24]

As we've seen, inflammation occurs when recognition of not-self entities stimulates the production of antibodies; the number of lymphocytes rises and there is capillary activity and cell activation. The internal state of the organism has become energetic. This high level of internal activity is in stark contrast to the cancer process. Even the surface picture is noticeably different. The ill cancer patient looks wan, pale, unenergetic—as though there is not enough energy to sustain the continuing operation of the life forces.[25]

In contrast, in the patient who suffers from an inflammatory condition the face is flushed; elimination channels are opened and one sees a tremendous discharge of internal-milieu substances; there is usually an elevation of temperature. Overactivity is observed, as opposed to the underactivity seen in the cancer patient. This visual picture is, in fact, an accurate portrayal of the state of the biological system.

The cancer condition is a state of underreactivity. The application of damaging toxic stimuli over an extended period of time has taxed the body beyond its limits. While the tumor itself represents an inflammatory response, it is only a local and wholly insufficient response to the overall systemic condition. The body is no longer capable of producing an adequate or generalized inflammatory reaction in response to unwanted material.[26] The cancerous body is one that has become anergic—it can no longer either prevent cancerous growth, respond to it, or defend itself against it.

The medical history of cancer patients will most often reveal that this inhibition of the inflammatory response is not a new phenomenon; there has been a long-standing history of decreased inflammatory reaction. Many cancer patients are found never to have had the common childhood febrile illnesses (measles, chicken pox) with accompanying fever. Similarly, cancer patients show a remarkably low tendency to infectious or allergic diseases.

The cancer patient is one who seems to exist in a sea of unfeeling. Both body and mind respond with silence to the provocation of the deadly assault occurring within the body. Each of the defensive mechanisms available have, one by one, failed. The first available line of defense—the inflammatory response—is inadequate. Failing here, the organism regresses to the more primitive defensive maneuver of isolation and attempts to cordon off the diseased area; thus, the tumor. When even this attempt fails, in a last-ditch desperate effort the organism resorts to a still more primitive defensive tactic—as a misguided striving toward regeneration it produces massive proliferation—that is, metastasis. Once this level of somatic regression has occurred, death usually ensues.

In the mind, despair, resignation, and the hopelessness/helplessness syndrome have the analogous place—last-ditch, inappropriate, and finally destructive. Central to this complex of feeling is the perception of unavailability of emotional supplies on which, it is felt, happiness depends. Losses, real, threatened, or symbolic constitute powerful stimulating agents. Yet, as studies of healthy individuals show, the hopelessness/helplessness reaction is only one of many possible responses to loss.

Grief, for example, is accompanied by many of the same feelings that the hopelessness/helplessness complex evinces: sadness, depression, longing, loneliness, depletion, loss.[27] Yet, the perception is that this loss is irresolvable and one from which recovery is not possible. However deep the wound of the loss is, in grief, the healthy individual retains the ability to recover.

This difference is illustrated in a study of grief in women whose husbands had been diagnosed with cancer. Responses were followed from the time of the diagnosis to one year following the death. While each woman experienced intense feelings of loss, only some manifested the hopelessness/helplessness syndrome. All those who did become either somatically or psychologically ill, while the others maintained health throughout the grief process.[28]

It is clear that neither affective nor biological states necessarily correspond to objective reality. These states simply constitute situational evaluations, and the internal makeup of the individual, rather than the external situation, determines whether this resigned state of body or mind will be evoked. These judgments are likely to be made only when the individual is already inclined in that direction.

The failure of normal defense mechanisms belies the superficial silence of both body and mind. Below the surface one finds that the interplay of forces yielding an integrated and harmoniously working system has been disrupted, and instead one finds dangerous systemic disarray.

Dysfunctions have been identified in all of the major physiological and psychological systems, including the tissues and organs involving respiration, digestion, elimination, hormone production, immunological competence, thermobaric pressure regulation, the nervous system, and psychological functioning.[29]

The cancer patient exists in a state of underreactivity on both the physiological and psychological levels, and this state of underresponsiveness has come to be experienced by the patient as normal. The generalized state of nonfeeling has become so much the rule that the patient no longer remembers the possibility of its having been different. Genuine health is a condition that if it ever was experienced in the past, is now long forgotten. The satisfied acceptance of this pathological condition constitutes the largest threat to the continued survival of the patient. He doesn't know he's ill until it's far too late.

The Viral Conditions

Viruses have presumably been around for millennia, we can document incidences going back about 3,000 years. The mummified face of Ramses V reveals that he was a victim of smallpox, and in all likelihood, died of it. It wasn't until the nineteenth century however, that scientists began to take an active interest in separating out this disease agent from others. They had begun to suspect that there were infectious agents of disease even smaller than the bacteria which were by now easily observed through the microscope. They passed contaminated solutions through filters which blocked even the smallest of the bacteria and found the solutions still infectious. The optical microscope was too limited to detect any material smaller than the wavelength of visible light. Viruses were hypothesized; even some of their properties could be surmised; but it wasn't until the invention of the electron microscope in 1931 that viruses, from ten to one hundred times smaller than the typical bacterium, finally were rendered accessible to the human eye.[30]

The virus always seeks a host to attach itself to. It represents the most extreme form of parasitism; left on its own, it will die. This tiny creature is equipped, however, with brilliantly adaptive techniques to compensate for its shortcomings. It makes itself into a precisely matched complement to any number of cells in the human body. The rabies virus has on its surface a protein that is shaped in such a way that it meshes precisely with a receptor protein found in brain cells; the surface proteins of the AIDS virus are exact matches to the helper T-cell receptor; the polio virus matches certain nerve cells in the spinal cord; the hepatitis virus matches liver cells. Once implanted within the host organism, the virus is made abundantly welcome. The host cell envelopes its membrane around the virus, and cooperates to reproduce millions of copies of the original invader.

Viruses have, of late, been blamed for a number of diseases having devastating, sometimes lethal effects. These include AIDS, herpes, Epstein-Barr, Legionnaires' Disease, and mononucleosis. Many of the viruses identified seem to be first cousins to one another, but exact understandings of their relationships are not yet known. In spite of this attribution of unilateral power to the virus, it is likely that any of these viruses—even those that are the most lethal—cannot cause irreparable damage to any host organism that maintains a state of health.

Research into, and treatment of, these diseases has followed the single etiology theory, and assumed the relationship of virus to disease as causal. The association of AIDS, for instance, with the retrovirus HTLV-III has been well documented. Not every victim of AIDS has produced antibodies to the virus, and some who don't have AIDS do have the antibodies. Clearly, the relationship is more complex than a one-to-one causation.[31]

Further, experimental research shows that AIDS, like cancer cannot be induced in a healthy organism. Close to one hundred chimps have been inoculated with the AIDS virus. So far not a single inoculated chimp has contracted the disease.

In light of this and other findings, scientists have revised their earlier thinking. The HTLV virus has been downgraded from its original position as a supposed virulent virus, threatening to overtake us all, to a relatively weak virus, and not very contagious. It is true that measles, also a disease associated with the presence of a virus, still kills more people than AIDS does—two million children a year, most of them in Latin America and Africa. AIDS is also far less contagious than polio, tuberculosis, malaria, and cholera.

No researcher of any sort believes that correlation proves cause. In the formation of disease, determination of cause was defined years ago by Robert Koch, who denied that the presence of the tubercule bacillus in the sputum of tuberculosis meant that the bacterium caused the disease. Causal determination could only be made if experimental animals are injected with the bacillus and uniformly contract the disease. Koch's insistence upon laboratory reproduction of the disease was an attempt to keep medicine from committing false attribution of cause to agents or factors that are merely associated, or accompanying, phenomena.[32]

In spite of Koch's lesson, we have continued, since his time, to recklessly attribute causal power to the virus. When the polio virus was found in the throat, it was thought to be transmitted through the respiratory tract. There was mass hysteria and people avoided going to the movies or public meetings for fear of catching it from breathing in public places.

As the data have come in, it's become clear that the rules of AIDS are no different from those of any other infectious disease. Whether or not one catches the disease is much more a matter of host resistance than of exposure to any particular disease agent. Exposure to the virus may be a necessary condition; it is certainly not sufficient.

It turns out that contrary to the initial findings, a factor much more significant than homosexual promiscuity is drug use. It has long been known that intravenous drug abusers suffered from repeated infections. It was initially thought that these infections were the result of unsterilized needles and contaminated drugs. Recent research, however, shows that the drugs themselves depress the immune system. Morphine is shown to reduce the ability of macrophages (scavenger white blood cells) to handle invading bacteria, fungi, and viruses.[33] Additionally, morphine shrinks the size of the liver, spleen, and kidneys—organs that store these macrophages and other infection-fighting cells.

It has been shown that these severely damaging effects are not limited to the intravenous drugs. Marijuana, commonly thought of as a recreational substance of relatively weak potency, has serious debilitating effects on the immune system.[34] Its active ingredient, THC (delta-9-tetrahydrocannabinol), suppresses both macrophage and NK (natural killer) cell activity. NK cells, like macrophages, fight viruses, but have the additional task of seeking out and destroying tumor cells, helping to prevent the growth of some cancers and their spread to other parts of the body.

Studies have confirmed the drug use factor. In reviewing the Center for Disease Control data, two researchers found that drug abuse was the most common risk factor. At least 79 percent of AIDS patients had a history of using a recreational drug at least once a week.[35]

One class of drug has been specifically tied to AIDS. The use of nitrite inhalants has been particularly popular with homosexuals. In a 1981–1982 study of patients with Kaposi's sarcoma (KS), a cancer of the blood vessel typically found in AIDS patients, the use of nitrite inhalers was the most distinguishing factor.[36] Nitrites directly affect the blood vessels by causing vasodilation. Many homosexuals believe it enhances and prolongs sexual stimulation, and use it routinely in their sexual practices. Of the KS patients, nearly all had used nitrites.

In addition, psychological defensive functioning seems disturbed. A recent study of AIDS patients places them squarely in the category of the syndrome of too little psychic defensive patterns. Psychological coping styles included particularly intense denial and suppression of anger. Affectless defenses such as perseverance and emotional stoicism were frequent.[37]

It seems that in the case of AIDS, as with most other diseases, diata—life-style and whole mind/body functioning—resurfaces as the primary component in healthy resistance to disease.[38]

Physical Disease of Too Much

Coronary Heart Disease

Those of us who will not die from cancer will, in all statistical likelihood, be felled by coronary heart disease. It remains the leading killer.

Heart disease, like cancer, begins as a natural process of healing. Like cancer, it is a silent disease—by the time the signs of the disease are manifest much damage, often difficult to reverse, has already occurred. As in cancer, routine diagnostic procedures—the kind that most of us will be exposed to without overt disease manifestations—including analysis of blood, urine, feces, x-rays, and electrocardiograms—do not pick up the presence of the disease process. And the process of heart disease, like that of cancer, has its beginnings in the first years of life.[39]

The arterial system is like an extraordinarily complex map. There is no part of the body that is not touched or fed by these tunnellike vessels carrying blood. When these vessels to the heart become thickened and lose resiliency, various forms of coronary-arterial malfunctioning can result, including myocardial infarction (commonly called heart attacks), angina pectoris, and congestive heart failure.

It is thought that early damage to the coronary arteries occurs because of the innate complexity of the system. The fact that they have to go everywhere, and be everywhere all the time, means that the arteries are incessantly turning and twisting in order to accomodate themselves to the human body. Such gyrations have the potential for causing much damage. After just a few years of life, it is likely that these arteries have already received many tiny wounds or tears in their lining.

The body's natural healing capability ensures that these wounds do not ordinarily become a problem. As with external wounds of the body, the healing processes of regeneration, isolation, and inflammation take over, and these internal wounds are quickly healed and bridged over through the growth of new cells. These internal scabs are the arterial thickenings that are observed early in life. They are a natural process, one that need not and should not be interfered with, and are simply part of the payment that each of us makes living an energetic life in a complex body.

As these wounds heal and scabs are formed, often there is an accumulation of cholesterol and fats in and around the overgrown cells. During the growth years the addition of these new cells which have no healing function needn't be a problem. The whole collection of cells—regenerated tissue plus the cholesterol and fatty cells—can still disappear and be replaced by a tiny scar. The healing potential still exceeds the demands placed on it. This process can happily continue throughout infancy and childhood, all the way to adulthood, with no apparent health consequences.

Unfortunately, the outcome is not always so successful. When the need for these defensive operations exceeds the capacity of the defense system, the process of disease sets in. If the accumulation of cholesterol/fatty cells reaches a certain point, instead of disappearing and forming innocuous scars, further growth will be promoted. Cholesterol acts as though it were a carcinogen within the artery. It is not just an inert substance; it actually promotes a wild new growth of arterial cells. This now wildly overgrown collection of cells soon reaches the point where it can be called a tumor, and like its cancerous counterpart, begins to interfere with vital functioning of the body. As new cells join these tumors, they expand and encroach upon the main channel, the lumen, and begin to cut off blood supply to the heart.

The addition of still more cells brings this process to the point of irreversibility. These cells are responsible for the formation of large and distorted scars—arterial plaques. Once this plaque has formed, the defensive solution of the comparatively thin and innocuous scars is no longer possible. Once present, plaque remains forever in the artery wall, and the best that we can hope for is that it will remain quiescent. It often does, for years—even decades.

Plaque is living tissue though, and like all other human tissue, it depends on blood for the support of its cells. Eventually the excess cholesterol/fat blocks the way into the plaque tissue, resulting in an inadequate blood supply. Cells die and form necrotic (dead) tissue. As more and more cells are attracted to the area, the plaque gets larger and larger, and finally, the coronary arteries can no longer transport the amount of blood to the heart that is needed to sustain life.

Heart disease arises, then, when the defensive process of scarring becomes wildly exaggerated. Cholesterol acts as a foreign presence, and more and more cells are attracted to the area. The normal healing process turns into a gross perversion of itself; what was a local inflammatory response has now grown to the point where the functioning of the rest of the body is interfered with. In its exaggerated response, the defense has become the disease.

If cholesterol is the stimulating agent to an excessive defensive response, how is it that an accumulation of this toxic substance can arise?

For years researchers attributed the main contributory factor to be dietary. There is, indeed, a good deal of epidemiological data supporting the idea that coronary heart attacks are much more common in populations whose diet is rich in cholesterol, and relatively rare in groups whose diet is poor in cholesterol. Yet, there remained some disquieting exceptions which couldn't be explained. In the United States, women have developed coronary heart disease much less frequently than men, although research established that American male and female diets were not significantly different. An explanation was that there must be some protective mechanism in the females that was lacking in the men—possibly the female sex hormones—had that beneficial effect. Again there were unexplained findings. The same differences were not found in either laboratory animals, white men and women in other countries, or black men and women in the U.S. (In fact, black women in the U.S. were found to be even more susceptible than black men to coronary heart disease.).

It wasn't until the 1970's that researchers were finally able to tease out the missing variable. What had been overlooked was the question of how different organisms handle stressing agents.

Following suit with the psychological research on cancer patients begun in the 1950's, it was found that heart disease patients also had particular personalities that correlated with susceptibility to the disease. The type A personality was formulated, and research revealed it to be a configuration of behavioral characteristics that stood in sharp contrast to the earlier discovered type C, or cancer-prone, personality.[40]

Where the cancer patient is repressed, the heart disease personality is easily aroused; where aggression is noticably lacking in the type C personality, it is all too apparent in the type A personality; hostility is likely to flare up easily, and under diverse conditions. The cancer personality demonstrates psychological underreactivity, while the heart disease individual seems to be suffering from a chronically inflammatory condition of the mind. He is always in a hurry, unrelentingly competitive, and obsessed with acquisitions and achievements. In short, he is a man incapable of relaxing (as we begin by saying, it is much more likely to be a man than a woman).

Whereas the cancer patient is excessively concerned about relationships, the heart disease patient is intensely devoted to his work. In fact, relationships are often sacrificed in order to fulfill a seemingly compulsive urge to work harder and better. While cancer patients often manifest a sense of vulnerability and induce in others a compelling feeling of protectiveness, heart patients seem invulnerable and not easily approachable. Cancer patients seem to be most in touch with love and need, where the conscious feelings of heart disease patients have more to do with strength and independence and emotional distance.

And, the analogous relation between mind and body that was observed in the cancer condition is similarly seen in the heart disease situation. The absence of childhood infectious diseases in cancer patients, signifying the failure of an adequate physiological defense response, is paralleled in the emotional monotone of the psyche. Both the emotional and physical history of the heart disease patient, in sharp contrast, represent an excessive degree of inflammatory reaction. A significant predictor of heart disease is childhood scarlet fever. The personality of the heart disease patient, like the body, is volatile and reactive. In heart disease, both mind and body have overly responded; defenses on both levels have become excessive.

Many subsequent studies have validated and augmented the original description of the type A personality. First, correlation between intensity of type A behavior pattern and serum cholesterol was documented: as the severity of the personality affliction increased, so too did the serum cholesterol level. Next, research was designed to explain the male/female discrepancies. When white women were categorized according to type A instead of taken as a whole group, it was found that they exhibited the same serum cholesterol pattern as their male counterparts. The relative paucity of coronary heart disease in white women was revealed as a cultural phenomenon. The fact is that most American white women are not exposed to the kinds of demand that tend to produce the type A personality. And of those that are, as many suffer from coronary heart disease as their male counterparts. As women are increasingly joining the competitive job market, we are seeing a parallel rise in heart disease among them.

Finally, following the protocols of Koch, the rise in serum cholesterol needed to be experimentally induced for the findings to have true validity. This was accomplished through the infliction of damage to the hypothalamus, the emotional center of the brain, in experimental animals. The animals exhibited almost instantaneous behavior bearing remarkable similarity to the type A behavior pattern; even more interesting was the correlated elevation in serum cholesterol.

Lynch's 1977 compilation and interpretation of a wealth of accumulated data further refined the psychosocial picture of the heart disease patient.[41] Stunningly, just as the origins of the physiological dysfunction of heart disease were closely correlated to the biological beginnings of cancer, so too did the psychological origins of both diseases look remarkably alike.

Both the physiological and psychological dysfunctions of heart disease begin, as is true in cancer, in the first years of life. Because heart disease, like cancer, strikes so suddenly with few warning signs, there has been widespread belief that the physiological processes leading to the disease had developed rapidly. Yet, the truth of the situation is that the degenerative process begins in childhood. Autopsies of U.S. servicemen killed in battle in World War II revealed that even at their young age (most of them were in their teens and early twenties), a significant degree of coronary arteriosclerosis was in place.[42]

Psychologically, too, heart disease patients present an early picture of disturbance. Paralleling the psychological profile of the cancer personality, the heart disease patient is exposed to early loss, emotional deprivation, or difficulty in parental relations. While cancer patients show difficulty in their relationships with their mothers, heart disease patients demonstrate the same kinds of emotional conflicts in regard to their fathers. A significant number of coronary patients had fathers who had died prematurely, usually when the son was between five and seventeen years of age. In cases where early death of the father was not a factor, intense conflicts between father and son were exhibited. This conflict often resulted in either father or son leaving the household.[43]

The heart disease personality develops, then, as a defensive attempt to deal with an environment that feels dangerous and threatening. The defense is to be normal, competent, and firm; to pull oneself together under all circumstances, to maintain self-control and leadership, to be, in short, superadapted. Behind the impressive shield of invulnerability, however, is a personality that has been exposed to more aggression (both others' and his own) than he can comfortably manage. The defense, which is held in place at no small cost in energy, hides an easily injured self.[44] In spite of a hardened defense against admitting the need for love, there is an underlying desperation for just that—an acceptance which he is incapable of giving himself.

It is the discrepancy between these two fluctuating stances, of strength and vulnerability, of activity and passivity, that marks the greatest danger for the heart disease patient. Where there is too rapid oscillation between the two, or an abrupt change from a state of inflation ("I can do anything") to deflation ("I can't do anything"), there is the greatest danger of an acute infarction.[45] It is as though one were pushing both gas and brake pedals in a car simultaneously, straining opposing systems of the car, and going nowhere. The opposite psychobiological drive states (fight and flight) have been simultaneously activated, with severe repercussions in the physiological correlates of the mechanisms of activation and inhibition.

The final stimulating provocation in heart disease parallels the final stimulating agent in the cancer development. Both cancer and heart disease diagnoses are generally made some short time after a specific traumatic interpersonal event in the patient's life. The precipitant event in cancer has to do with the area of emotional investment for the cancer personality—that is, relationships—and may be the sudden death of a child, or desertion or rejection by a spouse; the provoking stimulus in heart disease will more likely involve a setback in work, loss in income, a decrease of prestige in his profession, or an emotionally equivalent loss of some substitute for human love or security gained from interpersonal contact.[46]

What has emerged with the integration of data from heart disease and cancer patients is that both diseases represent physiological and psychological dysfunctions with similar origins and causes. Yet, the defensive responses to those offending stimuli are diametrically opposed. The cancer patient's response is to not respond; the heart disease patient's is to respond excessively. And, for both diseases, body and mind operate in tandem—mirror images of one another.

Notes

1. There are many proponents of the idea that cancer is a systemic disease, arising from an inadequate immune response. A cornerstone reference for this chapter is J. Issels, *Cancer: A Second Opinion* (London: Hodden and Stoughton, 1975). Also, D. W. Smithers, *A Clinical Prospect of the Cancer Problem* (London: U. Edinburgh, 1960).
2. T. J. Scheff, "Decision Rules".
3. R. Schmidt, *Med. Klin.* 6 (1910), 1690 and *Therap. u. Prophyloxe innerer Krankh*, 2nd ed., 1948. Of 241 cancer patients, he found 99 who had never had a fever.
4. J. Issels, *Cancer: A Second Opinion*, 88–90.
5. Ibid.
6. J. McDougall, *Plea for a Measure of Abnormality*. While she doesn't offer an explicit classification of the "cancer personality" as fitting into the normopathic mode, her research integrated with others, suggests the pattern.
7. Personal communication from a variety of psychoanalysts, including Phyllis Meadow, Hyman Spotnitz, Stanley Hayden, Delores Welber.
8. Research on the type C (cancer) personality is voluminous. While most of the experimental studies were done in the 1950's, the last decade of clinical work has contributed greatly to our understanding of the mind/body interface in cancer. Most of the books on this work have excellent bibliographies, including: L. Le Shan, *You Can Fight For Your Life*, (NY: M. Evans, 1977), and C. Simmonton, and S. Simmonton, J. P. Tarcher, *Getting Well Again*, (Los Angeles: 1978). Also, a short, concise summary is found in P. Rosch, "Stress: Cause or Cure of

Cancer?'' in J. Goldberg, *Psychotherapeutic Treatment of Cancer Patients.*.

9. D. Goleman, "Midlife: Aging Brain Loses Cells for Anxiety," *NY Times,* 21 April 1987.
10. P. Rosch, "Stress: Cause or Cure of Cancer?" in J. Goldberg, ed., *Psychotherapeutic Treatment of Cancer Patients* pp. 39–71.
11. Ibid.
12. Ibid.
13. Ibid.
14. Ibid.
15. Ibid.
16. This is a speculative theory, held by a variety of holistic practitioners, including Leo Roy, M.D., a clinical oncologist who has treated cancer patients for thirty years. It is also referred to by Selye in *Stress Without Distress,* (NY: New American Library, 1974), 94.
17. The classic description of the inflammatory process comes from Celsus (first century A.D.), who characterized the main symptoms as *rubor, colon, tumor,* and *dolor.* See Husemann/Wolff, *The Anthroposophical Approach to Medicine,* Chapter VII, 163–92 for an excellent conceptual description of the inflammatory process.
18. L. K. Altman, *Who Goes First?* (NY: Random House, 1986), 286.
19. J. Nooth, *Observations on the Treatment of Scirrhores Tumors of the Breast* (London: J. Johnson, 1806), 13.
20. J. L. Alibert, *Description des Maladies de la Peau Observers a l'Hopital St.-Louis, Barrois, Paris, 1806–1814,* 118, cited in W. H. Woglom, *Studies in Cancer and Allied Subjects. The Study of Experimental Cancer. A Review.* (NY: Columbia University Press, 1913), 43.
21. L. K. Altman, *Who Goes First?,* 287.
22. Ibid. 283–6.
23. G. vonBergman, *Funktionelle Pathologie* (1932), 173, cited in Husemann/Wolff, *The Anthroposophical Approach to Medicine,* 189.
24. O. Warburg, "On the Origin of Cancer Cells," *Science* 123 (1956): 309–14.
25. An excellent comparison of the inflammatory process and the tumor process is found in L. F. C. Mees, *Blessed by Illness,* (Spring Valley, NY: The Anthroposophic Press, 1983), 135.
26. Husemann/Wolff, *The Anthroposophical Approach to Medicine,* chapter VII.
27. Freud discussed grief in *Mourning and Melancholia, Collected Papers,* vol. 4 (London: Hogarth Press,), 152.
28. For a review of literature on mourning, see L. D. Siggins, "Mourning: A Critical Review of the Literature," *Int. J. of Psycho-Anal.* 47:14 (1966).
29. J. Issels, *Cancer, A Second Opinion.*
30. A short but sufficient explanation of viruses is in E. Potts, and M. Morra, *Understanding Your Immune System.*

31. Biologist Peter Duisberg is so convinced that the HIV doesn't cause AIDS that he's willing to follow Nooth & Brittingham's lead, and allow himself to be injected with the virus. See *Discover* (June 1988), 63.

32. M. Friedman, & R. H. Rosenman, *Type A Behavior and Your Heart,* (New York: Faucett Crest, 1974), 81.

33. B. Dunnett, "Drugs that Suppress Immunity," *American Health* (November 1986): 43–5.

34. Ibid.

35. Dr. Herman Friedman did this study, cited in Dunnett, ibid.

36. C. Cacares, and T. Krieger, stated in *The Wall St. Journal,* cited in Dunnett, ibid.

37. H. Haverkos, *Sexually Transmitted Diseases,* cited in Dunnett, ibid.

38. Cacares & Krieger state in the controversial *Wall Street Journal* article, "It appears that most AIDS patients are not healthy people who got AIDS simply because they had sex with the wrong person. Rather, they seem to be people who were already sick in the sense of having a damaged immune system."

39. M. Friedman, and R. Rosenman, in their classic *Type A Behavior and Your Heart* (New York: Fawcett Crest, 1974), give all the background necessary with which to understand the biology of the process of heart disease.

40. Friedman & Rosenman also give the first, and again totally adequate, explanation of the heart disease personality and the research that led to its formulation.

41. J. J. Lynch, *The Broken Heart,* 30–87.

42. W. F. Enos, R. H. Holmes, and J. C. Beyer, "Pathology of Coronary Arteriosclerosis," *American Journal of Cardiology,* 9: (1962) 343–54; A. R. Mortiz, and N. Zamcheck, "Sudden and Unexpected Deaths of Young Soldiers: Diseases Responsible For Such Deaths During World War II," *Archives of Pathology* 42 (1946): 359–494.

43. R. S. Paffenbarger, and D. P. Asnes, "Chronic Disease in Former College Students, III: Precursors of Suicide In Early and Middle Life," *American Journal of Public Health* 56 (1966): 1036; C. B. Behnson, and W. J. Wodell, "Personality Factors Predisposing To Myocardial Infarction," *Psychosomatic Medicine, Proceedings of the First International Conference in the Academy of Psychosomatic Medicine,* (1966): 249–57.

44. J. Bastiaans, "Psychoanalytic Investigations on the Psychic Aspects of Acute Myocardial Infarction," *Psychotherapy Psychosomatics* 16 (1968): 202–9.

45. H. K. Heijningen, and N. Treurniet, "Psychodynamic Factors in Acute Myocardial Infarction," *International Journal of Psychoanalysis* 47 (1966): 370.

46. J. Groen, J. M. van der Valk, N. Treurniet, H. Kits von Heyningen, H. E. Pelsor, and G. S. S. Wilde, *Acute Myocardial Infarction. A Psychosomatic Study* (trans.) (Haarlem: De Erven F. Bohn, 1965).

7

The Diseases of Unfeeling (of the Mind)

Psychological Diseases of Too Little

Psychosomatic, Disaffected and Alexithymic Personality

Diseases of the mind that reflect underreactivity were not much dealt with until quite recently. There were patients who seemed to make little progress in psychotherapy, or more commonly, who avoided such a process altogether. While they did not describe themselves as unhappy, there seemed to be little internal material that suggested an interesting or conflictual internal life. They seemed abnormally normal—Joyce McDougall coined the term normopaths for them.[1]

It wasn't until the 1960's and 1970's that psychoanalytic researchers began to recognize a psychodynamic in these patients that had eluded them for years. These people, described by Joyce McDougall as "disaffected," seemed to be psychologically separated from their emotions.[2] They had apparently lost the capacity to be in touch with their own psychic reality. The dysfunction was noticed in the inactivation of the normal psychological defense mechanisms.

Freud's initial identification of anxiety as a signal to the defensive apparatus led psychoanalysts into research on the additional feeling states of pain, guilt, and shame, and it was discovered that the psychological defense system resides in the superego as well as in the ego.[3] Each of these feelings serve as a powerful warning that some destructive consequence is imminent, and as a call to action to correct the situation. Under ordinary circumstances, pain warns us to the danger of bodily destruction; anxiety is a warning of either physical or psychic annihilation; guilt warns the individual that he is not attending to the dictates of his conscience; shame suggests a disharmony of ideal principles with reality.

The first group of patients identified as consistently demonstrating this disconnection from their internal feeling life were the psychosomatic patients.[4] In these people, feeling signals appear to be dulled. Consciousness of psychic pain, anxiety, guilt, and shame are warded off, and without access to these alarm faculties, responses to danger become rigid and stereotyped.

Beginning around 1940, investigators from a variety of disciplines, including psychiatry, psychology, and medicine, undertook extensive studies of patients with chronic diseases of no known etiology. Their research combined medical and psychological approaches to what came to be known as the Chicago Big Seven: the diseases of hypertension, peptic duodenal ulcer, ulcerative colitis, thyrotoxicosis, neurodermatitis, rheumatoid arthritis, and bronchial asthma. The choice of diseases was purely artifactual, reflecting logistics of investigator interest and patient availability, but in spite of the limitations of the research, a great deal of information was gathered about these diseases. Among the findings was that groups of patients with the same physical diseases showed the same psychological characteristics— personality structure, nature of core unresolved conflicts, types of defense mechanisms characteristically employed, and the types of psychosocial situations apt to activate the core conflicts and to be associated with precipitation and/or exacerbation of the illness.

All this reached a dramatic peak in the 1950's. A few researchers targeted a new disease for study—one that struck the modern medical mind as a most unlikely choice. The disease was the most somatic of all, and in the light of the germ theory, which was utterly dominant, there was no reason to seek any rhyme or reason to the disease other than ill fortune. No reason other than the long neglected wisdom of the ages; and none except Freud's ideas on the integrative functioning of the human organism.

The results were startling, to say the least. Here was a very large group of people who apparently shared nothing but an organic diagnosis. Psychological research revealed, however, that the physical disease they had in common was only the tip of the iceberg. Not only were their bodies doing the same thing; so were their minds. The psychological profile of the cancer patient revealed similar ways of thinking, feeling, and behaving; they talked about their childhood memories in ways that revealed that their psychological struggles and pains and conflicts were remarkably parallel. The cancer personality, as a diagnostic entity, was born.[5-7]

Even though a great deal of research was generated exploring these notions, the idea of a cancer personality did not find its way into the thinking of either the general population or most of the physicians who were treating cancer patients for the organic manifestations of their disease—the cancer itself. Only a few clinicians attempted to put these research findings into practice, and these few had trouble finding cancer patients who were willing to consider a psychological approach, even adjunctively to their medical treatment. The frustration took its toll, and the notion of a psychosomatic cancer personality faded into relative oblivion for another thirty years.

Psychosomatic pursuit did not stop altogether, however. The French school of psychosomaticists delineated the particular mode of thinking and feeling they saw exhibited in psychosomatic patients in general. In 1963 Marty and de M'Uzan first drew attention to a utilitarian type of thinking they called *pensee operatoire* (operational thinking).[8] For these patients, relating to oneself and to other people is entirely pragmatic. Responses to inquiries about feelings are devoid of reference to emotions, and without affect. Fantasy and imaginative thinking is lacking. Instead, their thought processes have the quality of being mundane, unimaginative, and utilitarian.

One such man, when asked how he felt after an automobile accident in which he had seriously injured a woman and her baby replied, "Oh, there's no problem; I'm totally insured against accidents." Another patient, when asked how she felt after her parents and fiancé were killed in an accident, replied, "Well, I realized I'd have to pull myself together."[9] The striving toward denial and avoidance of feeling states, as demonstrated in these patients, is in stark contrast to spontaneous and emotional responses to reality that mark a more normal adaptation. Both these patients fell ill shortly after these accidents—one with ulcerative colitis, the other with severe psoriasis. While both of the diseases are generally thought to have strong psychosomatic components, neither patient was able consciously to link the traumatic events, and their calm in the face of them, with the subsequent onset of the psychosomatic illness.

The research in Paris gave rise to further studies on similar patients in Boston, and it was out of these investigations that the concept of *alexithymic* was developed.[10,11] Here reference is made to the notion that these individuals have no words to describe their emotional states. Inquiry into their feeling states results in parsimonious responses. When a word can be found to describe feeling, the patient tends to minimize affect and emotional involvement. Responses need to be doggedly elicited. At no point does the patient come forth with his own thoughts and fantasies. If there is, indeed, any internal life in these patients, they way into it seems to be impenetrably blocked.

The more recent research findings of the Boston and Paris schools of psychosomaticists gives us perspective on the concept of a cancer personality. It appears that the psychological makeup of the cancer patient varies little from those falling into the broader diagnostic category of psychosomatic personality. An even broader inclusion is observed by McDougall, who found that many of the psychosomatic and alexithymic phenomena are equally characteristic of addictive personalities, alcoholics, and drug abusers, many of whom did not suffer form psychosomatic manifestations.[12]

We are reminded of Selye's discovery of the phenomenon of "just being sick," and it seems as though on the level of mind, as with the physical diseases, there is a very general organizing principle. There is a whole class of individuals who suffer from the disease syndrome of too little psychic arousal. These patients cross a broad range of physical and psychological diagnostic categories. The common thread is that on the level of mind, they exhibit a striking absence of feelings— whether the dysfunction is a failure to generate them, or an inability to tolerate them and chronic repression, is not yet clear. Stimuli that produce feelings in others evidently produce symptoms instead in them.

Psychological Disease of Too Much

Hysteria

As researchers discovered the core psychological attributes of the psychosomatic personality, they began to wonder about psychological conditions that looked diametrically opposed. Whereas the psychosomatic patients seemed to suffer from too little emotional arousal and little or no alarm reaction, others showed a picture of being in an almost perpetual state of excitation, with persistent and intense alarm behavior.[13] The concept of hysteria, the disease of Freud's original inquiry, gained new meaning in the comparison.

Hysteria is defined by Bastiaans as disease characterized by behavior that is a persistent distress cry, much like a little child who has been left in the lurch by its parents.[14] It implies an exaggerated and inefficient strategy to obtain help, support, love, and attention.

The term has found its way into everyday usage, and it is not uncommon to hear someone described as having an hysterical personality. When we describe someone in this way, we are referring to a quality like that of the little boy who cried wolf. The pleas for help are so frequent, so intense, and so fraught with underlying dependency, that we soon lose sympathy for the demands.

When we compare the attributes of hysteria with the physic makeup of the psychosomatic personality, we see numerous areas reflecting polar opposite attitudes and behavior. The attitude of hysteria is histrionic; the psychosomatic manifests an attitude tied exclusively to reality. The hysteric exhibits continuous cries for help, while in the psychosomatic patient there is a chronic blockage of cries for help. The behavior of the hysteric is tinged with aggression, while the psychosomatic renounces aggressive reactions. The hysteric has no hesitation about attempting to get what he wants and will resort to manipulative maneuvers in order to do so, while the psychosomatic patient, instead, seeks harmony at all costs. The hysteric is fond of complaining, and has a vivid imagination about the numerous and various ailments he may be afflicted with; the psychosomatic, on the other hand, is non-hypochondriacal to a fault, and may even ignore true disease symptoms. The hysteric maintains an attitude of egotism, putting himself first, while the psychosomatic assumes a self-sacrificing posture.

The extent of these differences is impressive enough to suggest a meaningful relationship between hysteria and psychosomaticism. It has become clear, through analyses of these patients, that the psychosomatic mode of adaptation is, in fact, the result of a constant intrapsychic struggle of the individual to not behave in an overt hysterical manner. The underlying hysteria in cancer patients is repressed and largely unavailable to conscious thought or feeling. The underlying hysteria in the heart disease personality is sublimated, or channeled into an overly zealous commitment to activity. Whereas repression forces material into deep recesses of the unconscious, the maneuver of sublimation keeps the material relatively closer to consciousness. The hidden hysteria of the cardiac patient, thus breaks out often into overt behavior, and we see the alternation of moods and activity that is typical of the type A personality construction. In either case, the outcome of too forceful pushing away of the hysterical awareness of one's needs and vulnerability is tragic.

Notes

1. J. McDougall, *Plea for a Measure of Abnormality*.
2. J. McDougall, "The 'Dis-Affected' Patient: Reflections on Affect Pathology" *Psychoanalytic Quarterly* L111, (1984): 386–409.
3. S. Freud, "Inhibitions, Symptoms, and Anxiety," *S.E.* 20 (1926).
4. M. Schur, "Comments on the Metapsychology of Somatization," *Psychoanalytic Study of the Child* X (1955): 122–164.
5. R. Renneker, & M. Cutler, "Psychological Problems of Adjustment to Cancer of the Breast," *Journal of American Medical Association* 148 (1952) 833.
6. C. Bacon, R. Renneker, and M. Cutler, "A Psychosomatic Survey of Cancer of the Breast," *Psychosomatic Medicine* 14 (1952): 453.
7. R. Renneker, et al., "Psychoanalytic Explanations of Emotional Correlates of Cancer of the Breast," *Psychosomatic Medicine* 25 (1963): 106.
8. P. Marty, M. de M'Uzan, and C. David, "L'Investigation Psychosomatique," (Paris: Presses Universitaires, 1963).
9. J. McDougall, *Plea for a Measure of Abnormality*.
10. P. Sifneos, R. Apfel-Savitz, and F. Frankel, "The Phenomenon of 'Alexithymia' ", *Psychosomatic Psychotherapy* 28 (1977): 47–57.
11. J. C. Nemiah, and P. Sifneos, "Affect and Fantasy in Patients with Psychosomatic Disorders," *Modern Trends in Psychosomatic Medicine*, vol. 2, (Butterworth, 1970).
12. J. McDougall, *Plea for a Measure of Abnormality*.
13. J. McDougall, aludes to this dichotomy in "A Child is Being Eaten: I. Psychosomatic States, Anxiety Neurosis and Hysteria-A Theoretical Approach," *Contemporary Psychoanalysis* 16:4 (1980): 417–59.
14. J. Bastiaans, "Neue Psychodynamische and Psychobiologische Aspekte der Hysterie," *Praxis Psychotherapie* 19:4 (1974).

IV

The Mind/Body Predicament

8

Mind and Body Apart

The virtual elimination of communicative channels between body and mind in the major killer diseases of cancer and heart disease is curious. That mind and body are intimately and integrally related to one another is obvious. Stimulation on one level normally effects change on the other, and the flow of effect can be in either direction. The reactive connections between mind and body has meant that, historically, it has not always been easy to determine the true origin of diseases. The somatic diseases of syphilis and paresis were initially understood to be disorders of the mind because of their effects on the personality of the patient. Freud systematically explored how the interactive pattern can be reversed. Through his and his followers' studies on hysterical and psychosomatic patients, the process of mind creating bodily disturbance was detailed.

We now know, through Freud's efforts, that only part of the mind can speak to us in words. Both the body and the other parts of the psyche have languages which are not always translatable such that we easily understand their meanings. Freud's identification of the importance of symptoms arose out of his understanding of the communicative function of symptoms, and from this understanding, he discovered the unconscious.

Freud's particular interest was on the interplay of forces arising and remaining strictly within the psyche. What he observed was a complex channel of communications amongst various parts of the pscyhe— belying our experience of ourselves. We don't experience our psyche in parts, much less communicating amongst themselves. Ego, id, and superego—conscious and unconscious—all interrelate, each using the

145

language particular to its nature, telling one another about the condition and fate of each.

The language of the unconscious was Freud's early concern. The unconscious does not have the privilege of speaking to us directly. Freud explored the ways in which the unconscious communicates to us, and observed the methods to be humor, slips of the tongue, free association, dreams, and neurotic and somatic manifestations.

Since Freud's working out of this problem in his autobiographical analysis of his own unconscious,[1] analysts have followed suit in their work with patients, and the clinical literature is replete with examples of communications from the unconscious that reflect accurate understanding of the state of an organism—information rendered that has not yet become available to conscious awareness.

Yet, we are reminded of Freud's dictum that the ego is a body ego, by which he meant that our psyches are housed within a physical body, and that this is a defining factor in the determination of the nature of our psyches. If, as Freud has suggested, we are a complex, though wholly integrated, system then mightn't we assume that as the various parts of the mind speak to one another, the body also has the ability to address psychic awareness?

Such a premise has profound implications for our understanding of the conditions of organic diseases. If awareness of bodily disturbances can be had on the psychic level, then we are rendered a powerful tool for diagnosing, predicting, and treating organic dysfunctions. We can reasonably expect that the omniscience of the psyche will provide us with some clue, some suggestion that the body in which it is housed is not functioning properly.

This idea found sympathy in Carl Jung, Freud's most famous follower, who was known on occasion, to make startling diagnoses of organic diseases from dreams.

For example, a dream was submitted to Jung for interpretation:

> Someone beside me kept asking me something about oiling some machinery. Milk was suggested as the best lubricant. Apparently I thought that oozy slime was preferable. Then, a pond was drained and amid the slime there were two extinct animals. One was a minute mastodon. I forgot what the other one was.[2]

With no other information about the patient provided, Jung concluded that the dream indicated an organic condition relating to a damming up of cerebrospinal fluid.

Jung's interpretation came from an extensive and profound under-standing of both human anatomy and the nature of symbolic communi-cation from the unconscious. He began with the idea that the lubricat-ing of the machinery and the draining of the pond gave the dream an obvious mechanical aura which suggested pertinence to the mechanics of the functioning of the body.

Jung happened, as well, to be a Latin scholar, and knew that the Latin word for slime is *pituita*, from which comes the word pituitary. From the pituitary gland flow slimy, colloidal secretions, and this flow continues until the third ventricle is reached. It is here, in this cavern-like portion of the brain, that cerebrospinal fluid serves as both a lubricant and as a mechanical barrier against shock to the brain. Along the course of its path, this slimy substance encounters a series of aqueducts which regulate the flow of fluid; if cut off or blocked through the shutting of any of these aquaducts, there is, as in a real aquaduct, an accumulation of a pool of fluid.

Jung's knowledge of ancient languages led him to the further asso-ciative link between the milk suggested as the lubricant and the image of the mastadon. The element mast comes for the word *mastos*; odon refers to teeth, and comes from the Latin *odontia*. It was from these etymological origins that the mastodon got his name, his distinguish-ing feature among mammoths being the nipple-like projections on his teeth. Jung knew enough about human anatomy to know that within the human brain was an analogue of the mastodon. Lying at the base of the third ventricle are the *mamillary bodies*, breast-shaped arts of the hypothalamus, with nipple-like protrusions.

The medical diagnosis of the case was a neurological disturbance in the third ventricle.

While it is true that most of us are not the scholars of classic languages and anatomy that Jung and this patient were, we still retain the ability to receive communications from the unconscious.

Yet, in each of the diseases where the defensive alarm reaction is irregular, we fail to see the contact between mind and body that would alert one to the destructive leanings of the other. Material from the unconscious which would, under different circumstances, leak out to provide the conscious mind with a notion of the biological and psycho-logical state of the organism, seems to be unavailable or nonexistent. Analyses of dreams of precancer or preheart attack patients, or those with as yet medically undetected disorders, frequently reveal nothing unusual. Even stranger, it has been observed that immediately prior to either a cancer or a heart disease diagnosis, it is not unusual for there to begin a state of nondreaming even in people who had previously been prolific dreamers.[3] It is as though they had suddenly become shut off from their internal selves. Typically, once the disease is well entrenched and the patient has entered a stage of conscious awareness of the disease condition, the dreams return, in a deluge of vivid material that, repressed for so long, now overwhelms the patient with the need for discharge.

While the body is proceeding rapidly along its path towards self-destruction, the mind seems blissfully ignorant of this disatrous state of affairs. Body and mind seem to be split off from one another, dangerously out of touch.

In such a situation,we are left to the judgment of the experts who through their technological instruments, have come to know more about the state of our bodies than our own intuitive sense does. It is now thought that a leading cause of death is late diagnosis of the disease condition. Without acute sensitivity to he functioning of our bodies and minds, the disease has progressed to the point where it is either difficult or impossible to reverse damage.

Notes

1. S. Freud, *The Interpretation of Dreams,* S. E., (1900) 4–5.
2. Jung's interpretation of this dream, and the connections he was able to make in order to arrive at the interpretation is thoroughly and excellently, discussed by R. Lockhart, "Cancer in Myth and Dream," in J. Goldberg, ed., *Psychotherapeutic Treatment of Cancer Patients,* 16–38.
3. This is a conclusion from personal observation, and from discussions with colleagues who have observed similarly.

9

The Mind/Body Connection

It is on the level of hormones that the mind and body meet. Hormones are the physical representation of emotions. Any change in feeling is concomitant with a change in hormone release or inhibition.[1]

All emotions are received in the form of chemical stimuli by the hypothalamus, the organ lying at the base of the brain which is both directly over and intimately in contact with the pituitary. The hypothalamus processes emotion both quantitatively and qualitatively, and in doing so, allows for distinctions to be made between feelings. We recognize the difference between sorrow and anger, for instance, because of differences in signals that the hypothalamus will send out. Sorrow involves signals stimulating tear glands, blood vessels in the face, and nerve complexes in the lungs and heart; anger involves signals sent to most of the nerve endings of the sympathetic nervous system, which causes secretions of large amounts of epinephrine and norepinephrine (also known as adrenalin and nonadrenalin, or collectively, as catecholemines). In addition, the hypothalamus will stimulate the pituitary, which then stimulates its own production of hormones that are sent to various other organs, including the adrenal, sex, and thyroid glands, and the pancreas. These organs in turn produce their own characteristic hormones. Having feelings, then, entails massive activation of the endocrine system. An individual subject to an intense feeling will be exposed to large amounts of pituitary and adrenal hormones, the sex hormones of testosterone or estrogen, thyroxine, and insulin.

The hormone system, like the other systems in the human organism, has a natural homeostatic regulatory mechanism.[2] When sufficient hormones have been secreted to meet the need of the body, the hypothalamus notes this satiation point in the blood, and inhibits further secretion. Conversely, if there is an undersecretion, the desired physiological effect of the hormone diminishes, signalling the inhibition to decrease, and the gland once again begins pouring out its hormone.

Malfunctioning in this homeostatic mechanism occurs when exposure to these hormones becomes excessive. If a particular emotion persists over time, these hormones are required to do much more than respond to an emergency or temporary situation. Stimulation of the glands is now chronic, and excess discharge becomes chronic, as well.

In studying this malfunctioning, some remarkable congruencies were found that shed a great deal of light—at surprising angles—on the two great killer diseases. In experiments that began in the early 1950's it was found that, in the hormonal system, fear and anger produce essentially the same reactions, and that in a sudden emergency, the autonomic response of massive secretion of the hormone epinephrine is the same, regardless of the nature of the emergency.[3] Fear and anger seem to represent the same phenomenon on the level of the body.[4]

Yet the personality type that is in a state of perpetual fear, and that behaves in a way designed assiduously to avoid anger and confrontation, is what's known as the type C personality—a cancer-prone individual. And the type A, heart attack-prone personality demonstrates an excessive susceptibility to fits of anger and rage, and gives little indication of any underlying fears.

What this seeming contradiction leads us to conclude is that heart disease and cancer, at the biological level, are identical. Both these personality types are engaged in chronic, continuous struggles. Physiological defenses are overtaxed and overstrained, so that recovery to the preemergency state of functioning is no longer possible. With the defenses all but shut down, massive proliferation on the cellular level takes place, and tumors interfering with functioning result.

The detailed route of all cell proliferation stimulated by the hormonal system is now known for both cancer and heart disease. Excess production of hormones leads, in both diseases, to the intrusion of a death process into living tissue.

In heart disease, excess catecholimine production leads to increased deposits of the blood's clotting elements. These clotting elements fix themselves on the arterial wall, as does cholesterol. Through their precipitation, plaque is made even larger. Also, the excess cate-cholimines cause narrowing of the capillaries which nourish the coronary blood vessels. Not only are the still intact parts of the coronary arteries affected, but internal areas of the plaque that may still have retained viability are now threatened, as well. As has been noted, the state of internal decay and necrosis in the plaque represents as serious a danger as the size. And, finally, to add insult to injury, because of the hypothalamus-induced overstimulation of the sympathetic nervous system, excess insulin beings to accumulate in the blood.[5]

What began as a relatively local phenomenon of the hypothalamus has now, through prolonged stimulation of hormones, fanned out throughout the body and caused the systemic disorder known as heart disease.

The effect of excess hormone on carcinogenic growth was also observed clinically in the middle part of this century. A patient with metastatic melanoma was subjected to a lobotomy, a surgical invasion of the hypothalamus used, at that time, to treat mental illness, and, in cases such as this one, physical pain. Within a few days of the surgical procedure, the metastases had completely disappeared.[6] Other clinicians subsequently confirmed this experience,[7-10] and hypothesized that some forms of cancer cells thrive on hypothalamus-stimulated hormones, and that when the supply is cut off, the cancer cell dies.[11]

Experimental research gives further evidence that carcinogenic change can occur through a direct application of hormones. Stilbestrol, a growth hormone, has yielded an increase in cell division in the adrenal cortex a few hours after injection.[12] Testosterone (male sex hormone) has been shown to increase both cell proliferation and cell size.[13]

Other studies have measured psychological determinants as well as hormone activity in cancer. One researcher found psychological co-variance of hydrocortisone production in women with breast cancer.[14] Others found correlations between steroid excretion patterns and personality attributes in patients with lung cancer.[15]

The process by which excess hormones result in carcinogenic cellular changes was discovered by Otto Warburg.[16] Warburg's discovery, for which he won a Nobel Prize, was that the cancer cell is an oxygen deficient cell. Our normal respiration allows oxygen to reach every tissue in our body. The oxygen that we inhale allows us to burn nutritious substances, resulting in the byproducts of water and carbon dioxide, which we then exhale. However, the respiratory enzymes in the mitochondria of the cell can be damaged, with the result that the cell becomes unable to utilize the oxygen, and the combustion process remains incomplete. Rather than water and carbon dioxide being formed, lactic acid is manufactured. Warburg called this a suffocation of the tissues.

Cancer cells stop with the production of lactic acid. They have been damaged, and are no longer able to burn sugar efficiently—all the way to carbon dioxide and water. The process leading from sugar to the endproducts of carbon dioxide and water is complicated, involving over thirty steps. This process can easily be interfered with. Warburg stated that the stressors that would act to interfere with the normal respiratory process were radiation or chemicals. Of the chemicals, those produced by one's own body, the hormones, were often the culprit and could cause irreversible damage. The remaining cells that had not yet been destroyed by the excess hormones were forced to make compensatory adaptations. A new process emerges, which Warburg called fermentation. The hormonal cycle is now unbalanced, and the fermentation process represents the organism's stuggle to survive in the face of an ever-encroaching death process.

Warburg's work is important in yet another way. He concluded that the destruction of the respiratory capacity of the cell is the result of small, often repeated doses of the stress agent. His work is compelling confirmation of Selye's idea that it is the continuous application of noxious substances, rather than a sudden, infrequent burst of attack which results in cancerous growth. Research following this idea has demonstrated that normal cells can be converted into cancerous cells through intermittent deprivation of oxygen over a long period of time.[17]

Notes

1. For a thorough discussion of the mind/body interface, see E. L. Rossi, *The Psychobiology of Mind-Body Healing,* NY: W. W. Norton, 1986. For a specific discussion on the role of hormones, see H. E. Simmons, *The Psychogenic Theory of Disease,* (Sacramento, CA: Citadel Press, 1966,) Chapter 2.
2. The process of self-regulation of the hormonal system as well as the other systems of the body is the theme of A. Kaslow & R. Miles, *Freedom From Chronic Disease* (Los Angeles, CA: J. P. Tarcher, 1979) Chapter 4.

3. W. B. Cannon, *Bodily Changes in Pain, Hunger, Fear, and Rage* (NY: Appleton, 1920).
4. A. F. Ax, "The Physiological Differentiation Between Fear and Anger in Humans," *Psychosomatic Medicine* 15.5 (1953).
5. M. Friedman, & R. H. Roseman, *Type A Behavior and Your Heart.*
6. P. M. West, "The Psychological Variables in Human Cancer," in J. A. Gengerelli, & F. J. Kirkner, ed., *A Symposium* Berkeley: University of California Press, 1954), 92–93.
7. M. A. White, "The Social Significance of Mental Disease," *Archives of Neurological Psychiatry* 22:873, (1929).
8. A. E. Sheflen, "Malignant Tumors in the Institutionalized Psychotic Population," *AMA Archives of Neurology & Psychiatry* 66:145 (1951).
9. W. Freeman, "Biometrical Studies in Psychiatry—The Chances of Death," *American Journal of Psychiatry* 8:425 (1928).
10. L. C. F. Chevons, "The Correlations of Cancer and Death with Type of Insanity," *Journal of Mental Science* 77:562 (1931).
11. E. J. Sacher, J. W. Mason, H. S. Kolmer, K. L. Artiss, "Psychoendocrine Aspects of Acute Schizophrenic Reactions," *Psychosomatic Medicine* 25, (1963): 510–37.
12. D. B. Carter, & M. P. Stachs - Dunne, "Effects of Growth Hormone and Corticotropin Upon Adrenal Weight and Adrenocortical Mitotic Activity in Hypophysectomized rat," *Journal of Endocrinology* 12 (1955): 25–32.
13. F. J. Ebling, "Endocrine Factors Affecting All Replacement and Cell Loss in the Epidermis and Sebaceous Glands of the Female Albino Rat," *Journal of Endocrinology* 12 (1955): 38.
14. F. J. Sachar, ed., *Topics in Pscyhoendocrinology* (NY: Grune & Stratton, 1965).
15. Ibid.
16. O. Warburg, "On the Origin of Cancer Cells," *Science* 123 (1956): 309–14.
17. H. Goldblatt, & G. Cameron, "Induced Malignancy in Cells From Rat Myocardium Subjected to Intermittent Anaerobiosis During Long Propagation in Vitro," *Journal of Experimental Medicine* 97 (1953): 525–52.

10

Psychosis of the Body—Cancer of the Mind (The Isomorphic Relation between Cancer and Schizophrenia)

> *Although there are finer creations of the spirit than perversion and psychosis, in the long run it is better to be mad than dead.*
> —Joyce McDougall

As discoveries were made in psychological and physiological laboratories about the defensive strategies of mind and body, researchers were led back to earlier and earlier stages in human development, both of the mind and of the body. The emphasis on tissue change caused by alien invasion was replaced by an emphasis on the structure of the very earliest life form—the cell.[1] On the psychological side, it began to be understood that the stage of arousal and resolution of the sexual feelings was too late a point in the maturational sequence to hold final answers.[2] The importance of the earlier conflicts, arising both before the acquisition of language and before sexual feelings were attached to an "out-there" object began to be emphasized.

As this ontogenetic retracing was done, researchers found that investigations into the nature of disease were bringing them to questions having to do with the very beginning of life. The development of the physical immune system was completed by the first year of life; the positioning of the psychological defensive apparatus was also largely completed in this early stage of infancy.

However, the inflammatory process that Freud observed on the level of the mind in the diseases of hysteria and paranoia, and that Selye observed on the level of the body, can only take place in a relatively mature organism. Inflammation as a healing process can occur only when differentiation between self and not-self has occurred. If the disturbance arises before the point in maturation when this distinction is made, when self and not-self remained fused, recognition of not-self by self is impossible, and the inflammatory response to not-self can't be triggered.

With this understanding, researchers noticed that in these very early processes of differentiation there seemed to be the potential for biological and psychological disarray that would lead, eventually, to the most profound of all dysfunctions. Without the ability of the organism to distinguish self from not-self, the initial problem, whose successful solution ensured survival of the organism, would not be solved. It was the inability of the organism to recognize not-self entities, and consequent failure to call the forces of self-protection into activity, which would inexorably lead to life-threatening dysfunction.

Once again the parallel natures of mind and body were startlingly vivid. This problem of self/not-self distinction was addressed and resolved on both the biological and psychological levels in the same fashion.

Human life begins on the cellular level from a single cell, residing within which is the potential to differentiate into component parts that will eventually comprise the complexity of the entire organism. The process of differentiation determines that as cells reproduce, each will have ascribed to it a single, special function, and the expression of all other functions represented in the other cells, will, within that cell, be repressed.

As cellular differentiation takes place in utero, the structure of the human organism is created. Cell growth follows certain preordained laws of nature, and within these fairly rigid constraints, the cells will organize themselves to create the form of the human organism. By the time of birth the major work in this effort toward differentiation has already taken place. Cells have multiplied and stratified into heart, muscles, lungs, brain, and so on; through a control mechanism the cells normally reach their appropriate sizes and shapes, and then stop their process of growth.

In spite of whatever differentiations have occurred and are apparent by the time of birth, the newborn functions as a whole.[3] Reactions to stress—whether from internal sources such as hunger or thirst, or external, such as cold or heat, and whether somatic or psychological—

are generalized patterns of total responsive behavior. The infant cries, salivates, regurgitates, defecates. Let only one toe be uncomfortable, and every part of the body is galvanized into action. The skin becomes flushed and vigorous movement occurs in every appendage. The baby functions in an integrated manner, using everything he has available.

At this stage of relative undifferentiation, the infant has the highest degree of potential for development—but he has the highest degree of sensitivity, as well. If the stimulus is traumatic or damaging, at this early phase the entire organism—body and mind—tends to be affected. Later traumatic events, acting on a more organized structure or function, are limited in both site and localization of effect.[4]

This level of differentiation is inadequate to sustain independent life. The birth of the infant after a nine-month gestation period has positive survival value only for the mother. The particular timing results, however, in serious disadvantages for the newborn, who remains almost equally dependent outside the womb as he was inside.[5] He can breathe, move his muscles, suck, and his heart beats. All the other regulatory mechanisms are poorly developed, and external imitation of his intrauterine experience is necessary to stabilize his temperature, fluid balance, and so forth.

In particular, the physical and psychological defense systems are seriously underdeveloped at birth. It is only in the first few critical months of life that the completion of both the psychological and physiological defense systems is achieved. The infant who does not mature normally at this time, through either congenital or environmental deficiencies, will retain, often throughout the rest of his life, serious disabilities in the functioning of these defensive mechanisms.

On the level of the body, the immune system is only a potential at birth. There are a few antibodies present, of a type called IgG, but these are merely residual from the pregnancy, when they crossed through the placenta to the fetus.[6] Another important class of antibodies IgA, which combat intestinal infections, are nonexistent in the newborn.[7] Macrophages, the front-line defenders against infection which have the ability to stop cancer cells, have yet to be acquired. The infant, then, has little ability to defend itself against invaders. The colostrum in the mother's milk, a substance rich in antibodies, at first substitutes for an immune system. As many as 80 percent of the cells in breast milk are macrophages, which when ingested by the newborn, confer a passive immunity until the time, six months later, when the infant will have a more mature immune system capable of manufacturing its own antibodies.[8]

With the maturing of the immune system, the body has acquired the ability to differentiate a variety of not-self entities. These include objects (living and nonliving) of the external world, microbes housed within the body, organs or tissues transplanted from another organism, or body parts dislocated from one body location to another (e.g. skin grafts).

The human mind, like the body, has the ability to differentiate self from not-self. And as with the body, this capacity is, at birth, still only an inactivated potential. On the level of the mind, the infant is born into the experience of psychic and somatic fusion. He lacks the capacity to distinguish either his mind from his body, or his own body and mind from objects in the outside world. Freud variously described this experience as "oceanic," "limitless," or "unbounded," and it is in this objectless field that the infant's first sensations of himself and the world are received and recorded.[9] This stage of undifferentiation was termed *primary narcissism.*

From this state of undifferentiation, maturation proceeds in several directions. Maturation and increasing specialization of function proceed in the central nervous system and motor apparatus. Simultaneously, stabilization of regulatory processes and emergence of thought processes occur. The initial recognition of one's body as a distinct entity comes about because of the integrated qualities of perception, thinking, and awareness.[10] The sense of self we call the ego begins as a body ego. The progression of maturation of the ego is consonant with the maturation of the central nervous system.

Corollary to the recognition of self is growing awareness of not-self. It is through the tactile experience of the mother's body that the infant is first able to develop a sense of two different bodies, his own and his mother's. As the bliss of symbiosis is punctured, the infant comes to know that he is not the entirety of the universe. As it is the mother who represents the first object field outside himself, it is toward her that the infant directs all his feelings about this shocking realization that they are separate. Fenichel provides a good description of this process:

> In the development of reality the conception of one's body plays a very special role. At first there is only the perception of tension, that is, of an "inside something." Later, with the awareness that an object exists to quiet this tension, we have an "outside something." One's own body

becomes something apart from the rest of the world and thus discerning of self from nonself is made possible.[11]

Through being mothered, the child becomes able to combine and coordinate the experience of sucking, or food intake, with more general sense intake. Perceptual and cognitive progressions permit the child to focus his gaze by the third or fourth week of life. His increasing ability to see constancy in the external world—to perceive it as stable and reliable—further aids in movement towards recognition of self as distinct from the objects he perceives.[12] And this well-known developmental sequence proceeds until, somewhere at the end of the second year of life, if all has gone well, the basic idea—that one is oneself, and everything else isn't—is in place. It isn't until full maturity—past adolescence even in ideal cases—that the boundary between self and not-self is complete and distinct.

The recognition of not-self is not limited, however, to the field of the world outside one's self. Freud's investigation into the mind revealed that just as the body is comprised of the component parts of organs and systems, so too does the mind divide itself structurally into functional aspects. The existence of the mental entities of id, ego, and superego, and various levels of consciousness, permit parts to operate conflictually and invasively to one another. Dreams, for instance, are a manifestation of unconscious material pressing into consciousness,[13] and if the material is deeply embedded in the unconscious, as in a nightmare, the conscious mind—the ego—experiences this as an intrusion of not-self material into self.

By observing the ways in which this process can be thwarted on the level of the mind, Freud identified the disease of pathological narcissism. Parallel research on the level of the body revealed that the equivalent somatic dysfunction led to the disease of cancer. Each of these conditions reflects a state of dedifferentiation where the normally distinct boundaries between self and not-self do not exist. Either the normal growth toward differentiation has failed to occur and the immature stage of undifferentiation is perpetuated (fixation), or mature differentiation occurs but interfering variables cause a reversal back to the undifferentiated state (regression).

On the level of the mind, Freud's discovery of the psychosexual phases of development was essentially a formulation of the normal linear progression toward differentiation in the psychosexual apparatus. What he found is that if early stages of development are not mastered, the personality remains stuck—he called it fixated—at that level of functioning. When this fixation occurs at the very earliest developmental milestone of the infant, before self and not-self would normally separate and become distinct from one another, the consequences are quite severe. While physical maturity may proceed, the narcissistic adult remains an emotional child housed in an adult body (alongside an adult intellect, often enough). The primary narcissism that marked a normal developmental phase in early infancy has now turned into pathological narcissism—a self/object fusion that is no longer appropriate.

Alternatively, differentiation may have occurred, but the original self/not-self fusion reappears through the process of dedifferentiation. Normal maturation would have led to an increasing desomatization of reactions—that is, toward maximal use of integrated muscle action and toward replacement of action by talk and by thought; and to a concomitant reduction of vegetative discharge phenomena. Now in a state of regression, these advances are lost, and the organism once again responds with body and mind at once, and self and not-self fused.

The extent to which the self/not-self distinction fails to be made is both the extent of the regression, and the determinant of the degree of neurotic pathology. Carried to its most extreme state, the condition becomes manifest by the clinical condition we refer to as schizophrenia. This psychotic state is marked by a pathological fusion of self and object images—the same oceanic experience that Freud referred to in his description of the experiences of the newborn.[14]

Psychic disturbance in pathological narcissism is evident on the structural levels of personality integration—ego, id, and superego. These component parts refuse to operate harmoniously, and function as though they were not part of the same psychic system. The ego—that part of the psyche which maintains a vigilance on reality—is split within itself, appearing to consist of isolated islands of psychic configuration, seemingly not linked to one another.[15] The id, repository of primitive drives which, when channeled properly, can be a wellspring of creative and energetic potential, here is experienced by the ego as an intensely inimical foreign body, threatening to overwhelm the rest of the psychic apparatus.[16] The superego—that part of our psyche we generally refer to as our conscience—normally serves to aid the ego in its efforts to respond appropriately to both id impulses from within and to the demands of the outer world. Here the superego functions as a cruel tyrant, assaulting the unintegrated ego with its own unrelenting and unreasonable demands.[17]

The bizarre behaviors that we see exhibited in schizophrenia are attempts to force on the self, often in painful ways, a felt experience of the self/not-self distinction. The head-knocking and self-biting frequently observed in autistic children can be seen as pathological attempts to sharpen awareness of the body self and to reinforce boundary integrity. It is as though the feeling of the definition of self is so dull, so blunted, that only this terrible assault has the hope of stimulating the experience of self. Hallucinations, too, arise out of the fact that internal and external sensations are experienced as a continuum, rather than as discrete entities located in the alternative sites of self or object. The schizophrenic, then, has difficulty discriminating between false impressions and realities. Investment in order is abandoned, and perception exists unchanged in its raw, unfiltered, and unrefined form. The process of dedifferentiation rules.

Short of this level of dysfunction is the patient who maintains some amount of self/not-self distinction, and still suffers from the lack of a secure and well-grounded self.[18] The boundaries between self and not-self will remain blurred and indistinct. Commerce between self and not-self is still profoundly disturbed. The narcissist, then, having failed to bring objects (that is, persons whose separate reality is evident to one) into existence, is left with an empty psychic house, with no stable internalized objects to provide a sense of comfort and security.

Investigation into the process of self/not-self differentiation on the level of the mind had convinced researchers that the most profound of all mental disorders, schizophrenia, arose from failures at this early stage of development;[19] parallel research on the level of the body led to an understanding of the fundamental issues in the development of the disease of cancer.[20]

What emerged from the research on the body was the fact that the fundamental dysfunction in pathological narcissism was precisely the same one seen in cancer. The cancer cell, in fact, acts as though it were schizophrenic.

The boundaryless state of narcissism is mirrored in the nature of the cancer cell. This is the biological mechanism that leads to the change that is cancer's most characteristic attribute—that of unrestrained growth. A normal cell in a state of growth will be impeded through its contact with other cells.[21] It will hit up against the adjoining cell, and a separating membrane will serve as a barrier against intrusion of one cell into another. Thus, cells are normally permitted both to grow and, simultaneously, to maintain integrity of form and function.

The cancer cell, however, respects no boundaries. In a similar state of growth, it will continue to reproduce, unimpeded by cellular contact inhibition.[22] The adjoining cell, by allowing its normally strong barrier membrane to yield to this invasion, colludes in the enterprise.

As the psychic structure in narcissism has regressed to an earlier mode of functioning, so too does the function of the cancer cell reflect a turning back. Cancer cells begin as not qualitatively different from normal cells. Normal cells divide when young, but remain undifferentiated—just as cancer cells do. It is here, though, that the cancer cell begins to manifest its pathology. Instead of maturing into a specialized cell with a specialized function, the cancer cell remains in a state of undifferentiation. It has become stuck in an immature phase. Whatever may have been the original intent of that cell in differentiation into a specialized cell with a particular function, as a cancer cell it now defies the laws that would assign it to a rightful and ordered place in the economy of the organism.

Further research led to even greater clarification of the cancer condition. The discrimination between the two different types of lymphocytes, the T and B cells, was crucial. Both types of lymphocytes come from bone marrow, but the types differ in the particular foreign matter they attack.[23]

It was research on the B cell that provided the impetus that led to specific answers about cancer and the immune system. World War II suddenly provided researchers with a very large population in which to study the immune reaction. In treating severe burn cases, surgeons attempted to transplant skin from one site on the patient's body to another. They were confounded by lack of success. It was news that the body has a built-in mechanism for the rejection of any not-self intrusion into the boundaries of self. This ability was well known for combating such not-self entities as viruses and bacteria, and it was the B cell which battled these. The body was now found to react to another class of entity as though they were entities originating within the body, but abnormal in some way. Tissue transplants and the cancer cell were among these, and it was the purview of the T cell to fight off these entities, which remained foreign only in that they weren't exactly where they were supposed to be.

The body had doubtless been struggling against microbes from the external world since time immemorial. It was easy to understand how natural selection favored such a defense. But why would thousands of generations of selection have preserved a built-in reaction to tissue transplants? How had we come to have such a highly developed capacity for rejection of foreign matter of this kind?

Lewis Thomas proposed a startling answer which unified all of the previous findings. In line with past thinking, he said that the immune system has the function of policing the body from internal as well as external threats. The nature of the internal threat was, however, obviously not tissue artificially introduced through transplants; it was the spontaneous and daily production of thousands of cells which are abnormal, genetically different, and potentially cancerous.[24] Speculating even further, it is possible that cellular immunity may have evolved phylogenetically for its value as a surveillance mechanism against the cancer cell.

By the 1950's, the mechanisms of resistance to diseases had been formulated on both the psychological and physiological levels: the defense mechanisms protect us against intruding agents on the psychic level and the immune system protects us from intruding agents on the physical level. It is only when sufficient differentiation of self has been achieved that the organism has the ability to recognize the invasion of not-self entities. Inadequate discriminations of self/not-self entities on the psychological level characterizes the disease of narcissism, and the same inadequacy on the somatic level leads to cancer. The schizophrenic mind and the cancer body appear to be mirror images of one another. Cancer is a condition of biological narcissism.

All that remained for the reemergence of an integrated theory of mind/body involvement in disease was the scientific determination that the psychological defensive apparatus interacted with the physiologic immune system, and that dysfunction in one could cause disease in the other. Psychic factors can play a role in the contraction and progression of somatic diseases; similarly, physical factors can contribute to psychic disturbances.

Psychosomatic medicine is the name given to the relatively new discipline whose express purpose is the study of the interface of mind and body.[25] It was within this field of study that such a determination of mind effecting body could be made. The problem of how the psychological apparatus interacts with and effects the body was not an easy one to solve. Freud's initial work with hysterics raised some of the questions for the first time, but provided few answers because the hysteric only mimicked physiological involvement. These people clearly demonstrated that mental disarray could play a role in the body's integrity, through their symptoms of paralysis, false pregnancies, and the like. But Freud's analysis of these patients revealed that there was no real organic involvement. The physical manifestations were symptoms, created only through the defensive mechanisms of the psyche. As such, the symptom was an expression of emotional matter that was repressed, or cut off from consciousness, and was a symbolic representation of that conflict.

The idea of actual somatic involvement posed a somewhat different problem: some mechanism whereby the mental apparatus could effect physiological change needed to be postulated. While Freud did not apply himself to this problem, other psychoanalysts attempted to extend Freud's original concept of hysterical conversion to all psychogenic disturbances, including those which arise in the organs and tissues themselves. In one early conceptualization, bodily disturbances were symbolic of particular repressed ideas.[26] This concept has now been abandoned. There is no evidence that either the organs or the autonomic nervous system can actually express an idea; neither has any direct connection with the part of the organism which produces ideational processes. Thus it seemed unlikely that the aspect of symbolic meaning of emotionally charged psychological content, as seen in the conversion symptoms of hysteria, could be carried over into the dysfunction of the vegetative organs.

It wasn't until clearer understanding of the hormonal, endocrine, and central nervous systems was acquired that researchers were able to postulate the precise workings of a mind/body interaction that could explain psychosomatic illness. Early psychosomaticists observed correlations between specific organic illnesses and personality traits.[27] Understanding of the process of human psychophysical maturation advanced, and along with it, how difficulties in the process could lead to somatic, as well as psychic, dysfunctions. It was actually Freud's abandonment of the trauma theory—that developmental distortions must be the product of an externally imposed injury—and his discovery that the enemy is within and a part of oneself, that paved the way for an understanding of psychosomatic illness.

If neurosis is an internal disturbance that can occur at any point in the developmental sequence, then the particular point at which development is snagged may well determine, to some extent, the nature of the dysfunction. Inadequate mastery of any stage inhibits progress into the next stage. While Freud himself was primarily interested in the conflicts that are aroused at the age of seven or eight, when sexual strivings reach a peak, psychosomaticists looked earlier in the maturational sequence. The psychosomatic diseases are thought, then, to differ from the less serious psychoneurotic dysfunctions in the point of origin and dysfunction.[28]

Freud's theories of energy, conflict, and psychosexual development provide us with the groundwork for an understanding of psychosomatic diseases. Freud's concept of the human organism was essentially an energetic one, based on tension and release of tension. Impulses well up from the id, and with these impulses come conflicts. Tension needs discharge as too much accumulation of tension causes disease.[29] The behavior of the newborn can be likened to the model of the reflex-arc. As tension is augmented with the emergence of conflict, there is a consequent increase in the level of excitation to the point where pleasure becomes displeasure. The infants seeks methods to release the tension so that he can return to his former state of tension-free pleasure. But he has only a limited number of ways of doing this. His mind is still insufficiently developed to be able to use any methods demanding complex thought, judgement or perception. Language has not yet been acquired. Motoric discharge, through the use of his body, is the only means available to him.

When Freud attempted to understand why a patient couldn't remember the cause of his illness, he speculated that there was, at times, an intellectual incapacity. Some painful, disease-stimulating experiences could not be thought about because they had occurred before the age when speech had been learned. There were no words to describe these experiences because there were no language residues associated with them. What had not been able to be talked about early on could not, later, be thought about.

As the child grows, his mind becomes an increasingly specialized, differentiated, and sophisticated instrument.[30] He develops judgement, perception, thought, affect, fantasy. These tools, then, become valuable when conflict arises again. The child's now adequately developed mental apparatus will allow him to find a means of reducing the level of tension so that conflict does not reach a level of intensity that is painful and/or destructive. If psychological development is stunted, though, the child remains unable to reduce the level of tension through the use of his mental apparatus, and he may resort to an earlier mode of discharge. There remains an incapacity to reduce tension through any means other than the body itself.

Experimental research on the psychosomatic cancer patient confirms that there is, indeed, a dysfunction arising very early in the maturational sequence,[31-34] and that this psychological dysfunction parallels the difficulty on the level of the body. In the cancer patient, the psychological defense system, like the physical defense apparatus, is inadequately activated. The responses to dangerous stimuli that would normally act as warning signals to the ego either are never aroused, or are aroused with insufficient strength to generate a response.

We know that activation of the physical defense system means stimulation of autonomic chemical and hormonal processes over which we have little conscious control. When we refer to the psychological defense system, we think in terms of the psychological representation of physical processes. We think in terms of feelings. The first feeling that Freud identified which represented arousal of the defensive apparatus was the feeling of anxiety: "Anxiety is reaction to danger," he said. For Freud, danger included both real and present dangers, and anticipated dangers that may exist only in the mind. Freud situated this response in the ego.[35] Later, the feeling states of pain, guilt, shame, and anger were added.

In the psychosomatic cancer patient, these feeling signals appear to be dulled. This lack of acknowledgement of feeling states—which appears in analysis to be quite strenuously worked for—is in stark contrast to our more spontaneous and flexible responses to reality that mark a more normal adaptation.

It is this inactivation of the psychological defense system which the experimental researchers have isolated as the main component in the makeup of the cancer personality. Greer observed in many cancer patients an "inordinately pleasant personality;"[31] Schamie found a tendency for cancer patients to be lacking in their experience and expression of aggression;[37] Rennaker refers to the Pathological Niceness Syndrome, by which he means an indiscriminate, even promiscuous niceness.[38] Each of these researchers has found that cancer patients demonstrate a pathological denial and repression of both their own and others' negative emotions, particularly anger.

In the face of this disconnection from important parts of his inner self, the cancer patient is left to create a veneer of a personality—generally a pleasant, likeable persona, but one which, in its incapacity to recognize danger and thus mobilize its own defensive strategy against it, is supremely vulnerable.

This patient reminds us of the unfortunate "boy in the bubble," who was born without any immune potential. Any intrusion of a germ into his defenseless body would have meant death to him, and he was forced to live his short life completely enclosed in a sterile environment, cordoned off and protected from the living environment. Cancer patients are like that boy, but without his protective shield of glass. In the light of inadequate defenses, both psychological and physical, the situation seems hopelessly fragile and precarious.

Research has afforded us a comprehensive understanding of how mind and body normally develop. We have seen that, initially, mind and body proceed in seemingly parallel fashion; what one does, the other reflects. Both engage in the essential process of differentiation, and in so making an adequate self/not-self distinction, allow for the emergence of the immunological and defensive systems. Research has further given us a vivid picture of the pathological outcomes of interference with this process of differentiation: cancer, on the level of the body; schizophrenia, on the level of the mind. The cancer cell is like the schizophrenic mind—undefended, wild, dangerously out of control. The cancer cell appears to be in a state of biological narcissism.

But the mind of the cancer patient seems to be in stark contradistinction to the functionings of the body. Cancer within the body is a state of wild expansiveness, growth unchecked by any normal control apparatus. The mind of the cancer patient is, in contrast, characterized by constriction—a control too tightly held. The cancer patient lacks the freedom of mind normally afforded us by our dreams and fantasies and our ability to imagine options for ourselves. Feelings and thoughts lead to psychic deadends for the cancer patient.

It may occur to us at first to postulate a breakdown of communication between mind and body. But the very consistency of their opposition here leads us soon to the idea that there is, instead, some profound link between them. Indeed, it looks as though mind and body are operating in some compensatory fashion. The mind seems to want to counteract the excessive growth of the body; and the body seems to want to compensate for the excessive constriction of the mind. The very rapid change that is evidenced by the body is counteracted by the quality of stagnation in the mind. With the body out of balance and the mind inharmoniously integrated, the two seem to be making an awkward and surely ill-fated attempt at homeostatic restoration of balance and harmony by serving as complements to one another.

It is within the realm of the unconscious mind that this communicative link can be found. It has long been an established premise that on the biological level, consciousness is not an essential ingredient in communication. Within the human system, the autonomic functioning of both the neural and hormonal systems are examples of exquisitely complex mechanisms for transmitting the effects of what happens in one part of the body to other parts, independent of conscious awareness. Freud applied this principle to the workings of the psyche, and found that parts of our psyche communicate with other parts without our conscious participation or awareness. The very definition of neurosis is based on the idea of the functional separation between conscious purpose and underlying psychic intent.[39]

In fact, it appears that while the conscious mind of the cancer patient operates, as we have seen, in a manner inversely related to the functioning of the body, the unconscious mind incorporates the very characteristics of the cancer process. This is to say that the mind of the cancer patient embodies certain characteristics of the cancer itself. Rorschach responses of cancer patients, for example, tend to follow the formal characteristics of the cancer.[40] On the cards where isolated images are presented, cancer patients, contrary to the more usual response, ignore the segmental and restrained presentation of the image, and instead, see the picture as one large, expansive image, attempting often to incorporate the entire card into the one image; we are reminded of the invasive nature of the cancer cell, threatening to subsume the whole body through its manifestation of a pathological expansiveness.

Further, when there was obvious symmetrical configuration of form in the Rorschach, as in the cards where the blots appear to be the result of paper being folded over on itself to produce a symmetrical, mirror image, the usual response is to see these figures as related and interacting with one another. Cancer patients saw them as separate and unrelated. Here we are reminded of the incomplete communicative capacity found in the cancer patient. Where body and mind should be connected, they seem to be dangerously out of touch with one another; where the intrapsychic and social worlds should mesh to allow for the possibility of intimate interaction between self and other, the cancer patient seems isolated and alone, cut off from meaningful contact.

Additional research suggests that this isomorphic relationship between the body and the unconscious aspects of the psyche pertains even to the detail of the formal characteristics of the particular organ site affected. Patients with exterior cancers (e.g., breast) had substantially higher barrier scores on the Rorschach, and patients with interior cancers (e.g., cervix) had higher scores on the penetration scale.[41] The data is convincing evidence for the notion of a meaningful link between the physical aspect of the cancer in terms of its location choice, and the psychological analogue as represented by discrimination of intrapsychic boundary dimensions.

It would seem, then, that in a cancer situation mind and body operate such that both do not go wildly out of control simultaneously. This inverse relationship appears to pertain to the schizophrenic condition, as well. Just as the constricted psyche of the cancer patient demonstrates attributes diametrically opposed to the wild-growing cancer, similarly, the schizophrenic rarely contracts cancer. It has been estimated that schizophrenics have a cancer rate two to four times lower than the rest of the population.[42-43]

There is one exception to this rule, and it is a telling one. In paranoid schizophrenics, cancer occurs four times as often as in the general population.[44-47] Paranoia is, of course, a state of exaggerated defensiveness.[48] It is the one form of schizophrenia where the defensive structure is too strong. It stands in sharp contradistinction to both cancer and all other types of schizophrenia, where it is precisely the weakened defense system that is the cause of the pathology.

It is perhaps the relative frequency of cancer in the paranoid condition that has made the alliance of these two dysfunctions a fertile area for speculation. Clinical observations on the waxing and waning of the paranoid state strongly support the theory of an inverse and perhaps compensatory relationship between psychosis and cancer.

All forms of schizophrenia represent a situation of severe psychological disorganization. The paranoid patient however, is the only type of schizophrenic in whom the response to the deterioration takes the form of an overreaction against this disorganization of mental life.

Elaborately detailed fantasies are constructed; often, there is enough contact with what's actually possible that the delusions can be quite compelling, even to normal individuals. There is a mere misinterpretation of environmental events—an arbitrary selection of perceptual experience—rather than the creation of a whole new delusional reality. Hallucinations are uncommon among paranoids. It might be the kind of accident of interpretation that any of us could make under conditions unfavorable to accurate perception, except that the mistake is so exaggerated, the process of error so elaborately and relentlessly pursued.

This holding on to a fragment of reality, tenuous though it may be, is in contrast to the other schizophrenic reactions where the disorganization (or, dedifferentiation) of mental life is more archaic and infantile. In profound cases, detachment and withdrawal from the environment is virtually complete.

The paranoiac, then, in having a closer hold on reality, wages a desperate battle between reality contact and disintegration of personality. The usual profuse verbalization of the paranoid, unlike the stonewall silence of the catatonic schizophrenic and the word-salad utterings of the hebephrenic schizophrenic, makes the extent of the hold onto and the slipping away from reality relatively easy to follow.

A number of clinicians working with paranoid schizophrenics with cancer have observed that as the psychosis becomes more apparent, the cancer regresses or goes into dormancy.[49] The converse also seems to be true: if the psychosis responds to treatment and the patient is brought back into the realm of reality, the malignancy resumes its activity. The interplay between physical and psychic disease manifestation is impressive, and suggests a possible survival function of psychosis.

Explanation for this fluctuating phenomenon is found in yet another attribute that the cancer cell and the schizophrenic mind have in common. Both are murderous. The cancer cell has the distinction of committing a double killing—first murder, by killing its host organism, and as the immediate consequence of this, suicide—for without its host, it must also die.

The schizophrenic, too, is caught in a web where it seems that the only solution is murder. The aggressive drive is thought to begin as early as intrauterine life, and its continuation is an attempt to maintain a homeostatic balance between tension and tension relief. Clinicians have observed the inability to constructively handle the arousal of these biologically innate feeling states in schizophrenics, and it is now thought that schizophrenia is a direct effect of precisely this maladjustment.

It is the dependency of both the cancer cell, on the biological level, and the human mind, on the psychological level, that produces this phenomenon.

The cancer cell cannot exist without a source of nourishment, and that source is the organism in which it resides. In its stupidity, it feeds off its host, homicidally invading and consuming as it grows, depriving its host of the necessities for survival, until finally debilitated, exhausted, and malnourished, the host ceases to be able to perform life-sustaining functions, and expires. The cancer cell, without the host on whom it depended, now succumbs itself.

The human organism has the capability of partnering itself in this same dance of death. We are born into a state of biological and psychological dependence incomparable to any other stage in our life. Though the cutting of the umbilical cord severs the biological connection of the infant to the mother, an equally strong, and equally vital, psychological bond remains. The infant quickly becomes aware that its survival is dependent on its mother's responsivity to its fundamental needs of food, warmth, and love. We now know that the intangible phenomena of feelings—a sense of security, of being lovingly cared for and attended to—are not luxuries; they are essential needs, without which the infant is susceptible to disease and death. These very early experiences, the development of feelings around the issues of feeding and love, determine lifelong characterological patterns, and how these feelings of dependence are handled in this initial stage will influence the way in which dependence is handled when that infant grows into an adult.

The kind of destruction that results from the parasitic relation between host and parasite in the conditions of cancer and schizophrenia are not, however, biological necessities. Under normal circumstances, nature does make other provisions. Nature is replete with examples of parasitic relationships where survival of both the host and parasitic organisms is ensured.

The example of maggots is a good one. Some species of maggots, like the cancer cell, depend on live tissue for food. These maggots will seek out a larger living insect, puncture its skin with their stingers, and lay eggs within the body of the larger insect. The eggs must be deposited in a live animal because the newly hatched maggots will feed on the flesh of this insect. If a vital organ were to be destroyed, causing the death of the insect, all hatching maggots would perish, as well. The intelligence of this relationship is that nothing of the living insect is eaten except parts not essential for its survival.

The condition of human pregnancy is an equally successful parasitic relationship. Pregnancy shares some attributes with cancer, for instance, that of unparalleled growth. The gestation period of nine months for the human fetus is a biological necessity if survival is going to occur. The rate of growth of the brain, and the consequent growth of the head size during the last phases of pregnancy, proceeds at a pace so rapid that continuation of the gestation period would render a later birth impossible. The expulsion of the fetus before its virtual entrapment within the chamber of the womb permits the survival of both mother and fetus.[50]

The implantation of the fetus in the mother's body is accomplished by a sort of trick the body plays on itself (similar to the trick that is artificially induced in transplants): The self—the mother's body— comes to believe that the not-self entity of the fetus is not a foreign being.[51] Precisely how this trick of illusion is accomplished is still only partially understood, but we know that it demands a joint effort between mother and fetus. On the one hand, the uterus of the mother is uniquely designed to allow the mother an immunity lapse for the necessary nine months. Additionally, the fetus cuts down on rejection potential by successfully hiding those parts of self which the mother's body would recognize as foreign.

It is proteins in the cells, called transplantation antigens, which permit the body to distinguish self from not-self. In each of us, some of these proteins are derived from the genetic structure of the mother, and some come from the father. The pregnant woman will recognize those proteins in her fetus derived from herself as being uniquely hers; those from the father will be recognizably foreign. To limit the provocation of an immune response, the cells derived from the father stay deep in tissue, away from the immunologically sensitive parts of the uterus.

The mother aids this process through a precarious balancing of her rejection response. White blood cells that hover in the uterus near the placenta become lazy, and don't respond to the normally immune-stimulating chemical interleukin-2. Killer T-cells remain quiet. As well, the HCG hormone is lowered.

The total suppression of the mother's immune system in the very early stages would be fatal to the fetus. Spontaneous abortion occurs for the same reason as the death of a cancer patient. Partial stimulation of the mother's immune system is necessary to prompt the protective defenses of the fetus. If the genetic material from the father is too similar to the mother, his contribution will not be recognized as different, the initial provocation will not take place, and the fetus never learns to defend itself. Subsequent inevitable attack by the mother's immune system results in the abortion and death of the fetus.[52]

This relative inactivity of the immune system, and the lowering of the HCG factor, are conditions that exist in only one circumstance other than pregnancy. This is the condition of cancer. Here, too, the body's innate ability to recognize this invasion of not-self (the cancer cell) is diminished, and as in pregnancy, this invading cell is allowed to reproduce and grow. In the pregnancy situation, after nine months the HCG factor spontaneously rises and the fetus is ejected through the process of birth. The outcome in the cancer situation is, of course, quite different. The host organism remains indifferent to the existence of the intruding cell, and the normal process that limits growth is never activated. The cancer growth is like an unending pregnancy, and unchecked, causes death—its own along with its host's.

The mind, though, rarely acts as stupidly as the cancer cell. The human organism is capable of consciousness, and the mind is able to perceive that murderous impulses discharged towards an object on whom it remains dependent for its own survival is, indeed, an act of suicide. Whatever life-preserving wish is present, not matter how slight, it is usually sufficient to prevent the human organism from engaging in an activity that would directly cause its own death.

It is not an accident that cancer is a disease which has its usual end in the death of the host organism, and that schizophrenia is not. It is the stimulation of the psychological defensive apparatus in the schizophrenic that permits preservation of life. The discovery and elaboration of the neurotic use of narcissism as a defense mechanism by Hyman Spotnitz in the early 1950's was the final clarifying point in understanding the malfunctioning of the defense systems in the cause of mental disease.[53] Recognizing the murder in narcissism was the breakthrough.

Early theories began with the idea that the self-absorption of narcissism was evidence of self-love.[54] A reason for this bias might have been that Freud only put the destructive drive—the death instinct—into place in his structure of thought in the 1920's, and not all analysts assimilated it then. Indeed some denied its existence, and some still do. So libido, the mental energy that flows from the life instinct, was the only motivating force that was seen.

Clinicians had noticed from quite early on the tendency of the schizophrenic to defend against murderous rage[55]—that is, to practice mental and emotional strategies to keep rage out of consciousness, evidently for fear that it would be acted on against those individuals upon whom they felt most dependent. These necessary objects might be the loved ones of the patient, or even, as the analysis progressed, the analyst himself. Acting on the murderous rage—killing the object—might mean losing the only object of the external world remaining to him.

As the defense takes hold, normal boundary demarcation between self and not-self ceases to exist. The schizophrenic can no longer distinguish against whom the rage is really directed. As one patient put it, "Instead of knowing you want to kill someone else, you wipe yourself out."[56]

In the 1940's, Melanie Klein referred to a splitting mechanism in the mind, allowing destructive impulses to be deflected away from the outside object, the "loved one" upon whom the dependency needs are lavished.[57] The destructive impulses are turned toward the ego, with the result that parts of the ego go temporarily out of existence.

The suicide that takes place for the schizophrenic is on the level of the mind. The ego functioning of the mind is obliterated, a sacrifice made in the service of object protection.[58]

It became clear that both the schizophrenic and cancer conditions arise out of the early, undifferentiated phase of development. It seems likely, since the earlier capacity of the organism to discharge aggression is on the somatic level, that the production of a potential cancer condition would come earlier than the organization of a schizophrenic nucleus.

In any event, this defensive maneuver remains relegated strictly to the realm of the unconscious. The schizophrenic assiduously avoids becoming aware of his own murderous rage, and gives ample demonstration of Freud's original precept that patients would rather be sick than know their own impulses. It is in this defensive maneuver, that ensures unconsciousness, that the psychological functioning of the cancer patient mimics that of the schizophrenic.

The unconscious mind of the cancer patient is replete with fantasies of revenge, destruction, and murder. It is only through the creation of the false persona of the pleasant, compliant cancer personality, and the disconnection between conscious and unconscious urges, that these impulses can be repressed and ignored.

What clinicians had been observing about the psyches of their cancer patients for centuries was provided with powerful experimental validation in 1946. Caroline Thomas administered extensive psychological and physiological testing to medical students in order to discover precursors to five primary diseases: hypertension, heart disease, cancer, mental disorder, and suicide. She had originally conceived of cancer as being a condition without psychological factors, and was startled to find that the personality profile for students who later developed cancer looked remarkably similar to the profile for those who became suicide victims.[59]

The dictum "out of sight, out of mind" stops making sense when the unconscious is brought into consideration. Where the destructive drive is inadequately channelled, its power to destroy is great. At its height, it seems to follow its inward path along alternative routes. When turned against the body, the result is cancer; when turned against the mind, schizophrenia results.

The destructive urges of the cancer patient are manifested overtly only on the physiological level—the cell runs rampant and takes in its wake anything that interferes with its unrelenting growth. Massive repression and denial of destructive urges are apparent on the level of the psyche. Locked away in the recesses of the unconscious, however, is the secret wish to kill. Unconscious suicidal and murderous wishes are revealed when the repression is lifted. The cancer cell knows, and lives out, the murderous intent that the cancer psyche has denied.

And so it is with the schizophrenic. The mind is destroyed in the service of keeping the murderous impulses hidden. On the level of the unconscious, a choice is made—insanity or death. Norman Mailer's thought that "cancer is madness denied" may contain as much scientific as it does poetic truth.[60]

Notes

1.   R. Virchow, *Die Cellularpathologie* (Berlin 1. Aufl: A. Hirschwald, 1858).

2. M. Klein, "Symposium on Child Analysis," *Contributions to Psycho-analysis*, (London: Hogarth Press, 1921–1945).
3. O. Fenichel, *The Psychoanalytic Theory of Neurosis* (NY: W. W. Norton, 1945), 34–39.
4. Ibid.
5. A. Montagu, *Touching: the Human Significance of the Skin.* (NY: Columbia University Press, 1971), 49.
6. C. Smith, *The Physiology of the Newborn Infant.* 3rd ed. Springfield, IL: Charles C. Thomas, 1960).
7. J. Pitt, "Breast Milk and the High-risk Baby: Potential Benefits and Hazards," *Hospital Practice* (May 1979).
8. Ibid.
9. S. Freud, "On Narcissism: An Introduction," *S. E.*.
10. O. Fenichel, *The Psychoanalytic Theory*, 39.
11. Ibid., 35.
12. M. S. Mahler, F. Pine, and A. Bergman, *The Psychological Birth of the Human Infant* (NY: Basic Books, 1975).
13. P. Meadow, and H. Spotnitz, *Treatment of the Narcissistic Neurosis*, (NY: The Manhattan Center for Advanced Psychoanalytic Studies, 1976), 94–124.
14. O. Kernberg, *Borderline Conditions and Pathological Narcissism* (NY: Jason Aronson, 1975).
15. H. F. Searles, *Collected Papers on Schizophrenia and Related Subjects*, (NY: International Universities Press, 1967).
16. Ibid.
17. Ibid.
18. O. Kernberg, *Borderline Conditions.*
19. H. Spotnitz, *Modern Psychoanalysis of a Schizophrenic Patient*, 2nd ed. (NY: Human Sciences Press, 1985), 57.
20. L. Thomas, "Cellular and Humoral Aspects of the Hypersensitive Statis," In H. S. Lawrence *Symposia of the Section on Microbiology*, (London: NY Academy of Medicine, Cassel, 1969).
21. W. R. Loewenstein, and Y. Kanno, "Intercellular Communication and the Control of Tissue Growth: Lack of Communication Between Cancer Cells," *Nature* 209 (1966):1248–9.
22. Ibid.
23. S. Locke, and D. Colligan, *The Healer Within* (NY: New American Library, 1986), 33–36.
24. L. Thomas, "Cellular and Humoral Aspects."
25. F. Deutsch, "Psychoanalysis and Internal Medicine," in M. R. Kaufman and M. Heiman, ed. *Evolution of Psychosomatic Concepts*, (NY: International Universities Press, 1964), 47.
26. F. Dunbar, *Emotions and Bodily Changes*, (NY: Columbia University Press, 1954).
27. Ibid.
28. H. Spotnitz, *Modern Psychoanalysis*, 84.

29. O. Fenichel, "The Psychoanalytic Theory," 11–13.
30. Ibid., 34.
31. B. Klopfer, "Psychological Factors in Human Cancer," *Journal of Projective Techniques* 21 (1957:331–40).
32. D. M. Kissen, "Personality Factors in Males Conducive to Lung Cancer," *British Journal of Medical Psychology* 36 (1963):27.
33. D. M. Kissen, "Psychosocial Factors, Personality and Lung Cancer in Men aged 55–64," *British Journal of Medical Psychology* 40 (1967):29.
34. L. Le Shan, *You Can Fight for Your Life* (NY: M. Evans, 1977), 64.
35. S. Freud, "Inhibitions, Symptoms and Anxiety," *S. E.* 20.
36. S. Greer, and T. Morris, "Psychological Attributes of Women who Develop Breast Cancer: A Controlled Study," *Journal of Psychosomatic Research* 19 (1975):147–53.
37. A. H. Schmale, and H. Iker, "The Psychological Setting of Uterine Cervical Cancer," *Annals of The New York Academy of Sciences* 125 (1966):807–13.
38. R. Renneker, "Cancer and Psychotherapy," in J. Goldberg ed. *Psychotherapeutic Treatment of Cancer Patients*, 146.
39. D. Bakan, *Disease, Pain and Sacrifice*, 29.
40. G. Booth, "Irrational Complications of the Cancer Problem," *American Journal of Psychoanalysis* 25 (1965) 41–60.
41. S. Fisher, and S. Cleveland, *Body Image and Personality* (NY: D. Van Nostrand, 1958). 301–6.
42. W. Freeman, "Biometrical Studies in Psychiatry—The Chances of Death," *American Journal of Psychiatry* 8 (1928):425.
43. A. E. Sheflen, "Malignant Tumors in the Institutionalized Psychotic Population," *A.M.A. Archives of Neurology and Psychiatry* 66 (1951): 145.
44. L. C. F. Chevans, "The Correlation of Cause of Death With Type of Sanity," *Journal of Mental Science* 77 (1931):562.
45. W. Freeman, "Biometrical Studies."
46. P. M. West, "The Psychological Variables in Human Cancer," in J. A. Gengerelli and F. J. Kirkner (ed.) *A Symposium* University of California Press, (1954) 92–3.
47. M. A. White, "The Social Significance of Mental Disease," *Archives of Neurological Psychiatry* 22 (1929):873.
48. T. Freeman, J. Cameron, and A. McGhie, *Studies on Psychosis* (NY: International Universities Press, 1966), 6.
49. P. M. West, "The Psychological Variables."
50. A. Montagu, *Touching*, 45.
51. J. Silberner, "Survival of the Fetus," *Science News* 130 (1986):234–5.
52. Ibid.
53. A. Sponitz, *Modern Psychoanalysis*, 41–46.
54. S. Freud, "Introductory lecture on psychoanalysis," *S. E.* 16 (1917).
55. H. Nunberg, "The Course of the Libidinal Conflict in a Case of

Schizophrenia,'' in *Practice and Theory of Psychoanalysis* (NY: Nervous and Mental Disease Monographs, No. 74, 1948).
56. H. Spotnitz, *Modern Psychoanalysis.*
57. M. Klein, "Notes on Some Schizoid Mechanisms," in M. Klein, P. Heimann, S. Issacs, & J. Riviere (ed.) *Developments in Psychoanalysis* (London: Hogarth Press, 1952).
58. H. Spotnitz, *Modern Psychoanalysis,* 49.
59. C. Thomas, and D. R. Duszynski, "Closeness to Parents and the Family Constellation in a Prospective Study of Five Disease States: Suicide, Mental Illness, Malignant Tumor, Hypertension, and Coronary Heart Disease," *The Johns Hopkins Medical Journal* 134 (1974):251–70.
60. S. Brody, "Psychoanalytic Experiences with Cancer Patients," *Archives of the Foundation of Thanatology* 6 (1977):9–10.

Part Two

How to Get Well

V

From Victim to Victor

11

Reversing Disease Psychologically

The hand of Another makes the mirror of
Narcissus tremble; this Other may be
allowed to remain, but on condition that he
confine himself to the role of Echo.
—Joyce McDougall

Words as Magic

Feelings kill.

Or, more precisely, the defense against certain feelings create a destructive imbalance in the psyche, a situation where what is conscious is too much of one set of feelings and not enough of another. In the case of the type C personality, only positive feelings—friendly, kindly, mild feelings—are allowed into consciousness; aggression and hate are relegated to the realm of unconsciousness in an attempt not to know them or to experience them. The type A personality presents a diametrically-opposed picture: aggression and hostility are apparent, and the softer feelings of patience, love, and compassion remain hidden.

It is insofar as these feeling responses occur without any conscious selection process that the psychic disease of neurosis exists. As these mechanisms are automatic, they are phenomenologically alien to the conscious ego. We do not have the experience of controlling our fears, worries, and anxieties; they seem to be unwanted entities and often we remain altogether ignorant of their origins and causes. On the experiential level, they are relegated to the world of not-self.

How, then, can we regulate our feelings so that the mechanisms of defense protect us rather than injure us? If the determination of disease is made on the automacity of response, a return to health would depend on an assumption of responsibility for these processes, by bringing them into consciousness and under the rubric of self. The experiential sense that these processes represent the functioning of not-self is a deceit; what we experience as "it," not-self, is really a part of us. Those parts that we have ejected from awareness must be welcomed back into their rightful home of the ego. "Where id was there shall ego be."

The discovery of the process that can bring this about was made inadvertently by a Viennese woman named Bertha Papenheim, immortalized in the psychoanalytic literature as "Anna O." When she took to her bed in 1881, she suffered from the diverse symptoms that characterized hysteria. During her treatment, Anna O. discovered that if she talked during her time with her physician, while in a state of hypnosis, her symptoms would remarkably abate.[1] She named her treatment the talking cure, and continued, with the cooperation of her physician, to follow this method of treatment until each of her symptoms had disappeared.

In coming to understand how her talking cure had worked, Freud made the first scientific exploration into the power of words to heal. He came to understand that it was in the act of talking that balance could be restored to the psychic system. Theories about precisely what in the talking brought about the cure have evolved since Anna O., in Freud's own thought and in that of his successors.

Freud's work had paralleled Bernard's research on the body, and he discovered that the psyche, too, had a homeostatic mechanism. With the forces of the id and superego in conflict both with each other and with the external world of reality, the ego serves as a stabilizer, a neutralizing force which enables the personality to maintain homeostatic balance. His early work on the pleasure-pain principle, and his later work on the life/death drives illustrate, as well, his concept of opposing forces seeking balance. The disease state is a result of the failure of the regulatory mechanism to achieve homeostasis, and the subsequent moving out of balance of opposing forces.

Through the mediating variables of the hormone and nervous systems, psychic imbalance can become bodily disturbance. Cure of the mind, then, can achieve bodily correction, as well. On the level of the mind, it is through the ego that we attempt cure. Freud learned that the language of the ego was words. Unlike both the id and the superego, which are comprised of primitive instinctual forces, and whose language might be actions, affective states, or even physical processes, the ego is rational, and susceptible to verbal, symbolic language, and reasoned thought.

Freud worked out his theory of how the talking cure worked through his studies of aphasia and hysteria.[2] In both cases it had been previously thought that the malady was strictly of the nervous system. Thus, treatment had remained strictly physiologic.

What was distinctive about how Freud came to conceptualize hysteria was precisely that he saw it as being "independent of the nervous system".[3] As in aphasia, where there is an actual cerebral lesion, in hysteria there is a lesion, but it is a lesion of the thinking process. This lesion of ideas comes about because of the occurrence of the trauma, an event which caused excessive excitation, and which couldn't be adequately integrated into the psyche of its victim (having been incompletely "worked over associatively").[4] The trauma gives rise to some thoughts that the person finds unacceptable to his conscious mind, and so he turns away from them.[5] These thoughts thus fail to find their way to discharge in verbal expression, and reappear in the disguised form of symptoms.

The treatment Freud was to discover, then, was a treatment that was comprised strictly of words. Words themselves seemed to have almost magical properties that would enable the patient to get well:

> Words are the essential tool of mental treatment. A layman will no doubt find it hard to understand how pathological disorders of the body and mind can be eliminated by "mere" words. He will feel that he is being asked to believe in magic. And he will not be so very wrong, for the words which we use in our everyday speech are nothing other than watered-down magic. But we shall have to follow a roundabout path in order to explain how science sets about restoring to words a part of their former magical power.[6]

The talking cure was a treatment of remembering. The memory of the trauma and the feelings associated with the event are called to memory and put into words. Freud's early description of this phenomenon, relating to hysteria:

> . . .if he sees things before him with all their original actuality, we shall observe that he is completely dominated by some affect. And, if we then compel him to put this affect into words, we shall find that, at the same time as he is producing this violent affect, the phenomenon of his pains emerges very markedly once again and that thenceforward the symptom, in

its chronic character, disappears. . .It could only be supposed that the psychic trauma does in fact continue to operate in the subject and maintains the hysterical phenomenon, and that it comes to an end as soon as the patient has spoken about it.[7]

The symptom, then, is an expression of lost words. A disruption has occurred in the associative link between the original event and the subjective meaning to the patient. As a result of the refusal to follow the associative links as they occur naturally, the words find their material locus in the body, rather than in the sound of language.[8]

Freud's search for a treatment method was essentially a search for ways into the unconscious, ways around the blockages between conscious awareness and the suppressed memories that appeared to be the root of the current dysfunctions. Hypnosis proved to have serious shortcomings for the purpose, beginning with the fact that not every patient could be hypnotized, and so it was eventually discarded.

The classic free association was a product of Freud's staunch belief in the intelligible infrastructure of the mind. The random products of such an organized mind might be unintelligible to the ego and thus allowed into consciousness uncensored, yet no products of such a mind would really be meaningless; they could be analyzed, and meanings could be discovered where none appeared on the surface.

The ego was not so easily fooled, and as a method of tricking repressed material directly to the surface, free association soon failed, too. But free association nonetheless proved the key that allowed Freud penetration into the unconscious. Patterns were seen in the kinds of material that refused to be brought to light, and the concept of resistance was born. Defensive structures began to be discernible by the shadows they cast. And finally what emerged unannounced was the phenomenon called transference—the real medium of psychoanalysis as therapy.[9]

It was discovered that when patients said whatever came into their minds—that is, when they were allowed to relate to the analyst in whatever fashion came naturally to them, free of the constant directions and cures provided by everyday relationships—they would inevitably begin to talk to the analyst as though the analyst were some other person. That is, the patient would seem to be making assumptions about the analyst that revealed basic misunderstandings of the analyst's character that couldn't be accounted for by anything in the analytic setting. Under analysis, these distortions were clearly seen to reproduce remembered perceptions of a person who was significant in the early history of the patient's life—typically, a mother, father, or important caretaker—or sometimes a kind of piecemeal conglomerate of several persons.

When this process was allowed to flow unimpeded it began to feel as though the present was being obliterated and the patient was living in some past whose existence only the patient had access to. This was in fact the working of the repetition compulsion that Freud would later come to see as pervading all of life. It was, in a metaphor unavailable to Freud but clear to us, returning the needle to the same groove, playing the same passage over and over, not to come to the end of the record and to lift off into the unknown.

In the analytic setting where it could proceed undistracted, Freud called it transference, for the phenomenon of transferring perceptions and affects from their real object to the present one. It served the patient as a resistance to remembering of repressed material; but for the analyst it was a brilliantly illuminated pathway into the past—that is, it allowed the analyst not just to see there, but to go there with the patient. Freud's theoretical contructs of the topology of the mind and the functioning of its parts were now imbued with clinical significance. Transference and resistance became operational principles and psychoanalysis became an effective method of treatment for neurotic disorders as well as an investigative, or diagnostic, procedure.

Words and the Nervous System

In 1895, shortly after Freud completed "Studies on Hysteria," he began work on a project whose ambition was no less than the full explanation of the mental apparatus in physical terms. Had he succeeded, Freud would have accomplished making the study of the mind a true natural science, where the physical basis for all psychological phenomena would be articulated. Just six months into "The Project for a Scientific Psychology," Freud abandoned the work unfinished. The degree to which he succeeded or failed in his attempt to reduce psychical processes to "specifiable material particles" is a matter of some controversy,[10] but the ideas he first developed in this brilliant inductive exploration have taught every neurologist and every philosopher since how to think about the mind.

Modern neuropsychological theory confirms many of Freud's basic ideas on neuronic functioning:

1. The neuron is the integrating unit of the nervous system.
2. The primary activity of the nervous system is the inhibition or excitation of neurons which are connected to one another through synapses (Freud's term was *contact barrier*), and neurons grouped together form elaborate neuronal networks.
3. The messages that are passed as a result of electrical changes (potentials) in the neurons seem to be related to highly complex psychological processes.[11]

Freud's hope in attempting to explain neurological phenomena was that the principles of neurological functioning would turn out to parallel many of the fundamental principles of psychological functioning;[12] in point of fact when we look at Freud's description of the psychological life of the human, we do recognize the similarities between the phenomenology of emotional life and the functioning of the nervous system.

The mind of the infant is still insufficiently developed, and so the only method of discharge from the tension states that arise from an uncomfortable level of excitation on the neuronal level is through the body—motoric discharge. When the child acquires the use of language, his words supplant his motoric actions in providing release from the instinctual demands. Words (the thoughts and feelings that they carry and evoke) make direct contact with the neuronal structures. Words that we hear can stimulate or calm the nervous system: words that we speak can serve either function, as well. Freud, early on:

> Let us suppose that a man is insulted, is given a blow or something of the kind. This psychical trauma is linked with an increase in the sum of excitation of his nervous system. There then instinctively arises an inclination to diminish this increased excitation immediately. He hits back, and then feels easier; he may perhaps have reacted adequately—that is, he may have got rid of as much as had been introduced into him. . .The most adequate reaction. . .is always a deed. But, as an English writer has wittily remarked, the man who first flung a word of abuse at his enemy instead of a spear was the founder of civilization. Thus words are substitutes for deeds, and in some circumstances, e.g., in Confession, are the only substitutes. . .[13]

If the development of the mind lags behind, though, the child may be unable to reduce the level of conflict through the use of the mental apparatus. An impulse may arise, but along with the desire to discharge the impulse comes a resistance. The control apparatus that normally "organizes, leads, and inhibits deeper archaic and more instinctual forces" is interfered with, and thus the economic stability of the entire system is threatened. Neurotic phenomena are understood, then, to be based on insufficiencies of the normal control apparatus. The insufficiency can be attributed to different phases of the transaction. Excitation that is more stimulating than the ego can master can enter the mental apparatus; such experiences are traumatic. Or, there can be a blocking of discharge, whereby tensions dam up, and normal excitations are experienced as traumatic.

In the particular case of the psychogenic and psychosomatic diseases, it appears that a large number of interneurons are committed to the task of inhibiting discharge, rather than facilitating discharge, of neuronal energy. The system seems to be one that has inadequately developed methods of processing and reducing the amount of stimulation, and thus pools of undischarged energy collect and cause an overloaded interneuronal system.[14]

Further, to the extent that the psychosomatic patient is able to sufficiently discharge energy, he remains immature in his ability to do it without damage. Without words to aid him, his only recourse is turn the blocked energy against himself—against his body.

Words As Cure

As the theory needed to become increasingly more complex in order to include additional disorders, the notion of cure changed. At first, it had seemed that the hysterics needed simply to relive the forgotten experience, and through the recapturing of the memory, the symbolic meaning of the symptom would be understood. The reexperiencing of the trauma would be relieving, or as Freud came to call it, cathartic.

Yet, in the psychosomatic disorders, there was no apparent connection between the symbolic symptom and the mental ideation. Because the vegetative organs are connected to the ideational processes through the nervous system, any notion of cure for the psychosomatic diseases would necessitate a theory implicating the mediating mechanism of the nervous system.

Freud never specifically addressed the issue of cure in "The Project." Yet, in spite of that omission, the theoretical working out that Freud attempted on the connection between the nervous system and psychic phenomena remains the best stepping-stone for the articulation of the curative process—what cure is and how it comes about—that we have. In describing in quantitative and physical terms how the mind works, Freud allows us to expand into the notion of how, in working through the mental apparatus, change can occur. And in positing the integration of mind/body processes through the nervous system, we come to see that change is both mental and physical, and that one can affect the other.

When we understand that thoughts and feelings are embedded in the actual physiology of the organism, we come to a clearer understanding of the strength of character patterns and their resistance to change. From this perspective, psychological (emotional) change involves a kind of rewiring—nervous system restructuring. It is not an easy task to accomplish.

It seems that pure discharge, in itself, is not ultimately curative. It relieves an overloaded system, and thus reduces stress momentarily. But discharge without ego integration, as in catharsis, doesn't provide full impulse discharge. At times, cathartic discharge can even provoke disease. This seems to be attributable to the fact that even the most primitive—the most narcissistic—ego is to some degree connected to others—*object related*, in the lingo of psychoanalysts. Given that, and given that characterological patterns are neuronally entrenched so that sheer force of will cannot be sufficient to create change, some intervention from without must take place to permit the nervous system to reorganize itself.[15]

It is the analyst, and the formation of the transference relationship, that serves as the source of this intervention. This is to say that the impulses get attached to the analyst. The transference relationship is a replication of an old relationship. In neuronal terms, it represents the activation of neuronal pathways that were established in the very early stages of the patient's development.

The analytic injunction ''to say everything'' is an effort to return the patient to the state of mental development before patterns had become quite so physiologically (neuronally) entrenched, and to the time when thoughts and feelings were more freely responsive to stimulation. The phenomenon of regression, on the physiological level, is a retracing of the steps that were involved in the establishment of the particular neuronal pathways.

The emergence of resistance—the patient comes to a block, and can't follow the direction to say everything—is witnessed. Because the impulses are now connected to the person of the analyst, it turns out that the transference itself becomes another form of resistance. The patient not only will not say everything because of resistance, but he won't say everything to the particular person of the analyst because of a transference resistance.

Through the analyst's study of resistance, both the patterns of thought and the blocks to new thoughts and feelings are discovered. The blocks continue to come up repetitively in the sessions until the analyst understands them well enough to know what to say to resolve them. In saying the right thing at the right time and with the right feeling, the analyst is able to resolve the patient's resistance to saying the next thing that he needs to say, thinking the next thing that has to be thought, or doing the next thing that has to be done. That is, the analyst has helped the patient to say whatever was necessary to mature him beyond whatever level of fixation he was stuck on.

In the resolution of resistance, old and nonconstructive neuronal pathways are deactivated, thus allowing the neurons to form new and more desirable pathways. In the topographical map of the psyche what has happened is that integration of the ego has taken place through the patient coming to know what he is feeling, thinking, and saying. As words are said, and they are integrated with the proper affect (the appropriate *feeling*), ego is created. Words, with affect, create ego.[16]

When resistances are successfully resolved, the patient comes to feel that he is in a different kind of relationship with the analyst because the analyst is, after all, quite unlike the original parent (or other significant object) in that he (the patient) has, for the first time, been genuinely understood. The damage from the original parental relationship is reversed.

In spite of the fact that the method of psychoanalysis is talking, the treatment is also physical. The disease (neurosis) has physiological representation in the nervous system, and the cure is an intervention that effects change on this same level.

Words Before Language

Freud's first serious consideration of the limitations of psychoanalysis as a treatment came out of his work with obsessives. Here, he discovered that their endless dissections and analyses, done defensively rather than constructively, rendered the analysis sterile. The success of the endeavor was directly tied to the establishment and resolution of the transference. In the presence of the narcissistic neuroses, where the extent of self-preoccupation excludes meaningful involvement with others, the formation of a transference is virtually impossible. In short, the patient is simply not sufficiently interested in the analyst to form even the distorted connection of a transference.

The pessimism Freud felt about treating the most severely narcissistic patients, and we include here the psychotic disorders, never lifted. Many years after his original work with obsessives he returned to the same problem, and again warned analysts that psychotic patients were resistant to the analytic method, and here, went even further than in his earlier thinking, and opined that these states might even be exacerbated by psychoanalysis.[17]

Contemporary schools of thought, in particular the modern psychoanalytic system, propose otherwise. Extensive work with severely disturbed patients reveals that these patients are indeed susceptible to the analytic process. New concepts, however, needed to be formulated to address the problem that led Freud to believe in the hopelessness of these cases—that is, the apparent lack of a transference relationship.

Modern psychoanalysis is an operational theory that was initially formulated by Hyman Spotnitz for the treatment of schizophrenic patients.[18] It adheres to the Freudian framework in its understanding and utilization of transference and resistance phenomena. It differs from the classical analysis, as formulated by Freud, in its reconceptualization of the meaning of certain phenomena, and, as a result of reformulation, it sanctions an extensive range of interventions, rather than the wholly interpretive method.

Modern analysts came to understand that severely regressed patients do, indeed, form a transference with the analyst (they are, after all, equally under the sway of the repetition compulsion). This transference relationship has the form of the early relationship, and as that relationship was characterized by narcissistic failure to distinguish the self from the other, ''I'' from ''not-I'', so does this one. This is called the narcissistic transference, to distinguish it from the object-related transference of less regressed patients, the transference that Freud first observed and identified.

As classical psychoanalysis was formulated and is still practiced with some patients, interpretation was the curative intervention of choice.[19] These patients have developed sufficiently that intellectual insight is possible and useful; the ego is developed enough that instinctual needs are not pressing for instant release and an alliance can form between patient and analyst. The patient can lead the analyst to insights about his functioning which, when verbalized to the patient, he can then process and integrate into his emotional life. But even with these patients, whether it is the insights themselves that are curative, or some other aspect of this patient/analyst transaction, is not precisely clear.

In any case, the use of interpretation is not helpful to patients whose conflicts have their origins at the level of development before the acquisition of language. Insofar as the pre-oedipal, preverbal conflict still holds sway, the patient lives emotionally at that age. This can be true of people whose intellectual development is quite normal, and who are capable of some normal social relations—so the temptation is powerful to treat them as capable of integrating intellectual and emotional spheres. But in fact, at that early stage, communications were made not in words but through the exchange of feelings, often in ways that did not involve the conscious ego at all.

Successful analysis of these preverbal states demands therapeutic interventions that replicate the form of communicating that took place in those early years (or months), when words were meaningless.[20] The analyst, assuming the psychological infancy of the patient, takes full responsibility for the progress of the treatment until the patient has achieved a level of development where he can assume his share of responsibility for the success or failure of the work—where he can join in a "therapeutic alliance."[21]

Words of the Body

Research in the last few decades has taught us a great deal about the particular psychological makeup of patients suffering from a variety of diseases. This data has led to increasing sophistication of psychological treatment techniques designed to reverse specific pathological processes.

Research indicated that the core problem in psychosomatic conditions is twofold: first, there is a inhibition of particular constellations of feeling;[22] second, to the extent that feelings are stimulated, they are directed destructively against the body.[23] The treatment, then, needs to be one which first enables the patient to become conscious of the repressed feeling, later to permit discharge of it away from the self, and, finally, to reintegrate it into the whole of the psychic apparatus.

Early psychotherapeutic attempts to reverse psychosomatic dysfunctions, including cancer, followed Freud's initial thinking that pure discharge could be curative. A host of psychotherapies have developed based on this conceptualization, and patients have been encouraged to touch, scream, and hate their way to health.[24] These methods have proven to have some efficacy in the treatment of psychically underactive patients. Stimulation of the energic systems works to gear up an underresponsive organism into a more energetic mode of functioning. The limitation of these techniques, however, is that underlying, dynamic change has not occurred. Permanent eradication of destructive psychological patterns means deep characterological change rather than the transient states of feeling better that are achieved through discharge techniques. In personalities where there is already an established pattern of discharge, these techniques can be dangerously overstimulating.

More sophisticated techniques recognize that permanent restructuring of the psychic apparatus comes about only through destructive impulses being filtered through the reality apparatus of the ego. The process through which this is accomplished is by putting thoughts and feelings into words.

Integrating the theoretical contributions of Spotnitz with the empirical findings of researchers, we can make a vivid picture of the psychological and neurological patterns of patients. The interneuronal commitment to the inhibition of discharge seems to constellate typically around the experience of a particular feeling. In order to cope with the accumulated pools of undischarged energy and the experience of unfelt feelings, the psychic system attempts a compensatory reorganization. It represses, in the vain hope that a feeling not felt will disappear. But energy seeks an object to attach itself to, and in this case, the object becomes the body. These patients, then, go to great lengths in their determination both not to feel their own unwelcome feelings and, similarly, not to recognize offensive feelings of others when they are directed towards them—even to the extent of effectively killing off a part of themselves. Given the integrated nature of the psyche, the repression cannot always be as specifically selective as one wishes, and this pattern of denying, avoiding, and killing one's feelings generalizes to other feeling states, as well. Feelings not felt don't just disappear, they become nonfeelings, and as such, begin to putrefy and pollute the entire system.

While the entire psychic functioning of the patient is irregular, the fact that the systemic dysfunction begins with the repression of the feeling apparatus suggests that a treatment approach would, as the first order of business, address itself to this level of dysfunction. The treatment technique, then, will be one where the analyst aims to facilite the experience and verbal expression of whichever feelings are most aggressively repressed.[25]

Given the typically severe extent of the repression in these patients, it is no easy task to aid them in allowing feelings to come to consciousness. Freud's original discovery that patients would rather be sick than allow certain thoughts and feelings to consciousness holds particularly true for these patients. The tenacity with which psychosomatic patients typically ward off unpleasant feelings suggests a powerful conflict operating on an unconscious level.

However, the analyst's recognition and encouragement of the expression of the unconscious material is usually not sufficient to mobilize the movement to consciousness. The defense against such feelings often seems impenetrable. The patient holds on to his defense as though it were a life raft in a turbulent sea. The fact that the defense represents survival becomes piercingly apparent.

It is for this reason that it is precisely at the point of the defense where the analyst begins the work. As the patient talks in the session, the analyst notes the ways in which the patient defends himself against the awareness of feeling. The very deep entrenchment of the defense means that the analyst needs to be extraordinarily sensitive to the subtle ways in which the patient denies, represses, or avoids.

There is, initially, no attempt on the part of the analyst to change the defensive pattern. Such an attempt could be experienced by the patient as damaging, even at some level life threatening. Pointing out the pattern is often experienced by the patient as a criticism, a psychological attack. Rather, the analyst observes the repetitive ways the patient uses the defenses, the automaticity of the defensive response.

In listening to the patient, and in reconstructing the patient's emotional history, the analyst comes to understand the original survival aspect of the defense. Defenses are erected out of real or imagined threats. In taking seriously the perceived threats to the patient, the analyst communicates an understanding and acceptance that allows the patient to maintain the defense while at the same time observing it with a benign interest. It is often appropriate to implement treatment techniques that will serve even to shore up the defense, strengthening it against the vast accumulation of raw, unfiltered impulses that hide behind it, whose uncontrolled release would come like a violent explosion to the ego, both shocking and threatening.

Spotnitz and his colleagues and students have developed ways in which the analyst can aid the patient in both holding onto a necessary defensive pattern, and at the same time working to resolve it, such that an habitual defensive reaction, now unrelated to the original dangerous stimulus, can be transformed into a truly effectual protective device. These analytic procedures fall under the broad category of joining techniques.[26]

What is unique about the technical intervention of joining is that the analyst makes a communication to the patient that does not stimulate further defensive maneuvers. The analyst does not insist that the patient recognize either that he, the analyst, is a separate person, nor does he force a confrontation with those aspects of the patient's psyche that the patient experiences as foreign to his ego, that is, not-self aspects. Rather, he allows for the development of a transference relationship where the patient can experience the analyst as a part of himself, a self aspect.

It is a trick of deceit, analogous to the one that the unrecognized pathological cell plays on the body. In the establishment of a relationship where the patient can come to experience the analyst as like himself, or as a part of himself, the analyst is allowed entrance through the defensive walls of the psyche, and into the world of the patient's narcissism.

In effect, the stage of dedifferentiation has been returned to, but with the analyst on the inside of the conglomeration of narcissistic material. As such, he is no longer experienced as a not-self entity from whom the patient needs to muster up his habitual defensive patterns. It is now with the acceptance of the analyst as self that the transformative therapeutic work can be done. This is not by any means always pleasant for either patient or analyst. The analyst is more often than not experienced as a hateful self-object, and can be the target of extremely negative feelings. But these feelings are tolerable to the patient, as experiencing the analyst as a separate person is not.

As the patient comes to experience the analyst as like himself, the rudiments of a working relationship have been established. It is only then that the analyst begins the difficult and painstaking task of differentiation.

The analyst begins on the level of ideas; feelings are still much too threatening for the fragile ego to tolerate. As part of the patient's narcissistic frame, the analyst now has somewhat more freedom of movement around the internal world of the patient's psyche. He can roam around the mind of the patient fairly unobtrusively, now that he has insinuated himself within the defensive structure, inside the walls of the narcissism.

While the defense remains intact and the repressed feelings are still avoided, there emerges the idea that there is more operating than had been apparent. The patient is encouraged to speculate, to guess as to the nature of the repressed material. The technique of free association, saying whatever comes to mind, has another contribution to make here.

At this point in the dissolution of the defense, the material emerging consists purely of ideas. There is still no affect attached to these thoughts, and most of the time, the patient will offer a disclaimer, and emphasize the hypothetical nature of his ideas. Yet, it is precisely through these hypothesized ideas that the patient leads the analyst, cautiously, into that world of confusion, pain, rage, or yearning that his defenses had attempted to seal off from consciousness forever.

The analyst works as slowly as the patient requires him to, and stays close to the emotional readiness of the patient to tolerate new thoughts and feelings. Objections to the hypothetical feelings are explored: "What if. . .?" "Suppose it were true that. . .?" Whenever it appears that the exploration is too stimulating to the patient and old defensive maneuvers reemerge, the analyst returns to his posture of entering into the patient's narcissism. The pattern of growth, then, is a fluctuating phenomenon, alternating between progress to new levels of self/not-self differentiation, and a regressive return to old patterns, not quite ready to be surrendered. In this fashion, the patient is allowed to move at his own pace toward that part of the self that he has, in the past, defined as not-self and has so strenuously avoided coming to know.

It is at this point in the analysis that the patient and analyst begin extremely delicate work. The long-repressed impulses are beginning to emerge, and the process of translating these impulses into words has mobilized the growth of the ego. Psychologically toxic material has begun to be unearthed, and to the extent that the newly strengthened ego can serve as a container for the experience of these impulses, the patient will benefit. This movement from unconsciousness to consciousness is essential for cure. Yet, the impulses being stimulated are powerfully destructive, and their arousal carries with it the possibility of backfiring. If the ego has not yet expanded enough to contain these powerful drives, then the old destructive pattern of turning the impulses against the self is resorted to. Improperly handled discharge can make the patient sicker. Thus, the analyst must carefully monitor the level of stimulation of the impulses, and ensure that the patient's ability to integrate feelings through verbalization keeps pace with the pressing need for discharge.

How does the analyst do this? The medium through which the analyst controls the stimulation and release of repressed material is the same process that the patient himself uses—words. Through the analyst's regulation of the quantity and quality of his talking to the patient, he is able to monitor and control the fluctuating defensive maneuvers.[27]

The analyst has studied the interaction between the patient and himself as the patient has been randomly and at times, seemingly pointlessly, saying whatever comes into his mind. The analyst has noticed that there are particular ways in which he speaks to the patient that arouse feeling. He studies the effect that he has on the patient, from both the quantitative and qualitative views. He will find that too little talking will arouse a certain kind of feeling, and too much talking will arouse another feeling. Similarly, talking in a particular way, with a certain tone, or about certain topics will effect the stimulation of feeling.

Once the feeling emerges, it becomes the guide for both patient and analyst. Feeling, uninterfered with, will lead to regression—a return to the point in the maturational development where the conflict first emerged, and where that feeling is still attached. The patient has, in effect, returned emotionally to the point at which the defensive pattern was first activated, and where feeling was first buried.

Through this kind of delicate exploration, which is neither over-stimulating nor frightening to the patient, the defenses are gradually softened. Finally, the actual feeling experience of the uncovered material is permitted. When emotion is tied to verbal expression of thoughts, the patient has allowed himself to know his authentic self.

He has reached a point of emotional openness such that previously unacceptable thoughts and feelings are now allowed into full consciousness.

The emergence of these newly discovered feelings creates the need for an outlet. The pattern of discharge of feelings needs to be redirected away from the body of the patient. The analyst encourages the flow of feeling toward the external world, thus reversing the direction of the destructive energy. Nonrecriminating and safe objects toward whom feelings can be attached are sought out. Sometimes strangers—such as shopkeepers or taxi drivers—with whom there is no emotional investment (but perhaps a recent encounter which may have stimulated feeling and which the patient has mentioned in passing)—provide ideal objects as the ground for exploration. The event may be of little importance to the patient, but every subtle nuance of feeling is explored and persistently encouraged. The exploration serves as a paradigm for the patient, a lesson that feelings are permitted.

More hidden are the underlying feelings toward the people with whom the patient is more intimately involved—family members especially, but also friends, work associates, superiors, and subordinates. It is to these people that the compulsion to repeat has most firmly affixed the perceptions—the transferences, in fact—belonging to the most important figures of his earliest development. These are the people whose relations with the patient call upon the very feelings his defenses have been erected to suppress. There is, then, good reason for his reluctance to know about feelings toward these people. These are the feelings most likely to be translated by such a patient into destructive psychosomatic action.

And when these feelings—let us say that they are angry feelings—have been redirected outward from the patient, the danger is scarcely less. The patient will now consciously resist having these feelings for fear of acting on them (this is classically the fear that masks a wish, of course). Action would be inevitable, the patient will explain. And this threat of action serves as a resistance to the full recognition of the underlying murderous rage. The patient can't come to know how profoundly angry he is because such feelings would lead him to get a divorce, disown his children, quit his job. Symbolic murder may seem to be the only possibility to the patient.

On the other hand, when the feeling that is repressed is love, and this feeling comes to consciousness, the patient will proclaim that he is in grave danger. He will be quite convinced that any softening of his defense will render him all too mortally vulnerable to others. He will express fear of being taken advantage of, of being dependent, of being hurt.

It is at the point in the analysis that the analyst engages in emotional reeducation, and teaches the patient a fundamental principle upon which the entirety of the treatment, and his cure, will be based. This is the idea, the full meaning of which is news to these patients, that feelings and behavior are independent of one another, and that one need not necessarily lead to the other. One can have an impulse, one can allow the full recognition of a powerful feeling, and still make the decision not to act on it. Murderous rage need not lead to murder; vulnerability need not lead to hurt. Repression or action are not the only two options. Feelings, when translated into words, serve as their own containers. As long as we continue to talk, and allow the full expression of feeling into words, there is no danger to ourselves or to others.

Ultimately, in order for full integration of feeling to take place, the object of the feeling must become the analyst. The psychoanalytic cure works through the development and resolution of the transference neurosis, and eventually the patient comes to have all of the thoughts and feelings that represent his core, unresolved conflicts, within the universe of the analysis. What is finally required is that the patient experience the full intensity of feeling and put it into words in the presence of the person (the analyst) to whom the feeling is directed.

The analyst facilitates this process by embodying the aspects of the patient that the patient had previously resisted knowing, but now has come to experience as part of himself. In so doing the analyst articulates the self/not-self differentiation that has occurred. Spotnitz refers to this method of intervention as the toxoid response, and it is through this process that the patient is immunized against any future dysfunction.

The patient who reaches this point will have achieved an emotional freedom that permits full acknowledgement of one's internal life. He is one who has come to live in his emotional present, rather than being bound by his ties to his past. And he is one who can appropriately, without being destructive to himself or others, discharge all the psychic toxins that are a natural product of emotional life.

How the Process Works

What follows are reports on two cases, one a cancer patient of mine, the other a heart disease patient of a colleague who has specialized in such cases (as I have with cancer patients). Each represents a fairly typical personality pattern for his disease, the type C pattern and the type A. Not all cases are so typical, but there are elements in each of these cases that can be applied to the work done with most patients, no matter how far from the normative work they may fall.

Sweet Sally and the Hate That Cures

Sally's personality was as sweet as cotton candy. She was emphatic that there were no real emotional problems and no particular stresses in her family life. It was just that she had this unexpected cancer that worried her.

When Sally talked to me her stories about her family felt stilted, too entirely devoid of negative feelings to be believable. I did not initially question this behavior. I joined her perception that, indeed, it sounded as though her family was being wonderfully supportive through this ordeal of her cancer; that she was lucky to have them; one could hardly ask for more.

It began to look, at this point, as though the treatment was going to falter. It seemed as though there was little I could do in terms of the perceived problem of the cancer and she insisted that not much else was wrong. We discussed whether or not psychological treatment was even something that would be useful for her. We discussed terminating, and I agreed that if there were no psychological problems, termination certainly seemed to be the appropriate step. I suggested, though, that since she was already there for the appointment, she might as well use the time in whatever way she wanted.

She allowed herself a mild complaint about her daughter. She said that she felt her daughter was not quite sensitive enough to her condition of cancer, and expected her to be operating at the same energy level as before she had the disease. We discussed this, though very gingerly, as Sally seemed to feel that it was a defect in her makeup that she experienced these feelings toward her daughter. I joined her narcissistic self-attack, agreeing that her daughter was doing the best she could under the circumstances; the experience of her mother having cancer must be a difficult one for her.

Sally felt comfortable with this kind of interaction, and she decided to continue the treatment. My communications reassured her that I would not force her to assume emotional postures toward those she loved that she was not ready for. Her complaints continued, always with the same apologetic tone, though they extended to include her other child, her husband, and her own mother and father.

The first intervention that I made which represented a puncture in the container of narcissism that now included both of us was an exclamation of surprise: "Really?" She had just finished describing a scene in which her husband had shown a level of insensitivity to her that any normal person would have reacted to, and she had reported the story in an affectless state. My response came as a shock to her. She asked what I meant by it. I disavowed that it had any great importance. I said that it's just that I had thought that from what she had told me about her husband that he would have been a little more sensitive to her. She defended him, and said that I completely misunderstood. I agreed that that was probably the case.

In spite of Sally's stated objections to my interpretation of her husband's behavior, the quality of her stories began to change. There was still no affect attached to the stories, but they became increasingly pointed in the content, toward complaints. It began to seem as though there was no one in her family who had a genuine understanding of the depth of her emotional conflicts, and no one who demonstrated a caring stance toward her. As the vituperative quality of her stories increased, I became convinced that there was an unconscious aware- ness on her part of both the hostility that was being directed toward her in her home life, and her own aggressive response to it. It was as though she were providing me with the information from which I could come to the conclusions that she herself resisted knowing.

I gradually became more emphatic about my perceptions that her family was not treating her well. I exaggerated any minute suggestion of aggression she made and voiced the outrage as my own. If she would tell me a story about her daughter, Leslie, acting negatively towards her, I would respond in a disbelieving voice, "Leslie did that? You're kidding. She really did that? The nerve of the girl. Whatever can be in her mind? That girl's got real problems." I told her, in

response to a story about her husband, that he was a "creep"—
"insensitive, uncaring, inadequate, impotent."

While her initial reaction to my by now very emphatic and feelingful
attacks on her family was to object, there was never any real enthusiasm in her objections. I asked her if she could allow herself to think
such horrible thoughts about her family if it would help her to get well.

As her objection to knowing that she was angry with her family
dissolved, her response to my attacks on her family was to take a
childish delight in them. We might be doing something bad by having
all these terrible feelings toward her family, who probably didn't
deserve these hateful feelings that she was having, but at least we were
being bad together, and there was some fun in that.

Related to the idea that Sally could not allow herself to experience
aggression toward others is the corollary idea that she did not recognize aggression when it was directed toward her. The question of
treatment was the first issue around which this conflict became manifest. As Sally began to be able to use her sessions productively, she
wanted to increase the frequency of her sessions. Her husband objected, saying that the sessions cost too much money, and that she would
have to make do with what she had. Sally had not yet been able to
experience the full range of her own feelings, and this story was told
without apparent rancor. But equally important was that Sally was
unable to recognize that this stance of her husband's was one that was
destructive to her, and reflected his own unconscious aggression toward her. The idea that if he wanted to be helpful he would pay for the
treatment that had the possibility of aiding her, and that if he didn't
have the money he would do his best to find it, was not an idea that
occurred to her. In order to not know her own rage at being deprived of
something that she wanted and that might help her, and his rage as
evidenced by his depriving posture, she made herself emotionally
stupid, and accepted at face value his objection to her proposed
intensified treatment (Sally was not at this stage at all ready to allow
herself any anger with me for requiring money for my service.).

As Sally began to uncover her own aggressive inclinations and to
experience those parts of her personality with comfort, and eventually
even with a great deal of pleasure, she was able to more fully recognize
and tolerate the aggression of others toward her.

In one session she told me that she had started a new sculpture. This was a sculpture of a woman, and she described her ambivalence about whether to make the woman pregnant. I thought to myself an obvious interpretation—that the ambivalence about the pregnancy stood for her feeling about her organic condition—that is, not fully prepared to give birth to life, and perhaps, as well, ambivalence about committing herself to this difficult analytic task of having feelings. Yet Sally was talking easily in this session, and while the sculpture certainly suggested unconscious conflicts, I did not feel that an interpretation here would further the goal of the resolution of her resistance to feeling. I refrained from making the interpretation, and let her continue with the story uninterrupted. She told me that she had discussed the idea with a friend who teaches an art class. She found out later, from another friend, that this art teacher had then assigned her class to do a sculpture of a pregnant woman. Sally asked me what I thought about this. I asked her what she thought, and she admitted that it bothered her; she felt that her idea had been stolen without acknowledgement or appreciation. I agreed with her view, and went considerably farther than she would allow herself to go in recognizing the aggression in the theft of the idea. Using information that Sally had given to me in previous sessions about this woman's destructive impulses toward my patient, I told her that the woman was a vulture—that she would probably take anything of Sally's that she could get hold of—and that if the woman ever asked Sally to give her any of her paintings, then she really better watch out, because that would mean that she expected Sally to die, and, if she expected Sally to die, it would probably be because she wanted Sally to die.

Ultimately, Sally even began to outdo me. Her very conscious aggression and recognition of aggression allowed me to implement the toxoid response, to ensure that the psychic restructuring that had occurred around this particular aspect of her personality was a stable one, and not susceptible to future breakdown. I played devil's advocate, and assumed her initial narcissistic defense of protecting the object. When she was uninhibitedly expressing aggression, I told her that she was being too hard on people, that they couldn't help it if they were so inadequate. She said that that was just too bad—that they had to get better. She needed them to get better. She wasn't going to let them get off the hook through an ill-placed generosity. She had had enough of that.

Angry Andy and the Love That Cures

I met Andy early in my tenure as the psychologist for a cardiac rehabilitation program. He was friendly, yet at the same time kept his distance with the use of sarcasm. He was engaging but elusive. Andy's behavior in group had the same seductive, inviting, yet elusive, quality. Compared with the other group members, who were extremely negative about the process, Andy evidenced at least a sense of humor about himself and toward my efforts to engage this very resistant group.

I saw Andy in group psychotherapy for approximately four months, after which he left the group to return to work. Shortly after his termination I invited him to come for a consultation. During this meeting I expressed concern about his health and his need for continued psychological treatment. I tried, unsuccessfully, to persuade him to attend one of my evening groups at another hospital. Later he would confess to discomfort with speaking in groups, and a feeling that what he had to say would not be understood or accepted by the other members.

At the end of this consultation I did not have a clear sense of whether or not Andy would return to see me again. But in his hesitance I sensed his conflict. Later Andy told me that even though I had invited him to meet, it was he, and he alone, who had made the decision to continue in treatment. We later were to return to this theme (that he was the one in control), and that, to quote him, "You could not make me come."

In later sessions Andy described his struggle with the choice to continue working with me. Traveling to sessions Andy reported often feeling that he should turn back; and he would find himself hesitating before ringing my bell. His ambivalence would take on other forms, too—he would forget questions that he wished to ask me, saying that "the words go out of my mind when I enter the building." Similarly my words, my questions, would flee as he departed my office. This forgetting signaled the forbidden, prohibited nature of his wish for involvement, for a relationship with another human being. It was as if his need for attachment, for love, had to be banished as the words of our contact had to be erased.

In the initial phase of his treatment, Andy talked only of mundane things (books, movies, politics), saying little about his health or his emotional self. I supported this form of engagement while at the same time questioning myself. "Is this an analysis? Am I doing right by him?" Andy's tone during these sessions was detached and uninvolved. At times of anxiety, he would resort to humor. I felt cut off, unimportant, and certainly not influential as his analyst. What I failed to realize at the time was that Andy rarely spoke to anyone at all and that his talking was a travail for him.

As the months passed, Andy revealed that one of the reasons why he came to treatment was his fear of acting violently. He had a history of this behavior and it was my sense that he hated this about himself. Andy would repeatedly tell me that he was not a likeable person and as the treatment progressed, the depths of his self-hatred became clear. His self-imposed isolation and his feeling that others would not like him served to reinforce his dislike of himself. It was at these times that I felt the urge to reassure Andy. Yet, I held back, for these assurances would have been rejected, suspected, and mistrusted. It was only after three-and-a-half years of treatment that Andy could even partially allow me to express positive feelings to him, telling me, "You know I can't take compliments, but I like hearing that."

One of the major therapeutic tasks in Andy's analysis was for me to maintain adequate emotional distance. Frequently I wanted to verbally reach out, to bridge what I felt was the emotional canyon between us. Yet I continued to maintain what I can only describe as an emotionally neutral but interested stance. My feeling was, and still is, that Andy had a strong wish to be loved and cared for, but this wish had to be negated—rejected outright by him. Andy similarly rejected and criticized his own feelings, saying that it was better not to feel anything for anyone, that it was "better not to feel." By "better" Andy meant safer, and the reasons for this equation became obvious as Andy began to relate his history.

In our working together nothing about our commitment to each other was acknowledged. Issues around which this subject is often broached, such as the difficulty of scheduling Andy's appointments (due to his changing work schedule) and my vacations, went undiscussed.

As we continued to work the reasons for Andy's self-hatred and emotional deadening became clearer. Andy's paranoia about people was based on multiple experiences of being rejected, beginning with his awareness of being an unwanted male infant. The theme of being punished, ignored, and rejected by women permeated his memories. His comments on my behavior revealed his profound distrust for women. What he would later applaud as my ingenuity in helping to talk, he originally labeled as my being manipulative and "sneaky." He would frequently comment, "Ah, you did it again."

I often wished, when I was with him, that I could escape from my womanhood, but I soon learned that even if it was not uppermost in my mind, it was in his. After his remarks on my "talents" or on some inconsistency in my behavior or words, I would simply reply, "What do you expect? I'm a woman!" Although he would then try to tell me that I was different from other women, I knew that he was comforted by my acknowledgement of my potential danger for him. Many of my interventions were designed to support his need for distance, for safety. When he would report to me, after recounting a very painful experience, that he did not feel anything about it, I would tell him "That's good, you are better off." Later, when he would protest that his denial of feeling was not human, I would reply, "It's better not to feel anything, you'll only get hurt."

Although consciously Andy knew that our contract was to help him experience rather than somatize his feelings, he felt unconsciously protected by my disavowal of his feelings. I believe that it was this stance, my refusal to allow him to be emotionally open or vulnerable, that built Andy's trust in me. Openness about, or any demonstration of, emotion was something that made Andy feel most vulnerable, and my refusal to elicit, or seduce, it from him symbolized my commitment to his, rather than my own, interests. Unlike other women in his life, I would not use his words or feelings to "stab him in the back."

While it might have appeared overtly as if we were solely acquaintances, my refusal to intrude upon Andy forged a strong bond. As I look back on this time I realize that my stance of neutral interest was invaluable to Andy's healing. The absence of exhortations to say more and the absence of "false" felicitations was felt as loving by Andy.

In the beginning of Andy's treatment I felt almost duty bound to inquire into his adherence to his medical regimen. My questions were often met with evasion or humor. We finally were to acknowledge that we both knew that Andy would do only what he wanted to do. Although he states this as fact, I knew that my concern and interest in his health meant a lot to Andy. As I suppressed my enthusiastic inquiries to the level of happenstance questions, Andy talked more and more of concerns about his health, and his fear of dying. What he feared most was not actually death itself, but dying alone.

As the months passed, Andy would inform me of his doctor's appointments and medical tests. When he was later to have a second heart attack, Andy called and waited for me to ask "Where are you?" before telling me that he was in the hospital. That I was to go to visit Andy in the hospital was, for me, expected and understood, but for Andy my visit was a priceless sign of loyalty and caring. I was only later to learn the real significance of my visit. In subsequent sessions Andy was to describe his "betrayal" by his wife. He stated that when he first became ill he felt incredibly vulnerable and out of control. His feelings of vulnerability terrified him. He stated that this was the one time that he needed his wife. When she finally came to the hospital, several days later, Andy stated that she looked as if she did not want to be there.

Although it has taken many years, it is now understood between us that if Andy becomes ill, he should call me. He is now able to acknowledge that I am the only one he would want to call. It is at these times, and at the approach of my vacations, that it becomes clear how much Andy relies upon and misses me when we are separated. Andy will talk almost as if he were scolding me at these times, and will tell me that I an the only one that he talks to, that he continually thinks of things to tell me, and hates the feeling that he misses me.

In my work with Andy, I have come to realize that cardiac patients have experienced heartbreak early in their lives. In discussions of our relationship, Andy often alludes to my eventual abandonment of him. From his communications I have realized that Andy's life has been a series of experiences with unrequited love. That he fears me to be the next is expected in his projection of the future. The theme of being profoundly and painfully rejected by women is recurrent in Andy's communications, as it is in my work with other cardiac patients.

Although Andy refused to discuss these rejections except in vague terms, he frequently forecasts my ultimate rejection of him. It has only been in recent months that he has been able to verbalize these fears with affect. In response to my happily reporting the moving of my office, Andy produced a dream where I was standing with his wife and daughter laughing at him, ridiculing him. The laughter, he told me,

signaled his having been fooled by yet another woman, and his abandonment was symbolized by my moving to a new office. In response to
these communications I told Andy that I had been in error by not being
clearer about the circumstances of my move and that "like it or not"
he was "stuck to me like glue" and would *have* to go with me to the
new location. Hearing this, Andy's face showed a marked reduction in
anxiety and his previously defiant and negative stance disappeared.

In my work as an analyst I have come to understand that analysts
often allow themselves to know only what the patient wants them to
know. While I am often curious about my surprise at being so important a person in Andy's life, it is by luck or coincidence (the unconscious?) that Andy picked as an analyst a woman who has few pre-
sumptions or expectations of being important to others. In this way my
failure to note my importance in Andy's life saved the treatment. I was
easily able to join his need to deny the strength of his feelings for me.
In this way we maintained a delicate emotional balance.

I am most aware of the severity of Andy's heart condition at those
times in which we are to be separated (changes in his schedule that
prohibit his coming to sessions, and my vacations). It is at these times
and at times when I am feeling effective as his analyst that I become
aware that Andy should have been dead long ago. Not only does Andy
have significant coronary occlusions but he has major difficulty with
the clotting factor in his blood. Of all my cardiac patients, Andy has
the most potential for self-destruction. He struggles continually not to
smoke, has a poisonous, hostility-laden relationship with his wife and
daughter, and has great difficulty controlling his eating and losing
weight.

We are now able to discuss Andy's self-destructive habits and to
label many of his behaviors as defiance. What Andy is telling me in
these behaviors is that no one has ever listened long enough to understand him. Consequently he has learned to appropriate (or misap-
propriate) attention by being difficult, by being different from others.
In accepting the defiance in his nature, I have reduced Andy's impulse
to act on it. Even in discussing his death and his wish to be cremated,
our dialogue communicates a comforting mixture of aggression and
affection.

One day Andy came to his session and informed me that he would
not be buried but cremated. This way, he said, no one would know that

he was fat. To this I replied, "Yes, but I'll have you put in a Buddha urn and write on 'He Died Fat!'" In this way I allowed Andy his fear of, and wish for, death without abandoning him to it.

The psychosomatic and analytic literatures are replete with evidence of the importance of verbalizing feelings for the medically ill (psychosomatic) patient. Andy's treatment has demonstrated to me the truth of that, and ultimately, the lifesaving power of psychoanalytic treatment for the heart patient. Further, my work with Andy has confirmed for me the importance of the need to respect the patient's defenses. If the patient is helped to maintain his defenses for as long as he needs them, he will come to prescribe his treatment for the doctor, and it is the doctor who must learn to listen to the patient.

Andy's treatment also required that I examine the role of aggression and the verbalization of aggressive feelings in the etiology and prevention of future cardiac illness. It was clear that Andy had a lot of aggressive feelings. What was not clear was whether the verbalization of these feelings would be curative. I have come understand that in patients with coronary artery disease, their facade of hostility and aggressiveness is a psychological defense, a means of self-protection from further emotional injury. In observing this aggressiveness it is important not to be distracted from the underlying, and therapeutically crucial, fact that it protects against the wish for a positive and loving relationship that has long been denied. What was curative in my treatment of Andy was my acceptance of his view of himself as aggressive, my acceptance of his need for distance, and my ability to help Andy be less aggressive and rejecting of his feelings, thoughts, and wishes. I respected Andy's need for self-protection without denying him the relationship for which he longed.

These tasks were accomplished not by my focusing on Andy's angry or suspicious feelings about me, but by allowing him to have these feelings, even if unverbalized, in the sessions, and by allowing him to verbalize the angry feelings and negativity toward people in his life. What was important was simply acknowledging the crucial emotional thread of Andy's history—that people, most notably women, have the capacity to harm him.

My use of parsimony in my emotional communications, along with an active stance toward an investigation of the ways in which I would surely ultimately hurt and abandon Andy, allowed his fears to be valued and respected.

I have come to understand that my neutral stance of consistent interest in Andy (regardless of his attempts to tempt me into negativity towards him) was another factor in this successful therapeutic process. I highlight consistency and interest because these two elements seem specific to healing the heartbreak of the cardiac patient. If these are provided within the context of a genuine communication between analyst and patient, the reparative relationship is formed.

Based on my experience with Andy and with other cardiac patients, I have concluded that it is the gradual unfolding of the positive and loving relationship that is curative in the treatment of the heart patient. In Andy's case, his forays into negative feelings signaled the testing of the relationship before the emotional acceptance of its veracity. In this process the negativity is the frame upon which the love is constructed.

Notes

1. F. Sulloway. *Freud, Biologist of the Mind* (NY: Basic Books 1979); 55.
2. S. Freud. "On Asphasia, a Critical Study," trans. E. Stengel (London: Imago, 1953)
3. S. Freud, *S. E.,* 169, (1893).
4. S. Freud, *S. E.,* III: 37 (1893).
5. S. Freud, *S. E.,* III (1894), 52–3.
6. S. Freud, *S. E.,* VII (1890), 283.
7. S. Freud, *S. E.,* III (1893), 35.
8. J. Forrester, *Language and the Origins of Psychoanalysis (Columbia University Press,* NY: 1980), 31.
9. S. Freud, "The Dynamics of Transference," *S. E.* (1924).
10. Three books that have lengthy discussions of the "Project" and its implications for modern neuropsychology are H. Spotnitz, *Modern Psychoanalysis of a Schizophrenic Patient,* F. Sulloway, *Freud, Biologist of The Mind,* and K. Pribram, and M. Gill, *Freud's "Project" Reassessed* (NY: Basic Books, 1976).
11. Ibid.
12. R. Wollheim, *Sigmund Freud,* Modern Masters Series (NY & London: Viking Press, Fontana Books, 1971).
13. S. Freud, *S. E.* III: 36 (1893).
14. H. Spotnitz, *Modern Psychoanalysis* 58.
15. Ibid.
16. Ibid.
17. S. Freud, "Analysis Terminable and Interminable," *S. E.* 23 (1937).
18. H. Spotnitz. *Modern Psychoanalysis* 37.
19. O. Kernberg, *Object-Relations Theory and Clinical Psychoanalysis* (NY: Jason Aronson, 1976).

20. H. Spotnitz and P. Meadow, *Treatment of the Narcissistic Neuroses* (NY: The Manhattan Center for Advanced Psychonanalytic Studies, 1976), 20.

21. R. Greenson. "The Working Alliance and the Transference Neurosis," *Psychonanalytic Quarterly,* 34 (1965): 155–81.

22. H. Friedman, S. Booth-Kewley. "The 'Disease-Prone Personality' " *American Psychologist* (June 1987): 539–55.

23. H. Spotnitz, *Modern Psychoanalysis.*

24. Fritz Perls was one of the first proponents of what has come to be called the "touchey-feeley" therapies. Ida Rolf, whose therapy attempts the retrieval of lost memories through muscle stimulation, has also been influential, as has Alexander Lowen and all those who similarly took Wilhelm Reich's idea of "muscular armoring" as the basis for therapeutic touch therapies. Pure discharge, through screaming, was popularized by A. Janov in *The Primal Scream,* and that too, found its culmination in Dan Cassels therapy, where patients were exhorted not just to scream, but to scream hate.

25. H. Spotnitz, *Modern Psychoanalysis,* 64.

26. Ibid., 263–72.

27. Ibid., 92–116.

12

Reversing Disease Physiologically

> *. . . we see flies on a manure pile, and
> other parasites also. Some of these
> parasites may be dangerous and capable of
> producing disease under favorable
> circumstances. If, however, we remove the
> pile of manure, the parasites disappear at
> the same time. Which do you think is the
> more intelligent: to fight disease by swatting
> flies or to remove the pile of manure?*
> —Dr. Julian Baldor

Health Means Immortality—Almost

It is probably the case that the cell is immortal.

Alexis Carrell performed a remarkable experiment to test the point. He took small pieces of heart tissue from a chicken embryo and immersed it in a solution from which the cells could obtain food. Waste material was secreted into the solution. Every day the solution was changed; the waste products were removed and new nutrients were added. For the twenty-nine years that this procedure was followed, the heart tissue was kept alive and it seemed as though the experiment would have no natural end. It was only through the forgetfulness of a lab technician that the experiment was prematurely terminated. He forgot to change the solution, and through the process of autointoxication, the cell died. Carrell concluded: "The cell is immortal. It is merely the fluid in which it floats which degenerates. Renew this fluid at intervals, give the cell something upon which to feed and, so far as we know, the pulsation of life may go on forever.[1]

Freud understood how this principle operates on the psychological level. He found what he termed "strangulated affects"—the idea that accumulated mental toxins cause a disease state, a psychotoxicity.

On the level of the body as well as of the mind, there is a regulatory mechanism governing the release of toxins. Clinicians have found that the condition of physical disease reflects a malfunctioning of these regulatory mechanisms of discharge of biological and psychological toxins. And on the level of the body as of the mind, the state of toxicity is intimately related to the defense system. With its excretory power, the defense system joins in with the other eliminative organs in a combined effort to rid the body of toxic waste.

What are the physiological consequences of damage to the eliminative organs of the body?

The eliminative channels are like the defense systems. Both the physiological immune system and the psychological defense system are multilayered structures, consisting of a series of backup systems. Should one line of defense fill, there are others waiting to step in.

The five eliminative organs—the skin, bowel, liver, lungs, and kidneys—all have this same ability to compensate for one another. Each organ will carry away waste material so long as the demands on that organ does not exceed its capabilities. If one organ is overtaxed, however, abnormal secretions will be discharged through one of the other channels.[2] The body will attempt, always, to find its way back to a homeostatic balance.

When, however, the organism has exhausted even its emergency procedures for ridding itself of toxins, and there still remains more to be eliminated, the body will try yet another solution.

In the case of cancer, for instance, it deposits the toxins into the part of the body known as the connective tissue, where these deposits will be stored. Although the function of this connective tissue was long ignored by scientists, its importance to the body is now known through the discovery of its role in cancer formation. Every tumor is surrounded by this connective tissue; wherever cancer establishes itself in the body, connective tissue is found.

When this storage capacity is exhausted, the connective tissue is rendered inactive and paralyzed, incapable of helping or protecting the body in defense or healing. The volume of unwanted material has now exceeded the body's capacities to deal with it, through either detoxification through the normal eliminative channels, or storage in the connective tissue. Toxins will pass into the blood and tissues, thus creating a process of autointoxication of the entire organism. This same process of toxic buildup occurs in heart disease, as well. The excess accumulation of cholesterol prevents the normal healing process of scarring. Toxic deposits of plaque are formed, and the disease state spreads from being a local and minor inflammatory response in the arteries to a life-threatening systemic condition.

We know that the accumulation of toxins in the body can also be reflected in psychological disturbance. Just as cure of the mind can achieve cure of the body in some situations, so too can cure of the body accomplish correction of psychic dysfunction. The mental conditions of schizophrenia, depression, and anxiety have all been found to respond positively to a cleaning out of biological toxins.

The immune system can function efficiently only if the organism is relatively free of toxic accumulations. The interdependence of the defense zones means that any blockage in one zone can affect all the other defense zones, and thus indirectly lower resistance. Similarly, the respiratory, digestive, hormonal, and nervous systems are all interdependently connected. Toxic accumulation in one system has implications for the functioning of all other systems. The disease process, then, beginning with toxic accumulation, can become manifest through the acute disturbance of any tissue or organ in the body; the circulatory system in heart disease, the joints in arthritis, the adrenal glands in allergies.

As Freud understood that restoration of health is dependent on release through the ego of pent-up thoughts and feelings, so too have clinicians working with organic diseases understood that regeneration of biological systems cannot be accomplished without a clearing out of the accumulated poisons which have exhausted the body's coping efforts and rendered the physiological systems inactive.

The physical reversal of disease begins in virtually the same place as the psychological reversal—release of accumulated poisons so that each of the physiological systems can be reactivated. Exposure to health-producing environmental conditions—food, water, air, and sun on the physical level and feelings, on the psychological level—is equally necessary. The ultimate goal of the treatment—reassigning integrity to the defense system—is the same on both the physiological and psychological levels.

Food That Kills

It is no great overstatement to say that the chief task of intelligence is to distinguish the wheat from the chaff. Both our minds and our bodies operate continuously, simultaneously, and on many different levels, to achieve this discrimination. Health resides in the ability to discern what is useful and what is waste.

Our mettle is tested in our attempts to discriminate among food sources and to choose those that will provide the nutrients we need. The human animal is unique in the breadth of choices available to it for food. Most other mammals limit their dietary repertoire to one category—either plant or animal food—and often to only a few selections within that category. The human animal, on both the anatomical and psychological levels, represents an admixture of both. Some of our teeth—the molars—seem to be phylogenetically related to herbivores, while the pointed canines have evolved from carnivores. The same is true of our intestinal system. The length of the large intestinal tract is necessary for the digestion of plant life, but the relatively short colon is more reminiscent of the meat eaters.

The advantage of being an omnivore has resulted in an unsurpassed ability to adapt to a variety of conditions. Eskimos, for instance, can subsist on a diet that relies heavily on meat without nutritional difficulties. A largely vegetarian diet, too, has been shown to be entirely adequate in providing essential amino acids and vitamins. But our omnivorous nature, and our unparalleled mobility, demands a certain degree of attention from us. Given the wide choices we have available, we must consciously distinguish between what is edible and what is not. The natural world is filled with plant and animal life that has no nutrient value, or is undigestible. Proper discrimination demands both intelligence and memory. All mammals other than man simply rely on their genetic programming to know what to eat and what to avoid. Our ability to make judgments provides us with lots of room for error.

Humans have always had the habit of swallowing almost anything that does not swallow us first. It has become an unfortunate fact of modern civilization that many of the substances that we eat as food have ceased to provide that one essential requirement of food—nutritional value.

How it is that we choose foods is as much a cultural decision as a biological one. Given that eating is a practice that all of us do repeatedly throughout the day, and every day, the foods we choose become a large part of our self-definition. The foods which comprise the most serious threat to our health in this country—meat, wheat, salt, and sugar—are almost as synonymous with America as apple pie. It is the overemphasis on these foods that is largely responsible for the fact that most Americans suffer from a subclinical and undetected condition of malnutrition. Analysis of the reasons for the cultural adoption of these foods shows that their predominance as food sources came about more from economic concerns than from any determination of healthy properties of the foods.

The emphasis on meat eating, for instance, has a history that shows its preference to be entirely unrelated to nutritional concerns.[3] Every culture has had foods which are scarce, and thus treasured above others. These foods generally came to be associated with the ruling class. Throughout history, until recently, the limited supply of animals made them expensive as a food source, and thus prestigious. Those animals which were more abundant were made artificially exclusive through the practice of the nobility denying them to the common people. In medieval Europe and Elizabethan England, venison and other game could only be hunted by the nobility. Even legislation attempted to limit the amount of meat eaten. Between 1563 and 1577 alone, six different edicts, called sumptuary laws, were given in France which attempted to put severe restrictions on the serving of meat. Meat was elevated above all foods, while most vegetables were disdained. Had those legislative attempts succeeded, vegetables would have come to play a more important role in European cuisine, and our present eating habits would, doubtless, emphasize meat less than they do.

Even more removed from health concerns is our current emphasis on the particular meat source of cattle. Beef is a relatively new substitute for horsemeat and pork, though it is superior neither in nutrient value nor in taste. The practice of eating horsemeat was common throughout Europe and Asia for centuries. Its phasing out as a main food source was done precipitately, evidently in response to religious stricture. Jewish, Buddhist, Muslim, and Christian edicts discouraged the eating of horsemeat. These religious declarations, however, merely validated what had already become an ecological necessity. Horses can easily survive and proliferate only where there is an abundance of land for grazing. With the industrialization of Europe, and rapid population growth, the raising of horses became a costly extravagance, and other food sources needed to be sought out.

Of the alternatives, a popular choice, and one which was preeminent in this country until the turn of the twentieth century, was the hog. Again, ecological concerns determined the choice. The pig is one of the most efficient convertors of plant life into meat. Swine produce twenty pounds of meat for every hundred pounds of feed, a figure which is twice that of poultry and three times that of cattle.

With the opening of the western part of the United States, however, cattle demonstrated one great advantage over hogs. Cattle, unlike hogs, have the ability to digest the tough cellulose of grass. The move west opened up vast grasslands which gave forage to the cattle. The subsequent development of railroad transportation and refrigeration, and the effective extinction of the major competing animal, the bison, were factors that converged to yield a way of providing to markets, anywhere in the country, fresh beef at a price lower than pork.

The mass introduction of white bread came, similarly, through cultural practices. White flour was regarded as a high status food for thousands of years. The advantage of the white flour was its ability to stay fresh much longer than the unmilled wheat. If flour is not milled, the large amount of fat in the grain will quickly turn rancid. The disadvantage, however, was that the milling process separates out the flour from the germ, thus removing the most nutritious part of the wheat. The difficulty of milling by hand ensured that not much white bread was available, and whatever nutrients were lost to the milling were made up for in other foods and through the larger quantity of breads made from unmilled wheat. The invention of new equipment in the 1870's enabled millers, for the first time, to separate out the white flour from the germ in mass quantities. The germ became seen as worthless, and was used then as fodder for barnyard animals. The large quantity of white flour that is eaten today, in the form of breads and pasta and cereals, and its national predominance as the representative of the wheat family, has now begun to be accountable for dietary deficiencies. White bread, as compared to whole flour bread, is 70 percent poorer in vitamin B6, 58 percent poorer in pantotenic acid, 47 percent poorer in folic acid, and 60 percent poorer in potassium. Comparable losses are accrued in vitamins and minerals, and the "enrichment" is comprised merely of calcium—hardly compensation for the losses—and sodium—which is downright harmful.

Salt, like white bread, was long a treasured commodity because of its ability to preserve meat and fish. Its scarcity, and the infrequency of eating the food it preserved, meant that its use was limited, and presented no health consequences to our ancestors. Over the years, the North American palate has become so accustomed to highly salted foods that an average of five teaspoons a day are consumed. Not only is salt added at the table in generous amounts, but it is hidden in a variety of packaged foods not usually considered salty, including ice cream, most processed wheat products—breakfast cereals, breads, puddings, pancake mixes—and most canned goods, including virtually all canned soups and juices, vegetables, and fish. The added salt is wildly out of proportion to what is naturally present in foods: canned peas have more than one hundred times the amount of salt of their fresh counterparts from the garden.

Excessive intake of salt has serious health consequences for the human body, which evolved in a world where sodium was scarce, but potassium, found in fresh fruit and vegetables, was abundant. The modern diet reverses the ratio, and potassium, a much needed mineral used in the contraction of muscles, including the heart, is in short supply. Excess sodium causes an accumulation of water, bringing about an increase in blood volume, blood pressure, and heart rate. The contribution of excess salt to both cancer and heart disease, kidney failure, and stroke has been abundantly documented.

Sugar is the nation's leading additive. The taste for sugar is innate, but our ancestors were able to satisfy their sweet tooth through the consumption of fruit, the naturally sweet food. While dental decay is only one of the damaging effects of sugar, it is one that is easily traceable through our various cultures. Aristotle asked why figs damage the teeth. At that time, there was a heavy consumption of honey and dried fruits. Similarly, during the Roman occupation of England, sweets were eaten in large quantities, and toothlessness became a common problem. During the subsequent Anglo-Saxon period, when abrasive grains and tough meat replaced the sweet foods, cavities practically disappeared. The opening up of trading, however, reversed the pattern again, and by the fifteenth century ships were bringing into England over a hundred thousand pounds of sugar each year.

The cultivation of cane and sugar beets meant that sugar achieved the same breadth of consumption as wheat. The ability to extract sugar from its whole food source at a price that made it affordable to the common man radically changed eating habits. Purified white sugar has had everything taken out of it except the sucrose. Any other ingredients—such as molasses, which is rich in minerals, iron, calcium, and trace elements—have been removed. And there is apparently some protective substance in the whole food that is no longer available when it is refined; the eating of as many as four stalks of sugar cane results in better than average teeth, rather than dental caries.

Sugar is most dangerous, however, in its effect on the general metabolism of the body.[4] The amount of sugar we have in our systems determines whether or not we feel hungry. Reduction of hunger normally occurs when sugar enters the bloodstream. When we eat processed sugar, we meet our craving for food while satisfying none of our body's need for nutrients. All of the vitamins, minerals, fats, and proteins that would have come from the food in its natural state are still needed by the body. These nutrients will, then, be pulled from the body's own reserves in order to support the metabolic activity stimulated by the sugar. A condition of a nutrient debt has been created. Sugar is a major contributor in many diseases, and is a more important factor in heart disease than the widely recognized factor of animal fat.

Even more remarkable as an example of our modern maladaptive diet is the general acceptance of a food substance which our biological system has seemingly evolved to reject. Coffee is initially unpalatable, and has many adverse effects, including insomnia, bad dreams, and increases in urination and anxiety. Its taste is an acquired one, and its bitterness is most often diluted with milk and sweetened with sugar. In addition, coffee contains at least one pharmacologically active component—caffeine, a highly addictive substance which, were it to be subject to governmental regulations, would doubtless be restricted in use.

The evidence for food as a stressing agent in the promotion of disease is now overwhelming. As many as 60 percent of human cancers have been attributed to dietary practices, and for the cancers involving the digestive organs, even this figure is probably far too low.[5] Diet has also been implicated in the diseases of arthritis, allergies, schizophrenia, depression, heart failure, and high blood pressure.

We have now become accustomed to using the term ''food'' to broadly indicate anything edible which goes into our mouths. The foods which comprise the diets of most humans, however, are complex mixtures of chemicals which may have been, and in this country usually are, modified by a series of events that have occurred between the field and the table. These events—packaging in the form of dehydrating, freezing, canning, homogenizing, pasteurizing, transporting, storing, and adding other substances to either preserve or enhance flavor or maximize salability—all change the chemical composition of food. We have invented a host of substances which look, taste, and smell like food, yet fail to meet the most basic definition of food. That is, the finished product that we typically have before us on our table is no longer comprised of chemicals that can be converted into use. We have invented nonfood food.

Changes in our cultural dietary practices have occurred most dramatically since World War II. Even a cursory look at these changes reveals the relationship of typical American dietary habits to disease.

Any of a number of foods could be singled out as exemplifying how great the changes in our everyday food supply have been, but the white potato makes a particularly dramatic example. For thousands of years, it provided a wide range of desirable nutrients, and had the additional advantage of being easily cultivated. Today, only half the crop is shipped as raw tubers, but even these have been chemically treated to prevent sprouting, and may have been waxed and colored, as well. In the last thirty years, there has been a five-fold increase in the per capita consumption of french-fried potatoes. About one-fifth of the crop is destined for potato chips, the end product of a complicated process which involves the use of gases to prevent darkening in color, exposure to high heat, and the addition of oils, salts, and often flavoring and preservatives. The common potato, in the form of a chip, has been robbed of any nutrient value, and is not much more than a paper-thin sponge for the retention of oils and fats.

The conversion of the potato into potato chips and french fries is only part of a trend toward a much greater intake of foods crisped by exposure to heated fat or to extreme dry heat, including fried snacks, crackers, and ready-to-eat breakfast cereals. Many of these foods, as well as byproducts resulting from frying and broiling, have been proven to cause cellular damage in the laboratory, and thus, must be considered deleterious to health.

Additives and Contaminants

In this country the question of food additives is as much a legal issue as one of health.[6] We depend upon the Food and Drug Administration

(FDA) for regulation of food safety, which is strictured by the Federal Food, Drug, and Cosmetic Act. This act has had many recent amendments, the most important of which was passed in 1958. Until that time the regulation of food additives paralleled the criminal law—a substance was innocent until proven guilty. Companies using the substances had little inclination to perform the research, and so it was left to the FDA to make whatever, if any, determination of safety. The 1958 amendment, however, required that safety be proven *prior* to the use of a substance. Because this change would have placed heavy burdens of time and expense on manufacturers to test hundreds of substances already in daily use, the term "food additives" was redefined to exclude many classes of substance, among them approximately five hundred ingredients listed as GRAS (Generally Recognized As Safe), about one hundred other "unpublished GRAS substances," approximately 1,650 flavoring agents, previously sanctioned food ingredients, and about thirty color additives. So, of the 2,700 substances intentionally added to foods, only four hundred are considered additives under the terms of the FDA regulations.

Growing concerns about cancer sparked another amendment to the Federal Food, Drug, and Cosmetic Act. The Delaney Clause prohibits the FDA from approving for use any food additives found to cause cancer in humans or animals. Again, though, only four hundred of the intentionally added substances are covered by this clause.

Larger groups of food constituents include 12,000 substances that are introduced unintentionally during processing, and an unknown number of contaminants that are inadvertently added to the food supply. The first group includes byproducts of processing, such as machinery cleaners, packaging components, caustics used in potato peeling, and residues of pesticides and drugs given to animals. The second group contains accidental contaminants. While there is some regulation of these contaminants, the statutory provisions governing food safety are more a patchwork of divergent, offhand legislative policies than a carefully considered monitoring system which might truly control our exposure to these ingredients. The vast majority of ingredients added to our foods have, in fact, never been tested, and their potential for carcinogenesis or other disease induction remains unknown. But where tests have been performed, many of the components have proven to be carcinogenic, and since these are not substances our species has come to earthly prominence eating, we should suspect that many, if not most, would similarly prove to be disease inducing.

Even where disease induction is demonstrated, there is no guarantee that the substance will be altogether removed from the food supply. Cyclamate sweeteners remained on the market while debate raged over whether they were cancer producing; they were finally taken off the market through governmental regulation. Saccharine, too, was found to be linked to cancer. The FDA attempt to ban it was overruled by Congress in deference to objections by diabetics and others.

The case of DES is another appalling example. Until 1978, it was routinely injected into beef cattle. As a hormone, it served to slow down the metabolism of the animal, fattening it up for slaughter, thus increasing the sale price per animal. It was, as well, routinely given to women to prevent miscarriage, and the children of these women are now battling rare forms of cancer induced by this medication. Its identification as a carcinogen took it off the market both as a human medication and as an injectable substance for the cattle. Farmers, interested in continuing to reap the economic advantage the substance bestowed, began adding the DES to the cattle feed, thus circumventing the legislation.

DES is only one of many drugs and pesticides whose residue is found in meat and poultry. Of the one hundred forty-three that have been identified, forty-two are known to cause cancer. In fact, synthetic products—DDT, PCB's, TCE, and 2, 4, 5-T are just a few examples—have been created much faster than either our ability or inclination to test them for long term effects. Sixty thousand tons of PCB's found their way into our environment between 1931 and 1971, when they were finally banned. A similar story can be told for DDT, and countless other chlorinated hydrocarbons.

What makes these substances particularly dangerous is that they are very stable and they are fat-soluble. The final reservoir for these chemicals is animal fat—the flesh of a cow eating grass laced with pesticide or feed spiked with DES, a fish eating algae two miles deep in the ocean contaminated with PCS's, or the breast tissue of a human female who has consumed either of these meats.

The poultry situation is no better. In spite of the recent popular shift from beef to chicken consumption, the meat of a chicken hardly fares better. Standard chicken farming means that the animal will live its entire life confined to a small cage. This animal never sees the light of day, never walks freely—never walks at all—and never has social interaction with its fellow animals. It is exposed to an abnormally long day, defined by fluorescent light. Its waste products are taken from under its feet by a moving conveyor belt. The bird is filled with antibiotics and progesterones (female hormones). When it is finally slaughtered for meat, this debilitating life has rendered it barely alive, and scarcely worth eating for any possible nutrient value which has surely, by this time, been lost.

The fact that N-nitrosodialkylamines are strong carcinogens under a variety of conditions and in many species means that pork and cured meats are suspect, as well. Bacon and ham are regularly treated with nitrates and nitrites as preservatives, and these can interact with other dietary components such as amines or amides to produce the cancer-inducing N-nitroso compounds. The average U.S. diet provides 75 mg of nitrate and .8 mg of nitrite daily. Within twenty to thirty minutes following the intake of pork, white blood cells undergo chemical changes which correspond to the changes that occur when blood is saturated with cancer.

Deficiencies

The problem with our food today, though, is not only what we have put in, but what we have taken out.

We have gotten into the habit of eating fragmented, partial food. What we take out when food is processed and removed from its natural state are essential nutrients. Pigeons fed exclusively with white rice, within four days lost the use of their legs and would fall over backwards. When their diet was supplemented with rice polishings—the part of the rice that is removed in making it white—they were able to stand within three hours and achieved complete recovery within twelve hours. Even when they were brought to the point of death, rice polishings were able to revive them. Similarly, chickens fed white rice lost the ability to hold their wings in place and eventually died.[7] The disease causing these symptoms is beri-beri, the first deficiency disease discovered.

With the quantity and variety of foods that we have access to, it is difficult to believe that the vast majority of us suffer from nutritional deficiencies. Certainly the kinds of deficiencies we have today are markedly different from diseases like beri-beri. Changes within the last few decades in our ability to transport and store food means that a wider variety of foods are available to us more of the time. Florida oranges are available to snowed-in New Englanders in the dead of winter. Thus, deficiencies of a single food component are not likely to develop.

Yet, an analysis of food quickly reveals that a diet consisting of partial and fragmented foods will not easily sustain human life. Let's look at a typical American breakfast. Orange juice: the fact that the food is eaten in juice form is already a problem. The calcium balance of the fruit is in the pectin of the pulp, which has been separated and thrown out. The pulp would have provided bulk necessary for the healthy functioning of the bowel. If the juice is made fresh from oranges, in order to allow transporting time without spoilage, the fruit has been picked six weeks before it has ripened. The acid content of the unripened fruit is green citric acid, which stirs up more bodily acids than the kidneys can carry off. Orange dye is generally injected into the fruit to change it from its natural green color, which marketing research has shown to be offensive to consumers. This food coloring is, most likely, one of the untested GRAS substances, and may have a direct carcinogenic effect. If the juice is canned or packaged, to all the adverse consequences of the fresh juice must be added possibly toxic chemical residues from the process of converting the juice into a form that has a frozen shelf life of years, or a refrigerated shelf life of weeks.

After the juice has been downed, the bulk of the breakfast will generally consist of wheat—toast, French toast, pancakes, muffins, or cereals. In whatever form, what remains as our food is only a fraction of what the original plant was; the germ and the berry, both highly nutrient parts of the plant, have been removed and the nutrients which were present in these parts of the plant are now lost. The process of cooking further debilitates the food. Vitamin E, lecithin, and natural oils—all present in bread and essential for health—are altered and ruined because of the heat that the wheat is exposed to. Lecithin heated above 212 degrees, the boiling temperature of water, is destroyed, and its valuable nutrient contribution to the glandular and nervous system is lost.

If we add bacon, or ham and eggs, we will have rendered a meal which may have been merely deficient into an outright carcinogenic factory. In addition to the nitrites, heated oil used to cook the meats turns rancid, and, through the creation of free radicals, is itself potentially carcinogenic.

And so we begin our day.

The fragmentation of food occurs even in the very process which attempts to make up for deficiencies in the food source. Vitamin and mineral pills are the products of isolating particular components of food. In these fragmented supplements, such as calcium, selenium, or the alphabet of vitamins, components that are naturally found together are separated. All substances introduced to the body require intrinsic factors in order to be metabolized properly by the body. The missing elements, which have been artificially teased out through the processing procedure, are then drawn from the body's reserves; in particular, bone, teeth, hair, nails, and muscles are affected. In order to complete the metabolism, deficiencies are created.[8]

Vitamin C is a good example. Vitamin C can reduce copper in the body, which in turn inhibits the recycling of iron. This is an essential process, since we cannot obtain enough iron solely from our diet. This effect has been found in even as small a dose of 500 mg of C, and when the C was discontinued, reversal of the effect was achieved.[9]

Excessive use of vitamins and minerals places an additional burden on the eliminative organs to remove the oversupply. Too much of a substance is experienced by the body as waste, and is treated as waste. Many of us have reached our threshold of capacity for tolerating unfavorable substances. The body, in recognizing these foods as unwanted, excess, or foreign, deals with them much as it would any other waste material. The immune system is triggered, and white blood cells rush to scavenge for the foreign intruders. Habitual eating of these foods produces an almost continuous immune response, and a system meant to deal only episodically with emergencies is in a constant state of activation. Exhaustion is inevitable.

Food that Cures

Food is an essential requirement of being alive. It is through the conversion of food into energy that the chemical and electrical systems in our bodies are fueled. Without the energy source of food, our bodies would lack the capacity to ward off environmental forces and our systems would shut down in death.

Food, like germs, is recognized by the body as a foreign presence.

The process of breaking down this foreign entity is the process of digestion. This is normally completed without ill consequences when the chemical composition of the food is such that the organism has the ability to break down those chemical components.

It is a fact that digestion occurs in a part of the body that is not, topologically, inside the body.[10] The body can be seen as a thick, misshapen cylinder, the outer surface being what we see, the inner surface being the alimentary canal. This digestive system consists of a single convoluted tube, some thirty feet long, open at its beginning—the mouth, and its end—the anus. Various sites in the tube, such as the stomach, are enlarged enough to accommodate the task of holding food and mixing it with glandular secretions. Some components of food, such as the cellulose in bread and vegetables, enter and leave the digestive tract never having entered the body itself. It is only when food components are broken down into small particles, simple enough to be absorbed, that the surface of the cylinder is finally breached, and nutrients enter the blood and lymphatic systems which, in turn, will carry them to every cell in the body.

Crucial to the digestive process is the functioning of minute particles called enzymes.[11] It is these that are responsible for breaking down and eliminating twenty-seven million cells in the body every minute. These cell-destroying substances have the additional remarkable capacity of not acting on or affecting normal, healthy body tissues or cells. They act only on abnormal, worn-out, sick, or dying cells, and foreign cells including food. The functioning of the enzymes in the body is a superb example of successful self/not-self differentiation in the service of life preservation.

The release of the first digestive enzyme, pytalin, occurs in the mouth and begins to change (digest) starches to sugars. When the food has been chewed, muscles in the cheeks, tongue, and roof of the mouth all cooperate to form a kind of chute so that food can be pushed down into the pharynx, and then, through involuntary muscle movements, into the esophagus. From here the food passes into the stomach where the effect of hydrochloric acid will break the food particles into still smaller units. Large quantities of digestive enzymes are secreted so that the food gets converted into a semi-fluid state called chyme. This chyme now passes into the beginning of the bowel—the duodenum, the first portion of the small intestine, where more enzymes combine to further digest the food substances. It is here in the small intestine that

90 percent of the absorption of all food constituents into the blood stream takes place.

By the time the chyme has reached the end of the small intestine, all that remains of what started out as food in the mouth is water and waste.[12] This solid waste passes to the large intestine, the colon, for the final stage of digestion and elimination. The large intestine swarms with billions of friendly bacteria whose function it is to accomplish the final synthesizing of nutrients. Rhythmic motions of the muscles of this five foot long organ, called peristalsis, push the solid waste toward the rectum and anus where it is eliminated from the body. The walls of the colon absorb most of the water which will be evacuated as urine.

Disturbances in digestion, assimilation, and elimination of food can occur at any point in this process, beginning with the mouth. Insufficient stimulation of digestive enzymes will interfere with digestion at this early stage. The usual presence of a dry, coated tongue in sick patients suggests this initial interference. Lab tests reveal that these coatings produce mold, yeast, and bacteria, indicating a condition of lowered resistance.

Inadequate mastication of food can be one interfering factor. Starches and carbohydrates must have an alkaline base for thorough enzymatic action. Mouth saliva provides this alkaline base, but it is only through proper chewing that the alkali can prepare the food for the digestion which the enzymes will begin.

Food aversion can be another interfering factor at this early stage of digestion. Digestive enzymes are extremely sensitive, and will respond to sight, taste, smell, and even thought of foods. It has been shown, for instance, that the reputation of chicken soup as "Jewish penicillin" in curing colds is not unwarranted. It is effective in speeding up the secretion of nasal mucous, thus clearing out nasal passages. The benefit seems to be attributable to its distinctive aroma, which stimulates particular enzymatic and chemical secretions. Conversely, foods which are unappealing in taste, smell, or sight will inhibit enzymatic secretions.

The stomach, too, needs foods to be broken down into the small particles that chewing accomplishes. Improperly chewed foods require the stomach muscles to work harder and accomplish what the jaw muscles should have done, thus creating a strain on the stomach. The stomach needs to be a highly acidic environment; without sufficient quantities of hydrochloride acid (HCl) in the stomach, the large molecules cannot be broken down. Without a proper mucous coating on the lining of the stomach, the highly acidic HCl would virtually eat away the stomach, as well as its constituents. Improper balancing of these acids creates an internal environment where enzymes cannot do their digestive work in breaking down nutrients so that absorption and utilization by the rest of the body occurs. The small intestine needs to secrete a bicarbonate to neutralize this powerful stomach acid. Each of these organs, including the large intestine, must have muscles that are developed enough to follow the rhythmic pattern of peristalsis— alternating contraction and relaxation—in order to move the food along the length of the intestinal track—twenty feet of small intestinal tubing, and five feet of the colon.

Most disease states reflect a situation where the vital processes of digestion and elimination have been interfered with.[13] Elimination through the bowel system has become insufficient to protect the organism from an accumulation of waste material, and this waste has created an internal bowel environment of decay and putrefaction.

The amount of putrefaction depends on the length of time the food has been in the body, the adequacy of the digestive system, and the particular kind of food that has been eaten.

Both cancer and heart patients have generally eaten more protein than their bodies can handle and less fiber and nutritional foods than they need.[14] The typical heavy emphasis on meats and fats can immobilize even a relatively healthy digestive system. Excess protein is stored around the cell membrane, and, as with too much fat, can reach a level of density which blocks blood cell permeability; nutrients and oxygen cannot be absorbed competently.[15]

The general principle of healthy bowel functioning is that what goes in should come out. The number of meals one eats in a day should be the number of bowel movements, as well.

Even regular daily movements may not be sufficient, however, if the transit time is abnormally long. Normal transit time for food from the time of its ingestion to its expulsion through the anus is between twelve and eighteen hours. For the ill patient, this time is greatly expanded, sometimes to seventy-two or more hours.

Food inside the body follows the same rules of spoilage as outside the body. Fresh fruit sitting at room temperature will take several days to putrefy; fresh vegetables take less time. Refrigerated foods will keep longer than unrefrigerated; cooked foods spoil faster than food left raw. Because the temperature in the digestive system is around 100 degrees, the process of putrefaction within the body takes place more rapidly than at room temperature.

In addition, food cooked above 118 degrees has lost the potency of its enzymes. The digestive organs must then come to the rescue and furnish the digestive enzymes of protease, lipase, and amylase to break down the food. To do this repeatedly, however, the body must steal enzymes from other glands, muscles, nerves, and blood. These excessive demands will lead to an eventual deficiency of enzymes.

Without adequate enzyme activity, food passes through the digestive tract too slowly. Because of the lengthened transit time, material can lose its watery consistency and become dry and hard. It can then be difficult to expel and can become encrusted against the walls of the colon. This encrustation prevents the absorption of vital nutrients through the walls of the colon, and narrows the passageway of the colon. As a result of this blockage, food cannot move easily through; whatever paristaltic movement remains present can often no longer be felt through the thick encrustation.

The bowel wall has now become a breeding ground for unhealthy bacterial life forms. While a healthy ratio of friendly (lactobacilli) to unfriendly (e coli) bacteria is 85 percent to 15 percent, in the disease condition (where the colon has become polluted with undischarged waste products), this ratio is reversed, with the unfriendly bacteria greatly outnumbering the friendly ones. Blood capillaries to the colon pick up the poisons of the accumulated waste and circulate them throughout the body via the blood stream. All tissues and organs of the body have now begun to take on the poisons seeping out from the colon.

Whatever nutrients the food source may have originally carried can no longer be extracted by the organism. In attempting to cope with this large amount of toxins, the system has strained itself and depleted its natural ability to digest, assimilate, and utilize nutrients. Stimulation of digestive enzymes is inadequate, peristaltic movement is sluggish, acid-alkaline balance is disturbed. The process of autointoxication, culminating in a life-threatening situation, is now well under way.

The existence of putrefied material in the colon has the further effect of compromising the lymphatic system. It is this system which carries toxins from all body cells. Lymph vessels combine to form ducts that eventually empty into the bloodstream. Within the lymph fluid are the white blood cells, which have the job of fending off pathogenic entities, such as the cancer cell. If the lymph is toxic, this fluid becomes thick and viscous, and the mobility, and thus effectiveness, of these white blood cells is hampered. The disease condition usually involves stagnation and blockage of the lymphatic system.

Putting In What Belongs In

We have seen that on the psychological level, the curative release of toxins occurs through the process of discharging thoughts and feelings into words. Inhibition of the normal discharge apparatus comes about from the destructive impact of external and internal stimuli which the psychic apparatus cannot adequately handle. The psychoanalytic environment is one where nutrient communications are made to the patient to aid in the process of discharge through verbalization.

The first task in reversing the disease process physiologically is to remove the noxious stimuli which threaten to overwhelm the coping ability of the biological systems. These, of course, exist all around us, both outside of ourselves and within, and there are many ways in which we cannot control our exposure to disease-producing substances. We can, however, bring under control some aspects of our exposure to toxins, primary among these being in the substances we ingest—the foods we eat, water we drink, and all other not-self material that we put into our bodies—cigarette smoke, drugs, alcohol, and inorganic chemicals from any source. Since these substances are the main stressing agents of all of the diseases of diata, their elimination goes a long way towards permitting the body a chance to return to a more healthy mode of functioning.

When we exclude most of the food and water that have been identified as disease inducing, it seems as though there's not much left. We have eliminated most meats as they are commercially available, all packaged foods, all sprayed fresh fruits and vegetables, and most drinking water. In any given supermarket anywhere in the country, there is scarcely a single item which would qualify as a healthy food under these strict criteria.

But in spite of this apparent paucity of qualifying foods, there remains a vast quantity of foods—foods left in their natural state, food as food, rather than the adulterated nonfood foods invented by man. The nutritional principle which begins the physiological process of disease reversal is that foods should be eaten as close to their natural state as possible.

The process of leaving food alone begins with the soil.[16] The chemical elements of which food is made up—calcium, silicon, sodium, magnesium, and so forth—are all formed in the soil. The growth of any plant involves a process of absorption whereby these chemicals are transmitted to plant life. It is through these life processes that the chemicals originally present in the soil finally become food for man.

We know that virgin and chemically balanced soil produces the best crops. Healthy soil yields the healthy plant life on which our nutritional needs depend. Disease preys on an undernourished plant, just as it preys on an undernourished human. Unlike chemically fertilized soil which consists of dead material, natural soil is replete with living bacteria. These bacteria work vigorously on breaking down the decaying organic material of the past dead generations of the plant life. These organic elements are then available as nourishment for the next generation of plants. Life begets life, for both humans and plants.

Whole foods must replace those fragmentalized, partial nonfood foods. Whole grains include brown rice (with the outer husk intact), millet, rye, and corn meal. Vegetables and fruits should be unsprayed and without the addition of dyes. Protein sources should be without added hormones and antibiotics.

Food, however, often fails to have sufficient potency to reverse the kinds of serious nutritive dysfunctions that are present in most serious illnesses. Food in which the nutrients are made available in concentrated form are adjunctive tools in the diet. Fresh vegetable juices and soups saturate the system with organically combined minerals, vitamins, and live oxidizing enzymes. When the essential enzymes are extracted from foods in juice form, the need for the larger amount of enzyme production required to digest solid food is eliminated. The system is spared this extra activity, and is then free to digest and break down the pathogenic cell and its protective wall. Like food, juice requires saturation by saliva in order to begin the digestive process. Gulping juice has the same effect as gulping food—aborted and partial breakdown of food particles, requiring the stomach and the rest of the digestive system to take up the slack. Juice should be drunk imitating the jaw action of eating, an act which will stimulate the required saliva secretion so that sugars will be digested before they reach the stomach. Different juices provide nutrients to different parts of the body, and it is possible to devise a therapeutic menu of juices.

Pure water is another essential requirement for the body. The only water which we can be confident will not only not damage the ill patient, but even work towards a cure, is distilled water.[17] Distillation is a simple process of evaporation and recondensation that leaves an absolutely pure combination of H2 and O. All minerals and possible contaminants have been removed. For the sick patient, this water is ideal. Without its minerals, the water has a far greater capacity to absorb body toxins and waste.

There has been a widely held conception that distilled water leeches out minerals from the body, and as a result, this pure water has been avoided by many of the people who are most in need of its benefits. Any minerals which are a component part of the cells and tissues of the body cannot be removed from the body, through leeching or any other method, so long as the cells and tissues are alive. Such elements cannot be dislodged from their resolute anchorage within the cell.

Minerals which have no value to the body, however, can be re-moved. These elements, such as lime and fluorine, present in water supplies, are not absorbed into the structure of the cells and tissues. If they are not removed through the eliminative channels of the body, they, like all other waste products, collect in the blood and connective tissues. Distilled water has the ability to collect this debris, and to facilitate its removal through the kidneys and bowel.[18] Because of this waste-collecting property of distilled water, it is an essential part of the detoxification program for the ill patient.

Getting Out What Belongs Out

Simultaneous with the introduction of vital nutrients begins the equally important process of detoxification, the removal of material that has remained, needlessly, within the body.

Most cultures have had practices designed specifically to eliminate bodily toxins. Among the most advanced are the techniques of the yogis. Sivananda yoga teaches various *kriyas*—purification practices which cleanse parts of the body that have a tendency to collect unwanted debris.[19] Kapalabhati is a method of vigorous inhalation and exhalation that rids the lower lungs of stale air, making room for a fresh intake of oxygen-rich air, and cleansing the entire respiratory system. Neti involves cleansing the nasal passages. Vastra dhauti is a method of cleaning out mucous and waste that have collected in the stomach and esophagus. Basti is a natural method of cleansing the lower intestines, involving the controlled use of muscles to pull water up into the colon, and then, after churning the water around to dislodge old waste products, expelling the water and whatever it carries off with it.

Most of us will not feel inclined to perfect these demanding and culturally alien techniques. Luckily, there are other options available. Once begun, the lymphatic system, the colon and the liver will all be brought into the effort.

Aerobic exercise has much the same effect in cleaning out the respiratory system as the yoga techniques. The skin is the largest eliminative organ of the body, and its secretion, in the form of perspiration, carries off vast quantities of waste products.

Feeling is an equally important way of discharging chemical waste. Tear ducts, stimulated into action by the feeling of sadness, carry waste products to our eyes. These wastes are then eliminated through the act of crying.

Internal cleansing of the lymphatic system is essential because it is one of the body's primary defensive mechanisms. The lymph glands are like filters which absorb excesses of proteins from the lymphatic channels distributed all over the body. They tend to swell under a toxic condition. This is a sign that the body is overloaded with excess wastes. Daily dry skin brushing is a good way of stimulating this system into its detoxifying function.[20] Further drainage can be improved through the introduction into the diet of certain herbal substances, such as blue violet tea, and additional enzymatic supplementation.[21] Specific juice fasts will also speed up lymphatic drainage.[22]

This direct stimulation of the lymph glands is not sufficient, however. Lymph blockage cannot be entirely eliminated except through the cooperative aid of the colon. A colon which retains putrefied material will continue to pour its toxins into the body of even a perfectly functioning lymph system.

Colon cleansing is fundamental in the degenerative disease conditions, and without it permanent reversal cannot take place. It is, unfortunately, the part of the program of disease reversal that meets with the most resistance. It was not always so. Physicians in past ages showed a lively interest in the matter of human waste as another of the products of the body that could give an indication of the condition of health of the individual. Precise discrimination of waste material was important enough to the Middle Ages that they had specific terms for the feces of different animals: "the Crotels of a Hare, the Friants of a Boar, the Spraints of an Otter, the Werderobe of a Badger, the Waggying of a Fox, the Fumets of a Deer."

Even among physicians, the idea of colon cleansing is not a popular one, and American doctors have contended for decades that the number of bowel movements an individual has is unrelated to health. Considerable research indicates otherwise, and British and South African scientists have conducted elaborate experiments involving the clocking and weighing of feces of human volunteers. It has been confirmed that too few bowel movements and too little bulk in the stool is related to a variety of disorders, including heart and gallbladder diseases, diverticulitis, varicose veins, hiatal hernia, and cancer of the large intestine.[23]

Further scientific confirmation of the idea that toxic substances produced in the bowel can have damaging health effects comes from a study of over a thousand nonnursing women. Those women, who were severely constipated, had abnormal cells in the fluid extracted from their breasts. These abnormal cells are the same cells found in women with breast cancer. These cellular abnormalities occurred five times as often in women who moved their bowels fewer than three times a week than in women who did so more than once a day.[24]

The simplest way of beginning colon cleansing is to add bulk to the diet.[25] Dietary fiber is the part of food that is insoluble and indigestible. When present in the intestinal tract, it supports a multiplying population of the lactobacteria, and thus can be an important aid in digestion and elimination. The detoxifying powers of fiber were demonstrated in a study where rats were fed poison, and simultaneously put on a high fiber diet. These rats survived without harm, while other animals fed the same poison, but without the fiber, became ill and died.[26]

Fiber is present in all fresh, raw vegetables; cooking softens the fiber and renders it ineffective. Whole psyllium husks are a good addition to one's diet; this substance acts like a magnet in attracting old fecal material to the psyllium particles; as it moves through the intestinal tract, it accumulates waste and grows to much larger than its original size, attracting more and more waste material, until its final expulsion. It has the additional advantage of secreting a liquid, thus lubricating its passage through the bowel. The common practice of using bran for the purpose of adding fiber is not recommended. Bran is a part of the wheat grain, and, as such, it is a partial rather than whole food. It acts as an irritant to the lining of the digestive tract. The intestinal tract, to free itself of this irritant, attempts to rush the process of moving the material through. Decreased nutrient absorption results because of the rapid transit through the tract. Further, constant use can cause a chronic condition of intestinal lining irritation.

Cleaning out the colon through the use of water injected directly into the colon is an essential aspect of the detoxification program for the seriously ill patient.[27] The water shooting through the alimentary canal acts as a gentle stimulus to dislodge old encrusted fecal material. Modern methods vary, and include enemas, colonics, and colemas. Enemas are effective in reaching the low part of the colon, but have the disadvantage of not reaching the entire organ. Adding ingredients to the water in an enema can, however, greatly enhance its detoxifying power. Coffee enemas stimulate the liver;[28] flaxseed tea enemas relieve the colon of inflammation; bentonite, or clay water, greatly increases the absorption of toxins from the colon walls.

Colonic irrigation consists of a cleansing of the entire intestinal tract, small as well as large intestine. It has the disadvantage of requiring costly equipment, and is generally performed only by an expert.

The colema is a home unit that combines the ease of the enema with the thoroughness of the colonic, and is, often, the recommended procedure. It most closely approximates the technique of the yogis in that it is a gentle procedure, following the natural rhythm for retention and expulsion of waste. Here, the water enters into the intestinal tract, and it is the colon's own spontaneous contractions that pushes water back out. Pockets of putrified material embedded within the colon walls can be dislodged through this method.

Internal cleansing can be facilitated through the use of fasting, as well.[29] Fasting, or the total or partial abstinence from food for the purpose of purification, seems to be an instinctive animal reaction to harmful metabolic accumulations. Domesticated and wild animals will refuse food when in a state of illness and will rest and fast until they feel well again. Even healthy animals follow a program of periodic fasting. We commonly observe that dogs and cats will eat grass to induce vomiting. This behavior brings up excess mucous and purifies the lymph system of the animal.

It is through the process of *autolysis* that fasting has its benefits.[30] The word is derived from Greek, and means "self-loosing." It refers to the physiological process of digestion or disintegration by enzymes generated in the cells themselves.

The human animal does well to follow this biological principle of fasting. Enzymes, as well as all body organs, need rest from their constant activity. They work hardest when attacking protein, and less hard with fruit and vegetables.

In the case of a wounded animal, great quantities of blood are sent to the site of the wound. The nutrients in the blood represent a great quantity of "food" given to the injury, and aid in the healing. The process of autolysis ensures that this can happen. The torn or damaged tissues are first autolyzed by enzymes. The body then draws on its reserves of food material, and redistributes nutrients wherever in the body they are needed.

Fasting increases the power of the enzymes. The enzymes will attack whatever material is present. In the absence of food, they will turn their attention to attacking, digesting, and expelling infectious wastes.

Short, intermittent fasting has been shown to be particularly effective in aiding the reversal of a cancer condition. Cancer tumors consist of blood, flesh, and bone—the same kind of tissue as other body structures. They are, as is ordinary tissue, susceptible to this process of autolytic disintegration. The cancer patient who fasts will be forcing his body into cannibalistic posture. The body is compelled to use every unnecessary element contained within it for food, including tumorous growths, which are then absorbed and systemically integrated and expelled.[31]

While soft tumors are quickly responsive to the autolyzing process, hard tumors are more difficult to dissolve.[32] It will usually take a regular program of periodic fasting before a fast will cause hard tissue to be absorbed. Large tumors present difficulties. In these cases, the fasting patient may experience an uncontrollable hunger before the enzymes can have done enough of the work of autolysis such that sufficient tissue absorption occurs. Also, some tumors are situated such that they dam up the lymph system. Here, the tumors will feed upon the accumulated excess lymph behind them, and the process of autolysis will be slow to take effect. It is helpful, in this case, to prolong the fast to the point where the enzymes are forced to seek food elsewhere, and can cope with the tissues of the tumor.

Prolonged fasts for the nutritionally depleted patient, such as in a cancer condition, can be dangerous.[33] Fasting can deplete the body of potassium, and cancer cells are already starved for this mineral. Fasting, then, can turn into starvation.

Fasting as a method of disease reversal has a long history in the Far East. It is here that it has been subjected to the most intensive laboratory research to demonstrate its effectiveness in a variety of diseases. Japanese researchers have done extensive testing with fasting therapy on psychosomatic diseases, irritable colon syndrome, neurocirculatory asthenia, mild diabetes millitus, obesity, and borderline hypertension, with an efficacy rate of 87 percent. Brain activity is involved and it has been shown that during fasting therapy, alpha waves of the brain (the normal waking pattern) are slowed and the incidence of theta waves (associated with relaxation and meditation) is increased. It seems likely that fasting stimulates chemical detoxification and works, like the talking cure, to effect change of abnormally formed neural links in the brain.

In spite of the beneficial effects of fasting, many people have great resistance to carrying it out. Fasting is often associated in the mind with deprivation, and conjures up images of weakness and hunger. In point of fact, usually after the first or second day of a fast (as the process of autolysis takes hold) hunger is no longer felt. The sense of weakness is precisely correlated with the extent of the stimulation of toxins, and, rather than dreaded, should be welcomed as a sign of the body's successful efforts at detoxification.

The weight loss associated with fasting is usually the most frightening aspect of the process for seriously ill patients. If the patient has already reached the point where weight loss is an observable manifestation of the disease process, the fear of still further loss sometimes creates an impenetrable resistance. In these cases, it should be remembered that the weight loss does not cause the disease; it is only a symptom manifestation. The fasting is a process that can correct the causative disorder. Weight will be readily regained as soon as the body is sufficiently detoxified that it is able to return to a state when nutrients can be absorbed from food.

How the Process Works

What follows is the autobiographical account of a woman, Doris, who cured herself of cancer through the means I have described in this chapter. I chose her story because it illustrates so well how seriously ill one can become when biological reversal is still possible.

When I work psychoanalytically with patients who are physically ill, I will always analyze their resistances to taking an active role in their healing. When patients choose the method of biological reversal that I have outlined, it is imperative that they work with a practitioner who is experienced in the method.

Doris had several advantages, as will become clear in the reading of her story, which surely contributed to her cure. No matter how sick she became, she maintained a firm belief in God, and was unafraid of her death. Whatever stress she felt was only from the physical debilitation; her psyche was in good shape. Additionally, Doris had a loving husband who would have moved the heavens (and practically did) in order to keep her alive and well. And finally, Doris had, every step of the way, the benefit of expert guidance from a colleague of mine who specializes in working the cancer patients through a nutritional/ detoxification program.

Doris, Who Cured Herself of Cancer through Biological Reversal

Doris: My story begins in March of 1971 when I began to feel tired, depressed and irritable. My normally healthy appetite grew poor. Since my life was very busy, I thought my symptoms might just be fatigue or a delayed reaction to an automobile accident I had been in two years earlier. Although I was only thirty-seven, irregularities in my menstrual cycle made me wonder if I was beginning change of life. I had bleeding and an unpleasant smelly discharge both during and between periods. When I told my friends about the way I was feeling, they urged me to get to a doctor, but I was too nervous and afraid of what might be found and so kept putting off calling for an appointment.

Then one day in October of 1971, I discovered a lump in my right breast. Both my husband and my chiropractor told me it was important to see a medical doctor right away. Although it scared me terribly to think what he might find, I made an appointment. The doctor examined me and said that my breast appeared to be badly bruised. However, the look on his face convinced me that there was much he was holding back. He called my husband into his office and suggested that we find a surgeon and have a consultation immediately. He tried not to alarm us, saying that perhaps nothing was seriously wrong, but it was important to follow through with an additional examination.

A good friend of ours who was a nurse in the hospital recovery room recommended a surgeon that she knew to be very skillful and kind. When I went to see him, I really appreciated his gentle treatment. He said that my condition could be dangerous—a biopsy should be taken to see if the lump was benign or malignant. As most people know, the procedure, if malignancy is found, is to perform a mastectomy, or breast removal. I put this thought out of my mind. Because it took ten days before I was admitted to the hospital, I tried to fool myself into thinking that things couldn't be too bad or the doctor would have rushed me in sooner. But the day came and I settled into my hospital room. It was my first time there as a patient and the prospect of surgery was terrifying. As I walked down the hallways with my husband the evening before the operation, we talked about my fears. He lovingly assured me that whatever happened he would love me—I would always be his wife whether I had to lose a breast or not. His loyal, positive attitude helped me tremendously. And so too, the next morning, did my favorite scripture as I got out my Bible and read these works from Isaiah 41:13, "For I, your God, am grasping your right hand, the one saying to you, do not be afraid. I myself will help you."

Of course I was aware of what happened during surgery, but later learned that the biopsy confirmed the doctor's worst fears and so he performed a radical mastectomy. When I regained consciousness, my friend, the nurse in the recovery room, was by my side. She was a real comfort to me.

By evening I grew more aware of my surroundings and found myself back in my hospital room and realized my husband was there with me. I heard his voice telling me, "Don't worry, it's all over."

The next morning my doctor came in to see me. He told me he was very sorry that the mastectomy had been necessary. When I asked if he felt he had gotten all the cancer he said, "I'm not God—but I did my best." Though it would have been nice to have heard him say he was sure everything was all right, I respected him for being honest with me.

I had entered the hospital on Monday, and had expected to go home the following Sunday. However, a few days later, as I walked down the hall with a nurse at my side, my doctor stopped me. He took me aside and told me the shocking news that another operation was needed—a complete hysterectomy. He felt it necessary because of fears that the cancer might spread to my reproductive organs.

At first I was too taken aback to say anything, but when I was able to speak I told him that my husband would have to be consulted. When I got back to my room I wept and wondered, "What else are they going to do to me?"

When I talked to John, my husband, he assured me that the doctor knew what was best, and encouraged me to trust his judgement. After that operation, my husband's support was even more appreciated. He visited every day without fail. He ate his meals with me and walked me up and down the corridors to be sure I got my exercise.

I had a frightening episode one day. As I was walking, I experienced heavy vaginal bleeding. The nurses rushed me back to bed where I had to stay for three days of strict rest. Before I was released from the hospital, the doctor removed my stitches, causing pain and bleeding. He bandaged me quickly, shook his head and said, "You need a lot of rest." Finally after twelve days in the hospital I was able to go home, but I was very weak and in a lot of pain from both operations. Once I was home my condition got worse, not better. The area of the mastectomy continued to drain and bleed. Though I visited the doctor once a week, there was nothing he could do to stop this unpleasant situation.

After several months, in June of 1972, I was readmitted to the hospital for a skin graft to cover the affected area. Skin was taken from my right upper thigh and grafted to my chest. The pain was so intense it felt like a knife was cutting into me. I was given medication to relieve the soreness in both my thigh and chest. After fifteen days I went home, but paid frequent visits to the doctor's office as before. Despite the application of ointments to promote healing, the graft did not take. So, in July I went back to the hospital for another graft, similar to the first. Skin was again taken from my thigh and grafted to my chest. I felt very depressed and wondered when all this pain would end—but I never gave up.

During this difficult period, my husband's devoted care kept me going. He would use a syringe to irrigate the graft area, and tried to cheer me up, but despite constant efforts to keep the area clean, it kept draining a thick yellow substance with a very disagreeable odor. This second graft did not take either.

During this time I was given strong medications (like Darvon) to help me bear the discomfort I felt. Because my doctor wanted so much for the next treatment to work, he suggested a skin specialist. In October, I was once again put back in the hospital for the third graft, this time done by the specialist. Again skin was taken from my thigh, and I had to be in the hospital for fifteen days. From my medical records, I later learned that during this time I received radiation therapy, though I don't remember it myself.

After I returned home I saw the specialist twice a week. Though I felt very discouraged, my feeling of hope never gave out. My religion was a great comfort to me, and our Bible study meetings gave me the strength I badly needed. The pain and weakness were so extreme that I fainted several times. During some of my office visits, the doctor tried to cauterize the unhealed areas on my chest and thigh, but to no avail. I continued on strong pain prescriptions.

When, at their worst, my thigh and chest looked like raw meat, I was admitted for my fourth graft. I went in April of 1973, and this time stayed for eighteen days. I was put on a water mattress in attempts to keep me comfortable and to prevent my moving too much, to avoid reopening the wounds. There were tiny holes in the bandage on my chest so that a solution could be dripped through to help keep the area clean and moist. It was painful, and despite these measures it continued to drain. I needed strong pills for pain and pills to help me sleep and calm my nerves. I had lost a lot of weight, but still I was determined to get through. It was necessary to be very careful about how I moved—but despite my efforts this graft, too, never healed properly. The doctor said that it did take, but that the skin was very thin and delicate. I asked him if I could go for a prosthesis, but was told I was not ready for that.

Though I was still optimistic and felt things would soon get better, in actuality I was going downhill and getting worse. This became evident when I felt a small lump in my neck and started to feel pain and several lumps in my right abdomen. Because of these symptoms, the doctor decided to put me back in the hospital for a gastrointestinal series in December. The tests I went through were more difficult for me than all the previous operations, and made me feel terribly weak. My weight had dropped from a normal one hundred thirty-five pounds to one hundred eight pounds. I went home after fifteen days with the assurance that everything would be all right, but the doctor told my husband privately that the tests showed that there was nothing more they could do to help me. From this point on I continued to slip—it was only the medications that were getting me through.

I had to think of others beside myself as family problems developed. At this time, my mother-in-law became very ill following a heart attack, and after being hospitalized for a short time she needed care at home. My husband and I urged her to stay with us, and this she did until her death a few weeks later. It was very hard caring for her, since I was so sick and weak myself, but I loved her and was happy to do all I could. Since her death left my father-in-law alone, John and I moved into his home with him to help care for his needs. We were thankful to friends who assisted with packing and moving.

My condition continued to worsen. Even strong medications did not ease the discomfort I felt—my legs and back ached terribly. When I went to my chiropractor for adjustment, he was barely able to touch me because of my pain. Other alarming symptoms developed. I was only able to move my bowels with the aid of suppositories and it was even difficult to urinate. The abdominal pain was only eased by holding a pillow firmly against myself. The only thing strong about me then was my faith, and I prayed often, as the Bible urges at Psalm 55:22, "Throw your burden upon your God himself, and he himself will sustain you."

It was really impossible for me to care for myself and a household any longer, so in September of 1975 I moved into my mother's house so she could help me. My husband stayed with his father, but as I worsened, he could come after work each day to spend evenings with me. Both my husband and my mother felt helpless and distraught as they saw me slip more and more each day. When my mother called my medical doctor to see if he could make a house call, he said, "All I can do is give her stronger pills to make her comfortable." He also suggested we call the surgeon, but said there wasn't much more that anyone could do.

By now I could not get up or walk on my own. My weight had dropped to eighty pounds or less. I slept most of the time—probably due to my medication and pain—and no longer recognized friends or relatives when they came to see me. Knowing how sick I was, the woman I had previously worked for for fifteen years came to see me at my request [although I don't remember her visit at all]. She was very distressed at my condition and was sure I would die that very night. My family began to think about funeral arrangements. My sister told my mother to prepare for the worst, that there was no more hope for me. From the end of October of 1975 on, I was unaware of anything— so my husband, John, will take over my story at this point.

JOHN: It was not easy to see my wife in such constant pain and so close to death. All of our friends were terribly concerned, and one day one of them told me that she had heard of a young woman in similar circumstances who had been helped when she went to Germany for treatments. When I asked what had been done for her, she explained that it was mainly a diet of raw juices and fresh fruits and vegetables. It seemed inconceivable that a diet program could help my wife, but still I reasoned, "What could we lose by trying?" We were referred to an organization that disseminates information about nontoxic treatments for cancer. They suggested that I take my wife to a clinic for treatment, but I explained how desperate Doris's condition was, and that moving her was impossible. The response was a firm, "Then we will do our best, if you are willing to cooperate fully." I said, "I am so afraid of losing her that I will help any way I can. Let's start right away—I just hope it's not too late."

We started Doris on what we felt would be safe amounts of vitamins, and we also gave her freshly extracted carrot juice. Because Doris was unable to eat at all at this time, it was difficult to feed her even juice, but we used a straw and urged her to take a little at a time. She could get the vitamins down if they were crushed. She also drank, alternately with the carrot juice, a nutritional drink mixed in a blender of yogurt, ripe banana, diluted frozen pineapple juice, digestive aids, bonemeal and kelp powders, brewer's yeast, A and D capsules, and small amounts of honey and vanilla to taste. Eventually Doris progressed to a super-nutritious diet of freshly extracted fruit and vegetable juices, raw vegetable salads grated very fine, unsweetened concord grape juice, vitamins, herbs, and enzymes.

With the help of loving friends who volunteered to come two at a time, around the clock, seven days a week for at least three months, she very slowly began to improve. To see her progress inch by inch, from her lowest point along the road to recovery was exciting. However, at first she was in such pain, so weak, and still so disoriented, that her friends had to help her in many ways. She needed a bedpan for a while, then later had to be carried to the bathroom. She had to be constantly turned and adjusted in her bed, her hair had to be washed in her bed, and she had to be hand-fed. Constant encouragement and large doses of love were the order of each day. We were truly blessed that her mother, her sister, and her friends were so generous with their efforts.

We were surprised at first, but later grew to expect, that reactions took place that made it seem that she was getting worse, not better. Frightening things like an increase in pain all through her body, skin rashes, muscle spasms, headaches, back pain, elevated blood pressure, fever, disagreeable body odor, dark stools, hemorrhoids, flatulence, cramps, poor circulation, and dizziness. But we were assured that these reactions are all a normal part of detoxifications, as the body cleanses itself from years of disease, chemicals, and medications. We had to keep reminding ourselves not to be alarmed, rather to expect these things to happen, and to see them as proof of success, not failure. Healing was taking place, though it was very slow process. It was such a delight to see the gradual signs of improvement.

In the beginning of December of 1975, Doris began to smile again, to enjoy the foods and beverages she took, and to regain her strength. She became aware of her surroundings, her family, and her friends once again. And so, because she remembers her recovery from this point on, I will let Doris resume her story.

DORIS: Yes, it is true that I began to feel alive again. I could appreciate the value of my treatment and I knew that it was vital to cooperate fully. I wanted to live. As John has said, it was early December of 1975 that I began to smile—no doubt because I began to feel that I would get well again. The detoxification was not easy, but I learned that it was all part of the healing period. At one stage my neck, injured in the car accident I mentioned previously, became so painful that I had to wear a neck brace again. The arm on the side of my mastectomy went into muscle spasms at times, and I would actually need help to hold it down. At night, it was often hard to sleep and to breathe normally. It sounds odd, but my teeth felt as fragile as glass.

But despite all this I was growing stronger, and did not need as much help from my friends. They cut down to one person at a time during the days, and my mother lovingly cared for me during the nights. My husband's enthusiasm kept me from being pulled down by the reactions I was experiencing. He told me that they would lessen and gradually ease away. That hope kept me going. Another feature of my treatment was taking cleansing enemas, needed to flush out the toxins as they were released from the system. Since I was too weak to give them to myself, my mother administered them faithfully twice a day or as often as needed.

About this time a friend who had been through the same therapy three years before came to visit me. She looked wonderful and told me how well she felt. I asked her, "Will I ever feel that healthy?" She assured me that I would indeed, as did all those caring for me. Their faith in me and in the program made me work hard to make progress.

As I improved I adjusted my diet. I began to eat more solid foods. The grated fresh raw vegetables and fresh fruit combinations were a pleasure to eat. It was exciting to actually see my body respond. The scars on my thigh and chest began to heal. Hair even began to grow again under my right arm which it hadn't done since my mastectomy. Though I still had occasional reactions, they grew less frequent. When I did experience stomach pains or nervous upsets [the latter I suspect being due to withdrawal from the medications I had taken], herb teas and gentle rubdowns with warm castor oil were of great comfort. Everyone was careful to keep any bad news from me to prevent stress. It tells us at Proverbs 14:30, "A calm heart is the life of the fleshy organism."

I was overjoyed to discover one day that the lump in my neck was gone, and soon the lumps in my abdomen began to disappear. I had advanced from the stage where I had to use a bedpan to where I was now able to get to the bathroom with someone to lean on. John gave me more and more help as he saw me improve; at my worst he had been nervous about handling me. Although I still needed help during the daytime, I tried gradually to get on my feet by myself—especially in the morning after a good night's rest. It felt wonderful to be up, but by around 10 A.M. I would have to lie down again. When I got tired I would begin to cry—probably from weakness—and that was my cue to rest. But, by taking it a little at a time, my strength continued to grow.

It was a joy to feel so well, and not to be dependent on any medications at all. When I started the program I gradually eliminated my pills over a two-month period which wasn't easy as I had become addicted to them. I have been drug-free ever since, not even taking aspirin for all these years. Whatever aches and pains I have are treated naturally with herb teas, massage, rest, and enemas.

It had been a long winter for me, so when we had a lovely clear warm day in February of 1976, I asked my mother if she would help me get dressed so I could go out in the back yard. I had not been out of the house since October of 1975. After I was dressed and stood outside at last, I looked up and thanked God with all my heart that I was still alive. I had thought I would never see the beautiful sky again. After about five minutes I felt a little weak so I went back inside—it seemed as if I'd been on a long, long trip. From then on, when the sun was shining, my friends would take me out for short walks. I would come back tired but very happy. My husband was so proud. One day he asked "How about going on a date? Let's take a little drive in the car." Although the idea frightened me, I didn't want to let him down so I agreed. We didn't go too far, but as we drove along I felt as if I were floating on water. I was really light-headed. It was a wonderful feeling to feel alive again and appreciate all that one has.

Now I saw myself improve in even more ways. I was gaining weight and was able to graduate from sponge baths to a regular tub bath. Since things were coming along so well, I began to yearn to go back home to be with my husband. But it was a conflict—here at my mother's I was cared for and pampered—if I went home, would it be too much for me? I had to promise that if I went home I would be extremely careful not to overextend myself. I knew that my loyal friends planned to continue to help me, so I decided to go home. My mother was not happy to see me leave; in part because she lived alone and she had gotten used to having me with her, but mainly because she was afraid I might regress without her care. She had been so loving and worked so hard to help me in every way that I knew I could never repay her.

But I did return home and my husband was delighted. Here it was March, and when I had left in September, he had thought he would never have me home again. John would wake me up each morning and say, "Are you okay?" He just couldn't believe how well I was. I had to be especially alert to my body's responses from this point on as I was taking more and more responsibility for my own care. My friends were concerned, but when they saw me continue to improve, they were relieved. They continued that year to check up on me, help me, and encourage me not to break my diet program. It took at least eighteen months to two years to regain complete strength and be on my own. I realized that I had to stick closely to my natural diet and avoid undue stress. I couldn't cheat and stay well.

In my case, as mentioned previously, two clear-water enemas a day were needed to keep my body cleansed as it continued to detoxify. Besides the enemas, I also went for colonics beginning in September of 1976, about a year into my recovery, when I was feeling stronger. Even after I felt strong and well again, problems sometimes arose. Probably because of too much stress, or fatigue, or failure to follow the diet zealously, at times the body weakens again. This had shown itself in my case in various ways. I have had vaginal bleeding, lumps under my arms, poor vision, upset nerves, and jaw alignment difficulties. Specifically, three to four years ago, I had a very pink discharge which turned dark red for a day or so. I increased enemas and took bed rest. I passed large blood clots, but quickly recovered after several days of complete bed rest.

Recovery is an ongoing process. I can never say "I am cured," and return to my old way of life and poor eating habits. To feel well, I must be conscious of caring for myself everyday. My husband and I feel that it is completely worth the effort. Life is a treasure and it would be the height of foolishness to neglect it.

Notes

1. A. Carrell, in B. Jensen, *Tissue Cleansing Through Bowel Management* (Escondido, CA. Bernard Jensen, 1980), 27.
2. The idea that physical disease is related to a condition of psychotoxicity has been referred to in previous sections of this book. The idea that physical disease is related to a condition of biological toxicity has never received wide acceptance in traditional medical circles, despite Alexis Carrel's convincing experiment. Proponents of this idea of toxic bio-accumulation are J.H. Tilden, *Toxemia Explained,* (New Canaan, CT: 1976, Keats Publishing); Bernard Jensen, whose books are too numerous to mention, but one of particular relevance is *Tissue Cleansing Through Bowel Management*; N.W. Walker, also prolific, including *Colon Health,* and Are Waerland's *Health is Your Birthright* and *Cancer, Disease of Civilization.* As well, some clinicians treat disease from this theoretical prospective. Especially generous with his time has been Leo Roy, M.D., who has been treating patients for over 20 years. He has numerous unpublished monographs and booklets, and we have had many conversations. Much of the material from this chapter has been gleaned from those sources.
3. Much of the material on the history of food habits came from P. Farb, and G. Armelagos, *Consuming Passion.* (Boston, Houghton Mifflin, 1980)
4. Sugar has received a lot of attention in recent nutrition literature. Some of the most popular works are by C. Frederichs, W. Duffy, and R. Aitkins.
5. Committee on Diet, Nutrition and Cancer, Assembly of Life Sciences, National Academy of Sciences, *Diet, Nutrition & Cancer* (National Academy Press, 1982).
6. Most of the information on environmental carcinogens is found in R.H.

Boyle and The Environmental Defense Fund, *Malignant Neglect* (Alfred A. Knopf, N.Y.: 1979).

7. Bernard Jensen is a leading proponent of the idea that nourishment is sorely lacking in our present-day food supplies. This research is cited in *Nature Has a Remedy* Escondido, CA.: Bernard Jensen, 1978).

8. This theory—of the fragmented natural of many of our vitamin and mineral supplements—is utilized by many holistic practitioners in the clinical treatment of disease.

9. B. Jensen, *The Chemistry of Man*, (Escondido, CA.: Bernard Jenson, 1988).

10. R. Ballantine, *Diet and Nutrition,*(Honesdale, PA.: Himalayan Interntional Institute) 307–31. It remains a classic, and gives, among other things, comprehensive information on the process of digestion.

11. Most current holistic practitioners and nutritionists understand the crucial importance of enzymes to the process of digestion, and to overall health, and enzymes are mentioned in most nutrition books. For a book specifically on enzymes, see Carlson Wade, *Helping Your Health with Enzymes,* (West Nyack, N.Y. Parker Publishing, 1966).

12. R. Ballantine, *Diet and Nutrition* covers the process of elimination, as well. Also, see Bernard Jensen, *Tissue Cleansing Through Bowel Management* (Escondido, CA: Bernard Jensen, 1980).

13. Proponents of this theory of disease include Bernard Jensen, Leo Roy, Carl Aly, Charlotte Gerson-Strauss, Donald Kelly, and Nicholas Gonzoles, who are all clinicians specializing in the non-toxic and biological treatment of cancer. Also, this notion of disease is reflected in the writings of Ebba Wairland, *(Cancer Disease of Civilization; Rebuilding Health)*; Are Waerland *(Health Handbook; Health is Your Birthright)*; Sir W. Arbuthrot Lane *(The Prevention of The Diseases Peculiar to Civilization)*; Max Gerson *(A Cancer Therapy: Results of Fifty Cases)*; Max Warmbrand *(How Thousands of My Arthritis Patients Regained Their Health)*; John Tildin *(Toxemia Explained)*; Henry Bieler *(Food is Your Best Medicine)*.

14. R. Ballantine, *Diet and Nutrition* 116–21.

15. Research of Lothor Wendt, reported in *Cancer Forum*, 6:1/2.

16. For an excellent treatise on soil, and our use (and misuse) of it, and the dire implications of this for both our personal and planetary health, see Peter Tompkins and Christophe Bird, *The Living soil.*

17. N.W. Walker, *Water Can Undermine Your Health,* (Phoenix, Arizona.: Norwalk Press, 1974).

18. N. Carrino, "Distilled water," *In Health* (February 1987).

19. L. Libell, *The Sivananda Companion Into Yoga* (N.Y.: Fireside, Simon & Schuster 1983).

20. *Nature Has a Remedy,* Jensen, B.

21. Ibid.

22. Much has been written on fasting, and at least a section on it is included in most nutrition and holistic health books. One of the early proponents

(and his book is still a classic) was Arnold Ehret, *Rational Fasting.* *(N.Y.: Benedict Lust Pub., 1971).*

23. Research reported in *Cancer Forum*, 3:3/4.
24. Ibid.
25. B. Jensen, *Tissue Cleansing Through Bowel Management.*
26. B. Jensen, *Research cited in Nature Has a Remedy.*
27. B. Jensen, *Tissue Cleansing Through Bowel Management.*
28. D. Kelley, *One Answer to Cancer.* Kelley has developed an elaborate biological treatment for cancer, using massive amounts of digesting enzymes to "eat" the cancer tumor and cells. Crucial to his program is rapid detoxification of the liver, which he accomplishes through the use of coffee enemas.
29. A. Ehret, *Rational Fasting.*
30. C. Wade, *Helping Your Health With Enzymes.*
31. L. Roy, "Fasting", unpublished monograph.
32. L. Wade, *Helping Your Health with Enzymes,* op. cit.
33. L. Roy personal communication, 1986.

VI

Cure: Where Mind and Body Meet

13

Turning Back the Clock of Disease

Disease reversal on the level of the mind follows the same regulatory laws as disease reversal of the body. Freud found that in order for the psychological dysfunction to be corrected, the patient must go back in emotional time to the point at which the disturbance began. Spotnitz's contribution, that the analyst could control the pacing of the regression through his judicious use of a repertoire of therapeutic interventions, marked an important advance in the treatment of patients whose cure depended upon a regression to the earliest phase of development. The quantity and quality of these communications to the patient permit the analyst to control the depth of the regression. Selye's idea that the intensity and duration of the noxious stimulus determine the physical disease can be applied to the notion of treatment of psychological disease, as well: both how the analyst speaks to his patient—his tone, manner, affect — and how much, determine the extent of the retreat toward the point when the disease was established.

The analyst walks with the patient the tightrope of regression that is necessary for the cure but that simultaneously threatens to overwhelm the ego with impulses not quite containable within the still fragile psychic apparatus.

On the level of the body, various agents can be used to stimulate a return to health. Food is one, and it serves the same function as the analyst's words. Foods vary in both their nutrient (i.e., fueling and building) and detoxifying aspects. Fruits, in their ability to carry off acids, aid the body in cleansing; of the fruits, citrus fruits are the most stimulating, and can stir up toxic material most rapidly. Raw vegetables are next in line in their ability to dislodge toxins. Cooked foods have the effect of slowing down the detoxification process.

Here, too, there is a dangerous tightrope. The detoxification process will stir up old poisons, some of which had been tucked away in storage tissue. Toxic material from past illnesses which were especially serious or acute because of a greater accumulation of toxins are the ones most likely to emerge.[1] These toxins, aroused and circulating within the body, can cause a systemic toxicity.[2] Resurrected from their bodily storage graves, they can be dumped back into body fluids and the blood stream. Should the eliminative capacity of the body not keep pace with the stimulation of the poisons, the body can be thrown into a dangerously toxic condition. In this situation, the patient may show a sudden loss of weight, or become dramatically weakened. The physiological detoxification process, like the psychological regression which it parallels, must be carefully monitored and controlled. It is through the alternation of detoxifying foods with building foods that this process is regulated.[3]

The biological detoxification process parallels the psychological regression in that here, too, there must be a return to the point at which the disease began. Chemical toxins tend to be thrown off in sequential order, the most recent accumulations being the easiest to dislodge. As the body purifies itself, like the mind, it moves back in time, retracing the development of the disease and its causes.

The Healing Crisis

As this backwards movement occurs (it is never so perfectly orderly as this account implies, being subject to a variety of influences), eventually the body will return to a point when there was an especially intense accumulation of toxins. This will usually be a point where illness or disease manifestation was dealt with through suppression of symptoms.[4] Use of symptom alleviating drugs or medicines would have had the effect of interfering with the body's natural attempt to eliminate toxins. There will then remain, after many years, residual toxins which had found their way into storage tissue; and now, in addition, the toxins of the medication used will emerge. At this point, the symptoms of the original illness will be reexperienced.

This is a critical point in the detoxification process. It is in these crises that fever develops, the patient will feel quite ill, and it will seem as though he's getting sicker instead of better. This stage has the same appearance as the disease itself, yet it is a healing crisis.[5] It is at this point that many patients misinterpret the manifestation of these healing symptoms, and assume that they are ill. In a state of panic they will—as they did in the original illness—attempt to suppress the body's natural attempt at working through and ridding itself of accumulated toxins, often with symptom-suppressing drugs.

The healing crisis is, however, of quite a different nature from the original disease. In the disease state, elimination has become blocked. In the healing crisis, the succession of detoxification steps that the patient has taken has enabled the body to reach a point where eliminative channels can be open. Skin, bowel, kidneys, lungs, and liver all work smoothly in keeping pace with the detoxifying needs of the body. Wastes that have been stored in the body are now dissolved and free-flowing. Cleansing and purifying have replaced blockage and constriction.[6]

The healing crisis in the physiological detoxification parallels the point in psychoanalytic treatment where the regression has returned the patient to a core conflict central to his neurotic functioning. Here, too, it seems as though the patient may be getting sicker; feelings become frighteningly intense as the patient approaches the true origin of his illness. Patients at this phase in their analysis often fear that they are going crazy—as in a sense they are. The reliving of the emotional turmoil must be done, though it is done this time, as with the physiological healing crisis, in a different way from the original. The protective role of the analyst permits the patient to experience the gamut of his thoughts and feelings fully and consciously and helps him to put them into words. The earlier alternative, of relegating thoughts and feelings to the realm of the unconscious so that this material seeps out later as pathological symptoms, is now replaced by the opening of the psychological eliminative channel of talking.

These healing crises, like disease itself, may have the appearance of coming on without warning.[7] In spite of the feeling of suddenness, however, each of these situations comes at a predictable point. The disease made itself felt at the point at which toxic accumulations could no longer be contained without overt symptomology; in psychoanalytic treatment, controlled regression comes when the ego has acquired sufficient strength to tolerate the stress that the regression will stimulate; and in the physiological detoxification, the patient will generally have had a period of feeling quite good—it is only when there has been an exchange of new tissue for old, when the lifegiving foods and healthbuilding processes have fortified themselves, that the body will permit this physiological regression into disease origins.

This detoxification process, like the emotional regression, is curative. The presence of the fever, and the now satisfactory functioning of the eliminative organs are signs of the body's return to its natural healing and defensive capacity. On the psychological level, feelings that had long been repressed are now available to conscious experience. A proportionate admixture of love and hate replace the imbalance caused by the previous disproportionate emphasis of one over the other.

Formerly inactive healing potential has become activated. The disease process has begun its reversal.

How the Process Works

Two case studies are presented to illustrate what the healing crisis looks like and how it works. While not every example of disease reversal throws the patient into a dramatic healing crisis such as these two patients experienced, it is nevertheless not uncommon in the serious diseases.

While most patients will benefit from this form of treatment, there is one notable exception. The technique can work only if the eliminative system can be stimulated to release the full amount of toxins that are being stirred up. On the level of the body, where there has been a particularly intense accumulation of poisons (as we see in cancer patients who have been treated with chemotherapy or radiation), this precarious balance may not be able to be created. The system may be so overloaded with poisons that no amount of elimination is sufficient to carry them off. Once the toxins are stirred up, they become rapidly assimilated into the body. Systemic toxic poisoning, and even death, can ensue.

Both of the patients presented here had levels of toxicity—one physical and the other psychological—that were susceptible to reversal. Their stories are atypical only in the severity of their healing crises. More often than not, the method stimulates mild, and sometimes not even noticable, reactions. Reversal of serious disease means walking a fine edge, and it is only through careful and skillful supervision, such as these patients had, that such an attempt should be made.

Cathy, whose story illustrates physiological reversal, had the benefit of her daughter (who tells the story) who was already steeped in the concept and method. There were many times during the process that decisions could have been made differently—drugs administered, slackening off on the detoxifying juices and colonics—that would have yielded a different result. Each decision weighed the impact on Cathy's body, for both short and long term consequences, and on the level of discomfort that she was able to tolerate.

Irma's story, illustrating a healing crisis of the psyche, came close to being a disaster. Her family panicked at the sight of her newly emerging feeling states, and were convinced that she should take mood-altering drugs. She was tempted to believe them, and began to think of herself as sick, rather than as healing. It was only through the stabilizing effect of her analysis that Irma could trust enough in the process to allow it to unfold, and to tolerate her feelings until she could understand them better, and get more comfortable with them.

Cathy, Whose Physiological Healing Crisis Looked Like Dying

My sixty-one year old mother's blessing in disguise came without warning on Monday, May 21, 1984. It began with a severe headache for which she took aspirin, the granddaddy of all painkillers!

On Tuesday, she visited the doctor due to the persistent, unbearable headache for which she was prescribed an antibiotic, Vibramycin, in addition to Tylenol, a close relative to the "granddaddy." The antibiotic was to be taken as a preventative measure, in case she was to have the flu with possible secondary complications. That evening a high fever of 103.5 degrees began and lasted for three days. A blotchy rash and brutal itching which persisted tenaciously for two-and-a-half weeks accompanied the fever. The fever was the body's way of ejecting the accumulated endogenous and exogenous toxins along with the newly introduced medicinal toxins by autolysis.

On Wednesday, my mother was advised to double the antibiotic and Tylenol. As a family, we all agreed that this would do her more harm. One need only refer to the *Physicians' Desk Reference*, its 3,068 pages, to see the dangerous side effects of drugs. If one antibiotic could trigger such a violent reaction, could we afford to risk increasing the dosage?

On Thursday, upon reexamining my mother and suspecting possible pneumonia, the physician recommended chest x-rays. His diagnosis?

Mild pneumonia. Terribly worried, I confronted the radiologist and requested to know the severity of the respiratory infection. I was stunned by his uncertainty as to whether my mother had bronchitis or pneumonia and by his explanation: "It's difficult to determine since I have no previous x-rays for comparison."

On Friday, it was suggested that another type of antibiotic, Velosef, be given for the pneumonia as well as an antihistamine for the itching. Still unsure of the healing crisis phenomenon, we reluctantly yielded and permitted my mom to take five tablets of the antibiotic and then one antihistamine. Despite the drugs, there was no relief. The rash and itching only intensified. Seeing my mother's strength diminish day by day, I decided to consult a nutritionally oriented researcher who recommended Vitamin B liquid, cod liver oil, Vitamins A and D, and raw vegetable juices. I immediately referred to a book on raw juice therapy entitled, *Raw Vegetable Juices*, written by Dr. N. W. Walker, a well-respected centenarian. Luckily, my mother had a juicer and I juiced combinations of carrot, beet, and cucumber for the pneumonia and the itching. This was given morning, noon, and night.

On Saturday, the family doctor revisited and was pleasantly surprised to see an improvement in mother's lungs. What amazed everyone was that it improved without the constant use of medications. In fact, throughout the entire ordeal, we gained more confidence and reassurance in the nature cure as we consistently witnessed a relatively normal blood pressure and pulse. This was most gratifying as my mother had had high blood pressure for several years prior to the change in diet. Up to this point, the fact that my mother did not have any elimination of the bowel perplexed us tremendously. Knowing that her diet had relatively improved, I could not understand why her elimination was at a standstill. I feared the worst! She looked so bloated and her skin was becoming more and more discolored with red and purple. Suspecting the antibiotics as the culprit for the constipation, I called the pharmacist who confirmed my suspicions. He did, indeed, state that antibiotics are often responsible for the destruction of the intestinal flora, so necessary for proper digestion and elimination. Pursuing it further, I read in the *Physicians' Desk Reference* of the myriad of other side effects that could develop from Vibramycin and Velosef. They included skin rashes and renal toxicity, the former especially evident in a most severe form in my mother's case. The listing of adverse reactions to the drugs continued for at least three pages. Those deadly antibiotics! T. C. Fry, his predecessors, and contemporaries were so right:

> When an organism is overwhelmed by toxic substances beyond its ability to eliminate them in normal course the body institutes emergency action to effect expulsion of the toxic burden . . . which results in a healing crisis . . . Drugs . . . interfere with vital body purification and reparative functions and normal body functions as well. . . . (T. C. Fry, *The Life Science Health System*)

The intake of drugs to treat the symptoms only adds more toxins to the already toxic body, thereby causing a more severe reaction.

On Sunday, my mother's itching subsided somewhat. Soon, she developed excruciating arthritis pains in her joints. Referring to Dr. Walker's book, we juiced grapefruit for breakfast, carrot juice for a snack, carrot and spinach juice for lunch. My adorable mother drank all this with some reluctance but turned out to be a super patient. During her moments of utter despair, she did suggest that we take her to the hospital. All we could say to her was to try to think logically. What would they do for her in the hospital? Give her painkillers, tranquilizers, other forms of antibiotics, antihistamines? Nevertheless, in order to please my mother, we asked her physician what he thought about the idea of admitting her to the hospital. Upon seeing how my husband, brother, sister-in-law, and my father had kept vigil on a rotating basis for twenty-four hours, he felt that her home care was far superior to the hospital care that she would have received.

On Monday, May 28, 1984, the juicing of the organically grown carrots combined with the celery began. Her arthritic pains persisted for three days along with the itching. Temporary relief was to be had for the itching with the application of cold compresses, the juice of the aloe vera plant, and above all, an aloe-based moisturizing cream. When we realized that the cream could serve as an obstacle in permitting toxic elimination via the skin, we had no other alternatives; it was necessary to apply it for everyone's sanity and especially my mother's. Despite her sleepless nights and days, my mother continued to "hang in there."

My brother played "doctor" by taking mom's blood pressure with his newly acquired kit. We reported the result to the physician who said that it was normal. In order to help alleviate the arthritic pains, we tried to divert mom's attention to television programs; unfortunately,

the soaps and news were too depressing. If only they could have aired
more shows with "belly laughter" humor so highly recommended by
Norman Cousins in his book, *Anatomy of an Illness*.

Floral bouquets were sent by friends and family but they offered
only a few moments of relief. Our children created super-duper greet-
ing cards and put on a brief puppet show which cheered her temporarily.

On Tuesday, the vegetable juices continued. Thanks to our health
food stores who lovingly replenished our organic carrots, we incessantly scrubbed, peeled, washed, and juiced the adored, yellow and
green treasures. And then it happened! My mom finally had her first
elimination. Who ever thought that I would rejoice about the elimination of my mother's bowels? Now, I was convinced that my mom was
indeed experiencing a healing rather than a disease crisis. It was at this
point that my husband and I reread, reread, and reread Dr. Bernard
Jensen's *Doctor-Patient Handbook: Dealing with the Reversal Process
and The Healing Crisis through Eliminating Diets and Detoxification*.
This valuable book which was to become my "bible" was most
comforting, for it explained my mother's road to rebirth perfectly.:

> Symptoms . . . do not usually come at the same moment but move from
> one part of the body to another or wherever the body is placing its energy
> for cleansing, rejuvenation, and getting rid of the old tissue and acids that
> probably have accumulated over a period of years.

The arthritis pains were now being replaced by sciatica pains, both
of which were very prominent in her past. There was, undoubtedly, a
cleansing of the inorganic calcium deposits in the cartilage of the
joints, commonly known as arthritis. The cleansing was now traveling
to the sciatic nerve and/or surrounding muscle. The former condition
was due to the overconsumption of concentrated carbohydrates; the
latter state was due to the excessive uric acid-producing foods. All the
many years of bad eating habits were coming back to haunt my
mother! For our further peace of mind, we has asked our physician to
have my mom's blood chemistry tested. What a shock when we were
informed that the white blood count was 35,000! In the evening we
spoke to a naturopath from New York City who advised that she have a
blended celery and tomato juice three times per day; a blended salad
three times per day; fruit and an egg yolk.

On Wednesday, the diet continued. My courageous mother was still "hanging in." Needless to say, her weakened state worried us all. I was also disturbed about her overall bloated appearance. I began to read Dr. Ann Wigmore's Book, *Recipes for Longer Life*. After reading about the therapeutic use of wheatgrass and of her Hippocrates Health Institute in Boston and San Diego, I was ready to take my mother; the only problem was that since she was bed ridden and hardly able to walk, I did not know how she could get to the airport and especially endure the ride.

On Thursday, the doctor retook the blood test and he felt the white blood count (WBC) was an error. The blood pressure and body temperature continued to be normal. The severe itching persisted along with the deep purple discoloration of my mother's extremities. The latter worried me greatly; in fact, I even feared gangrene. The vegetable juices, blended salads, subacid fruit, and cooked egg yolk were still given. Her bowel movements were irregular and infrequent. The sciatica was beginning to subside.

On Friday, the doctor informed us that the WBC had now risen from 35,000 to 36,900. The WBC was not the only abnormal factor in my mother's blood chemistry. The LDH, glucose, uric acid, BUN, globulin, triglycerides, and potassium levels were all unusually elevated. The cholesterol, albumin, and sodium were also "out of whack," as they were abnormally low. The doctor insisted that my mother be hospitalized for a week of testing, as he suspected leukemia. We were panic-stricken! How could we permit her to undergo painful bone marrow tests? *No way!* Most fortunately, I remembered an organization which disseminates information about biological treatments of disease. It was they who recognized the symptoms as toxicity due to a healing crisis. They advised us to immediately refer to Dr. Walker's Detoxification Diet of three days, and the essential use of enemas.

On Saturday, the enemas continued as did the lemon-orange-grapefruit combo. In addition, epsom salt drinks were given, as we did not have the Glauber Salts or Seidlitz powders. My mother's weakness troubled all of us but in spite of it she listened and did everything we asked her to do. My exhausted father was great and a marvelous help with the enemas. I don't know what we would have done without him. Having been born and raised in Europe, he was well acquainted with the use of enemas.

On Sunday, in the early morning hours, a peculiar thing happened. My mother's body temperature ranged from 94 to 97 degrees. The strange thing was that the temperature was the same degree as the degree to which I had shaken the thermometer. I began calling the emergency units of different hospitals as I was worried and puzzled. Most said that there was no need for alarm but it would be best to bring my mother to the hospital. Throughout the day, my brother observed the same results for which we could not obtain any scientific explanation. The enemas and drinks continued but there was still not a tremendous amount of water that my mother could tolerate with regard to the enemas. As a result, colonics were suggested. We made several phone calls and finally found a clinic in Pennsylvania that administered them.

On Monday, we traveled with my mother, comfortably propped on pillows and blankets, for two hours to the clinic. She was some champ! Everyone boosted my mom's morale as they were sweet and gentle. She had a colonic and a medical examination. She still had the purple discoloration and rash throughout her body but the itching finally began to subside. The kitchen staff juiced her carrots and spinach and prepared her a soft-boiled egg yolk along with a green leaf salad.

My mother had a colonic on Wednesday and again on Friday. She slowly began to recover her strength. The worst of the best was soon to end. Since that week, throughout July, my mother was losing her old skin which was beautifully replaced by soft, baby-fine, new skin. The process is well described by Dr. Bernard Jensen:

> What becomes of the old tissue? It is not absorbed immediately; nor is it eliminated from the body immediately. It is exchanged by the blood stream over a period of months in a gradual process of reabsorption. This process of building up new cellular structure has been accomplished through good blood containing needed substances and through the circulation of the blood where it is needed.

The intense peeling of skin was an incredible sight. My father literally had to cut off the old, peeled epidermis which hung in excess from my mom's extremities. We were all in ecstasy and very thankful and grateful for the wonderful people that guided us.

*Irma, Whose Psychological Healing Crisis Looked
Like Going Crazy*

Irma was, from the beginning, a most unlikely person to be in psychotherapy. She had had a strict Catholic upbringing—two of her brothers had become priests—and was much more inclined to turn to religion and its support systems for help. The idea of her needing—and using—psychotherapy was sufficiently odd in her social and familial circles that she insisted on maintaining her treatment as a well-kept secret from everyone she knew.

For a long time Irma was quite unsure of how to use treatment. She had never really been good at expressing herself, and this difficulty made her sessions tortuously slow for both of us. In every session we struggled with trying to find things to talk about. Often there were silences, times when our efforts to talk failed and we simply had to endure the discomfort of being together without anything coming to either of our minds to say to one another.

During this early phase of treatment Irma's main concern, and what had brought her into treatment, was her daydreams. She experienced her daydreams as intrusive; she had no control over them, and they came to her unwanted and, at times, she was afraid they would begin to interfere with her work. Though Irma was fifty, she had never had an intimate, or even close, relationship with a man. Her daydreams were all the same: she fantasized about being with a man who she had recently met. With great reluctance, she confessed that the daydreams were largely sexual. She didn't believe in premarital sex, yet her impulses were pulling her strongly in the direction of wanting to have sex with him.

Some time after Irma started treatment, she was elected to be president of a social organization that she had been active in. She had spent weeks talking in her sessions about whether to run for president. She knew she was competent and a hard worker—both of which were qualities that would get her elected—but her shyness and her inability to talk easily scared her. She was afraid that she would feel too frightened to be able to successfully run the meetings. The idea of standing in front of a group of people and having to talk terrified her.

For the year that Irma was president of her club, her sessions were, relievingly, easier for both of us. The problems of the social club became her focus, and together, we hashed out all the issues. She went to each club meeting fully prepared, having thought out with me ahead of time how she felt, what she wanted to accomplish, and the best method of doing this. This emphasis on her presidency was a blessed distraction from the painstaking task of addressing the intrapsychic issues which were so steadfastly resisting being brought to light.

Though Irma's relationship with the man of her fantasies never developed, she soon met, through her involvement with her social club, another man who was taking quite a keen interest in her. This new relationship suffered from another problem: this new man, Mark, shared with Irma the affliction of shyness. He, too, had great difficulty talking. Their dates were strained and difficult; the only times that they could relax with one another was when they were performing activities—tennis or skiing—both of which they did a lot of, but neither of which required talking.

After dating for two years, and developing an increasing sense of comfort with one another, Irma and Mark married. The first year of their marriage was reasonably uneventful, and it seemed that the two were accomodating themselves to one another without too much difficulty. In the second year of marriage, however, there was an event which was precipitant. On a business trip, Irma fell down some stairs and broke her leg. She was laid up for months with a cast on her leg from foot to hip. The emotional fallout from this situation became far reaching, and what was initially a trauma for her body became a boon for her psyche. The efforts toward that transformation, however, were painful, arduous, and fraught with peril.

Shortly after a second operation to remove a pin, Irma found herself depressed, frightened, and frequently irritable. These were altogether new feelings for her, and she sought for reasons to explain them. She developed a series of theories: fear of pregnancy, menopause, her leg not healing properly. Each of these theories developed into obsessional thoughts, and each ran a course of a few weeks when these ideas filled her mind with terror: if she were pregnant, she couldn't have an abortion on religious principles, but she was too nervous to raise a baby, and the baby would probably be Mongoloid anyway because of her age; if she were going through menopause, she would need an operation which she wouldn't be able to handle emotionally; if her leg was not healing properly, she would have to have it amputated. None of these initial explanations for her feelings included her marriage:

neither verbal nor sexual interactions with Mark were mentioned (though as I was to find out later, she had stopped having both with him).

During the time that Irma was plagued with these upsetting thoughts, her outward personality, as would be expected, changed. While Irma's life before her marriage may have been devoid of intimacy, she had developed a strong sense of confidence in ability to care for herself, and an independence that went along with this self-assurance. Now, rather than being her usual calm self, she was frequently upset and cried often and easily. Her irritability was difficult to control, and she found herself, unexpectedly lashing out at people. These behaviors were so unfamiliar to her that she became convinced she was a "mental case." There was a rational part of her mind that told her that her thoughts and feelings and behavior were irrational and unfounded, yet in spite of her efforts to rid herself of them, they persisted, and their continued presence convinced her that she was going crazy.

And, as is often the case when repressed material begins its seepage out from the unconscious, Irma was not the only one who grew alarmed. Her family, too, became quite convinced that she was on the edge of having a nervous breakdown. Her brothers became concerned enough that they encouraged her to seek psychiatric help from a medical physician who could prescribe drugs for her.

I should say at this point that all through Irma's analysis, she had never really warmed up to me. We maintained a friendly, but distant cordiality with one another. I was, for her, merely a professional doing my job. That we could (or should) develop feelings for one another was a thought that never occurred to her. It was clear that Irma's whole emotional training had been to not put stock in feelings: the negative ones were avoided altogether, and the positive ones were regarded as nuisances. Though she talked little about her childhood, I surmised that she had had an early history where no one had taken an interest in her emotional life, and she had come to assume this same indifference. Even her marriage had been more of a practical affair than a romance. While she clearly was desperate enough to continue the treatment, I often felt that she would feel more comfortable talking if I weren't there at all.

So when Irma's family panicked at her condition, she was easy prey. I happened to be out of town at a time when she was having a particularly bad anxiety attack. One of her brothers was with her, and as he was a priest, she was used to deferring to his judgement. He encouraged her to call a psychiatrist friend of his. She must have, indeed, sounded quite distraught because this psychiatrist insisted that her husband take her immediately to a hospital emergency room.

The point at which a patient in a non-drug treatment decides to resort to orthodox medicine, with its arsenal of chemicals, is, of course, always a critical juncture. When the disorder is one that can be successfully treated through natural means, such an act displays a failure of confidence in the existing treatment, and it is most often a signal that the symptoms have reached a point of intolerability. This holds true for either mind or body. It is often a point of no return. In the physical conditions, the intrusion of the toxic drugs often renders further detoxification too dangerous to continue or to subsequently resume. In the emotional disorders, there is often a masking of symptoms that here, too, the process of detoxifying the feelings is no longer available to the psyche.

Irma had a natural aversion to drugs, and in spite of her family's and the psychiatrist's efforts, she chose not to proceed with drug therapy. This decision marked a turning point in her treatment with me; with this decision came an understanding of her reliance on me for her cure. Her efforts to find a solution where feelings didn't need to be dealt with had all failed: her Bible reading ceased to comfort her; her conversations with her family and friends no longer reassured her; and, she wouldn't do the drug therapy. All that was left was talking to me.

Irma threw herself into her treatment; she increased the frequency of her sessions and forced herself to talk to me, to say even the most innocuous or outrageous things. She determined to do anything to get well; even the idea of considering her own thoughts and feelings didn't seem too farfetched at this point.

Finally, shortly after making her decision to not take drugs, Irma developed a new symptom through which we got some clues about the true causes of her dysfunctional state. Irma had become insomniac. Her sleepless nights were causing her grave concern for her health and her ability to function during the day at work. She was desperate for relief.

I suggested she try writing a letter during an insomniac attack. It is a suggestion that I occasionally make to patients when I feel they need more sessions than they can afford. I tell them to allot the time period of the sesion, and to sit down and write all their thoughts and feelings—to in effect behave as though we were conducting a session.

Irma's letters were particularly revealing. There, alone with her thoughts and feelings, and finally with an uninhibited channel of expression, she let the floodgates of emotion open. She was plagued with guilt and self-recrimination. She was terribly pained that she was a burden to Mark. He had married an active, vital woman. They had shared sports; sports had brought them together and was the time that they spent together that was the most relaxed. Now all he had was a defective, overly anxious woman. And, beyond that, she had been in psychotherapy all this time and had never told him. She had hidden from him that she was a "troubled woman, possibly even a mental case." She felt she had deceived him.

Irma's letters marked the beginning of her psychic healing. As we processed this material over the next few months—and letters remained a crucial means of communication between us—we were able to dig even deeper into her conflicts. Irma didn't feel that she deserved to be loved. She had the idea that she could earn acceptance through hard work. This was her drive, and it was this commitment that she gave first to her work and then to her social club. At the time of her marriage, she felt confident about her ability to, similarly, devote herself to the task of being a good wife. But to be loved for just herself. The idea wasn't even in her mind.

The marriage to Mark had upset these preconceived notions about her value. With her broken leg, she couldn't work at being a wife. Even worse, she depended on Mark now in a way that she was unaccustomed to and unfamiliar with. And yet, in spite of her being a bundle of needs, Mark persisted in loving her. None of it made any sense to her.

At last, and most importantly, a piece of the puzzle that took months to fit in was the aggression underlying Irma's self-recriminations. Slowly, almost imperceptibly, the direction of Irma's aggression began to shift: she complained that she didn't feel that Mark was taking her situation seriously enough: "Mark is so wonderful to me. I have no right to feel the feelings I feel towards him. I get so irritated with him. He tries so hard, and his intentions are so good, but he often says things that only upset me all the more. When I get anxious and he tries to comfort me—he says things to reassure me—he tells me it'll all go away soon. But I only end up feeling that he doesn't understand at all, and that he's not taking the whole thing nearly as seriously as he should. He's too optimistic. When I feel that way, I don't want anyone's optimism." And finally, as a note of apology, a final confession, with perhaps a hint of pleading to tell her it's not true, "Aren't I terrible for having these feelings?"

Gradually, piece by piece, more of the real story came out. It was not just this that bothered Irma about Mark. It was the fact that he seemed to live in their house oblivious to his surroundings; they didn't have a proper shower, but her request for one went unheeded; the ceiling leaked, but he preferred using a bucket to fixing it. It was a thousand different little irritations—the kind that come with normal living together, but which she had felt guilty about having. Most of all, it was his endless, and, to Irma, tortuous silences. They would sit through dinner with barely a word exchanged. She would try to engage him—"a penny for your thoughts" had come to be a recurring proverb in her marital interactions, though it remained ineffective as a way of stimulating conversation.

As Irma's true feelings about her contemporary life came more to the surface, her anxiety attacks diminished, and finally disappeared. It was then that we could begin the very deep and luxurious reconstructive work of integrating the present with the remote past. Irma came to understand the characterological origins of many of her conflicts. They predated Mark, and could be traced back to her own family. Here, too, she initially exhibited strong defenses against knowing the truth. The commonalities between her and Mark made it easy for me to make communications to Irma while still respecting her defenses. I speculated that Mark's silences must have origins in his early history. I suggested that his parents must not have expressed much interest in his thoughts and feelings, and as a result, he developed a whole secret internal life. "What riches lie underneath his silence," I exclaimed, knowing all along that I was, as well, describing Irma and talking to Irma about herself. I ventured a little closer; I suggested that they were so alike—their discomfort with talking, maybe they even had similar early histories. Irma had an immediate defensive reaction to such a notion, and rejected it out of hand. She protested that she and her mother had often talked. "How? What did you talk about?" I asked. As Irma was able to reconstruct her memory, she finally had to admit that they didn't really talk at all: her mother talked and she listened. In fact, her mother had talked incessantly, and Irma had developed the trick of pretending to listen to her, but in reality, tuning her out.

Irma became interested in the kinds of unconscious messages that she had received from her parents: don't express aggression; if you feel it, try not to feel it and definitely don't let anyone else know you're feeling it; love is conditional and one must work to deserve it.

As Irma became entirely comfortable in allowing me access into her internal life she realized that Mark, too, needed to be let in. She was able, at last, to tell him of her needs, wants, frustrations, irritations, fears. He proved himself a receptive audience, and even ventured forward a bit into sharing more of his own history and his own feelings with Irma. They now have a marriage that works. And Irma didn't have to go crazy.

Notes

1. B. Jensen, *Doctor - Patient Handbook* (Escondido, CA: Bernard Jensen Enterprises, 1976), 54.
2. L. Roy, *Detoxify for All You're Worth*, unpublished manuscript.
3. I have had hours and hours of conversations between 1980 and 1990 with Ruth Sackman, director of The Foundation for Advancement of Cancer Therapies, and Leo Roy, M.D. on the nature of this biological reversal. Much of the material here is gleaned from those conversations.
4. B. Jensen, *Doctor - Patient Handbook*, 51.
5. Jensen coined the term, "healing crisis." It has come to be common parlence in alternative healing circles.
6. B. Jensen, *Doctor - Patient Handbook*, 51.
7. Ibid, 52.

14

Food and Feelings: Unconscious Meanings

Children never seem to tire of listening with fear, wonder, and a certain amount of glee to the Big Bad Wolf's threat to eat Little Red Riding Hood all up. As with most myths and fairy tales preserved over time, the story touches upon some primitive and yet still relevant issues for each of us.

The history of life is that all living things have always faced two fundamental tasks in their struggle to survive—eating and not being eaten.[1] Almost as soon as there was anything worth eating, things began to eat other things. By the time consciousness arrived, and these things developed into sentient beings, organisms with feeling and awareness, the world was rife with predators. With the threat of predators came, as well, the feelings they aroused. It is likely that the feeling of fear has everything to do with our primitive instincts about being somebody else's food.

As sophisticated inhabitants of a modern world, we generally seem to be free of such primitive concerns. Yet, just how close to the surface these fears lie becomes quickly evident when we unexpectedly perceive ourselves as the object of someone else's hunger. Consider, for instance, the recoiling that is typical of discovering on one's body that small, but horrifyingly persistent insect we identify as the tick. The idea of one's own blood being the food of another conjures up for us the most primitive of fantasies, the idea of being eaten.

And, as with most dreaded events, the idea eventually found its way into a therapeutic principle, as well (if it feels bad, it's good for you). Leeching, the application of insects with the deliberate intent to suck blood, was a commonly practiced method of healing in this country, but was met by its victims with great fear and dread.

The notion of being eaten up is powerfully felt by cancer patients. It is commonly thought that the hapless victim is being eaten up from the inside-out by the disease. It is not unusual to hear cancer patients describe the cancer process as a force that is consuming them. Dreams of monsters, fires, and any other dangerous entities which have the attribution of devouring are common in the patient who has become aware of the disease process in his body.

The importance of food is ever-present in the mind of the heart disease patient, as well. He will generally feel that the most powerful, and perhaps only, control he has over his disease is the way in which he eats. Eating concerns, then, become quite literally matters of which the patient makes the choice to facilitate or impede progress towards his own death. Food choices are usually made on the basis of one's ability to make conscious decisions about one's wish to survive.

The concern for survival having to do with food—whether the issue is being food for another, or having food for oneself in sufficient quantity and quality, is present in most serious physical and psychological diseases. In spite of the fact that it is now undisputed scientific thought that most of the killer diseases are related to nutritional difficulties, this is only a marginally valuable piece of information. In a survey of cancer patients who were asked whether proof of dietary contribution in the contraction of their disease would persuade them to make dietary changes, 54 percent said it would not.[2] The number should not surprise us. Smokers do not continue to smoke for lack of information about the deleterious effect of the habit. One cancer patient exemplified the inability to give rational consideration to the idea of making dietary change by retorting, ''I would rather die than give up eating meat.''

The human animal is unique in that it is the only species who eats; all other animals feed. Since the beginning of civilization, food has come to have emotional significance having nothing to do with nutrition. It is only in understanding the symbolic value of food that we can appreciate the resistance in making dietary adjustments that would lead to a longer and healthier life.

The most obvious ways in which eating has acquired symbolic value is in the ceremonial and religious rites in which food is used. The celebration of weddings and birthdays are never complete without a cake; glasses of wine serve as a way of formally communicating good wishes; bread and wine are distributed to celebrate the Christian rite of communion; and the unleavened bread and bitter herbs of Passover remind Jews of their historical past. In these ceremonial uses, food is elevated to a symbolic and treasured status. The use of foods which were already traditionally valued because of their scarcity made the symbolic meaning a relatively easy leap.

All human societies, be they simple or complex, share in the fact that eating is the primary way of initiating and maintaining human relationships. The derivation of the word *companion* is from French and Latin words meaning "one who eats bread with another." Our earliest experiences as newborn infants, revolve around food, and it is in this fact that unconscious concerns, as well as the conscious value attributed to food in ceremonial rites, come to play a role in the symbolic meaning of food.

The Original Feeding Paradigm

All human relations have their origin in the relationship to the original feeding object—the mother.[3] The desire for food is biologically innate, and indeed, the entire life of the infant is characterized by an alternation between hunger and sleep; hunger is the tension state which repeatedly interrupts the calm of sleep.[4]

It is through the feeding situation that the infant comes to accomplish the essential task of distinguishing self from not-self. Initially, intrauterine life consists of a biological unity between mother and child, where the placenta nourishes the growing fetus. After birth, the infant may continue to experience this unity during the act of feeding. The mother extends herself to the child, and the child accepts the breast as part of his own self.[5]

The feeding situation becomes the infant's most intense experience of a world outside himself.[6] He is, eventually, confronted with a puncture in his envelope of unity with mother. He learns quickly that the supplies he wants are external, that he must experience some frustration, and a state of unpleasure before his hunger needs are satisfied.[7] It is thus, through the tension state of hunger and the feeding situation with the mother, that the infant forms his first object relations.[8]

As the infant is compelled to recognize a world outside himself to meet his need, he finds that objects differ from one another. He learns that some objects which he puts in this mouth will satisfy his drive and thus reduce tension, while others will frustrate him and increase tension.[9] The first recognition of reality, then, is in the differentiation of whether to swallow the object or spit it out.[10] Swallowing represents the first positive instinctual behavior; spitting out represents the first negative instinctual behavior.[11] The decision to incorporate or expel is the infant's earliest judgement.[12]

The close contact the mother and infant have with each other means that there is an intense exchange of emotional communication; the feelings in one influence and induce feelings in the other.[13] The healthy mother and healthy baby induce positive feelings in one another. The baby who eats his food cooperatively and produces normal, healthy stool gives the mother a feeling of adequacy. She feels that she is emotionally in tune with her child, and she prides herself on her motherhood. The mother who is sensitive to the delicate balance of frustration and gratification the infant needs for maturation induces in the baby a feeling of pleasurable satisfaction with himself. He knows that he can sometimes have what he wants, and the gratification of his desire feels good. He also knows that sometimes he cannot have what he wants, or not always immediately on the asking, but he easily tolerates the frustration of either not getting or the delay of gratification. Later, with minimal ego development, he may even feel pride in himself for his ability to tolerate deprivation.

Situations can occur, however, which will prove to be overly frustrating for the underdeveloped ego of the infant.[14] The mother may not be able to read the communications of the child, and, in that way, may not understand the infant's needs; or, the child may have an inherently weak digestive system, and the mother may not be unable to alleviate the infant's discomfort. In these situations, the infant will continue to experience frustration. The mother may begin to question her adequacy. Or, her frustration at not being able to please the baby may turn into aggressive feelings toward the baby; the infant's frustration at not being able to be pleased will thus turn into aggressive feelings towards the mother.

Conversely, the eating situation may be overly gratifying for the infant. The mother, anxious about her role as caretaker, may act out these fears by being perpetually available to the infant, meeting his every whim. The infant is robbed of the valuable and necessary lesson of learning to comfortably experience and tolerate frustration. Such an infant may never come to know the feeling of hunger, and how to manage states of unpleasure without immediate gratification.

The infant and mother, sensitive to the emotional needs of the other, may begin to experience eating as an act filled with anxiety. Or, the eating may become so pleasurable that no other activity comes close to generating the same amount of gratification. In either case, eating, and those processes associated with feeding, may come to have meaning beyond its biological intent. Conflicts established at this early age around food and the use of food as solutions to psychological conflicts may become lifelong patterns.

It is through a disturbance in this early learning of self/no-self boundaries that fears associated with eating or being eaten can arise.[15,16] The fear represents a wish to return to a more pleasurable state of unity. Eating is incorporation, where two objects come to be one. The longing can be to incorporate, or to be incorporated—a yielding of one's own omnipotence to a larger, more powerful object,[17] and these can be associated with either pleasure or anxiety.[18]

The object that most readily banishes the state of unpleasure is the mother's breast, or, in later life, whatever object or activity has come to represent this. As such, she, or her substitute, comes to be experienced as omnipotent.[19] As the most important person in the infant's world, she is the object on whom fears and wishes are projected.[20] The relationship becomes ambivalent. Love and hate are both felt.

This may be a confusing situation for the infant, and one which his underdeveloped ego cannot handle. And so, he develops the mechanism we call splitting, by which we mean that the object is split into good and bad parts,[21,22] the good breast and the bad breast.[23] The introduction of this mechanism allows the infant to tolerate the fact that his nourisher is also his controller; he is both gratified and frustrated by the same person. Separating the good and bad objects allows him to experience his normal feelings of aggression toward the frustrating object without fear of destroying the nurturing object.

The fact that the infant continues to put objects in his mouth which do not provide physiological nourishment indicates that oral incorporation has become separated from the function of nourishment. Rather, the stimulation derived from the contact with the object is pleasurable in itself and becomes independent of the original tie to nourishment.[24] The effect of this independent is that objects can come to have symbolic significance.[25]

When the child begins to learn to feed himself, it is an indicator that his symbiotic dependence on the mother is changing to some modicum of independence.[26] Separation is, of course, an ongoing process that begins with birth, but the skill of learning to give oneself nourishment can be seen as a developmental milestone. This act can have symbolic significance in later life when the exigencies of the world demand from the adult that he maintain this self-loving, self-nourishing attribute.

Equally important is the infant's reaction to the change from breast to solid foods, the introduction of new tastes and consistencies. Here is reflected, for the first time, his leaning toward progression and adventureness, where new experiences are welcomed, or a tenacious clinging to existing pleasures, where every change is experienced as a threat and as deprivation.[27] Whichever attitude dominates here, too, will have consequences in later developmental roles.

The symbolic equation of mother equals food helps us to understand battles around food between mother and infant. The mother may experience every refusal of food as a personal rejection of her maternal care. The child may act out his emotions through eating: he may refuse to eat because of aggressive feelings (rejection of the mother substitute), or he may overeat (treating food as a substitute for mother love).[28]

These primitive and early emotional connections, linking food to mother, remain in the unconscious of the individual throughout his life. The object of the mother will eventually become an internalized part of the self. The emotional meaning that has come to be ascribed to conflicts around food will, in adult life, be experienced as conflicts between two warring factions of the self: "I shouldn't eat this food," vs. "I can't stand to deprive myself." The original link between mother as the initial object of involvement in the conflict, and food, has become lost in the complex maze of the unconscious. It is fair to say, then, that one never eats alone, for always present are the earliest eating experiences associated with the mother.

The Feeding Paradigm in Psychosomatic Disease

The development of life-threatening disease is a regressive experience. Severe psychological reactions have been noted and they include immobilization, depression, anxiety, paranoid responses, feelings of inferiority, aggression, isolation, increased dependency, suicidal thoughts, feelings of rejection, withdrawal, denial, and obsessive preoccupation.[29-31] The patient may already have early, unresolved conflicts, as the psychosomatic literature suggests, and this itself may play a role in the development of the disease. But even without this conceptualization, the contraction and treatment of the disease sets up situations which necessarily induce regressive feelings in the patient. It is not uncommon for patients to say, "If I have to die, I want to do it with dignity," or, "I couldn't bear to be a burden on my family." Such statements reflect the deep, unconscious material that is touched by the implications of the disease, and the strength of the desire to not allow themselves to be affected by these regressive tendencies.

The typical patient will initially feel quite helpless in the face of his life-threatening disease. He feels that his body is out of conscious control, and that he does not have the internal resources to reverse the progression of the disease.[32] This feeling of helplessness parallels the state of biological helplessness he felt as an infant, when he was dependent on his mother to provide the supplies necessary for life sustenance. It is with these feelings already activated that the patient seeks help in fighting for his life.

The Feeding Paradigm in Medical Treatment:
Medicine As Food

Cultural tradition defines the physician as the person from whom the patient can expect the most help. The physician, presumably, has superior knowledge and tools that are otherwise unavailable to the patient. All hope for cure in placed in the hands of the physician, and he comes to be endowed with omnipotent powers.

The omnipotence ascribed to the physician parallels the experience the infant has of the mother. Relative to the child, the mother is intensely more powerful. In this regard, the doctor/patient relationship is a structural recreation of the original mother/child relationship.

Evidence of this phenomenon can be garnered from observations of the affective responses of patients and their families toward the physicians. Some patients who have been informed of a poor prognosis will, even in the face of contrary evidence, still maintain the firm belief that their doctor will find a way to save them, or that medical science will make the necessary advancement in time. Or, conversely, some patients will be firmly convinced that no doctor on earth can help them, and will conscientiously avoid using them for any purpose.

The illusion of the patient that he is being eaten away is a myth that has its roots in this projection of omnipotence. All scientific evidence available thus far indicates a situation quite different. The physiological representation of such a notion would be of the pathogenic cell feeding on its host. In fact, the host and the invading cell (the tumor, in cancer; the plaque, in heart disease) have nutritional needs to ensure their survival, and they must compete for whatever nutritional goods are available. Tumor and host, then, are rivals.

Despite the horror of the progressive nature of the disease, the fantasy of being consumed is not always met with dread. The fantasy may include the idea that one will be eaten whole, as Jonah by the whale, and spit out without bodily injury. Or, the idea of yielding to a larger, more powerful force may suggest an intimacy that is thrilling, like the threat of the Big Bad Wolf: "All the better to eat you with, my dear." Some patients, upon diagnosis, have expressed relief that the long-dreaded event has actually come to pass. These patients may willingly submit to the will of the disease. The release from the struggle to ward off the feared event may be pleasurable. Some patients are pleased to finally have a good enough reason to give up self-destructive behavior (smoking, eating bad food, working until exhaustion), and use the disease as an excuse to reverse life patterns.

Because incorporation destroys the object, however, it gives the aim of incorporation an ambivalent character.[33] Accompanying the feeling of pleasure are feelings of anxiety. The patient fears the consuming nature of the disease, and awaits his own eventual destruction with dread.

The patient does not, however, limit the power of incorporation to the disease. Orthodox medical treatment ravages the body and can be experienced as intensely devouring as the disease itself. Chemotherapy and radiation destroy healthy cells as well as diseased cancer cells. Surgery is an intrusive invasion, and is often experienced as threatening annihilation of the ego. The feelings associated with the threat of this new object powerful enough to devour will largely determine the patient's ability to participate in his treatment program, and the success of the coping mechanisms he employs to deal with the fact of the disease.

The physician's devotion to treating the patient parallels the mother's commitment to providing life-sustaining nurturance to the child. Like the mother, he comes to represent life itself. Because his medicine is what will give the patient life, the medicine comes to have the symbolic meaning of food. The patient, like the child, hopes to share in the omnipotent powers of the superior object. Incorporation of the omnipotent figure, or its psychic equivalent, is the mechanism by which this transfer of power will take place.

On the level of the unconscious, where symbolism holds sway, it makes no difference whether the medicine is ingested orally, given through body absorption (radiation and injections of chemotherapy), or cutting (surgery). In conditions of regression, all sense organs are conceived as mouth-like.[34,35] Objects are not looked upon as individuals, but only as food, or providers of food.[36]

Incorporation has the effect of uniting the person with the object. The magical notion of communion, that one can assume the vital power of a desired object through the eating of the object, has wide historical precedent.[37] In many cultures the flesh and blood of dead men are eaten and drunk to inspire the qualities those men personified.[38] Bushmen refrain from feeding their children the heart of a jackal lest they become timid.[39] The ill patient, too, hopes that in eating the foods of the physician he will acquire the power the physician has come to represent—triumph over death. The patient whose childhood history included feelings of pleasure and safety in the hands of a competent mother will be more likely to participate cooperatively in a treatment regimen. The patient whose feeding history was one of overgratification may demonstrate a compliant willingness to submit to the ministrations of this new omnipotent figure, replacing the original mother whose powers were exaggerated. For the patient who experienced displeasure and frustration in early feeding, rebelliousness may result.

With or without pleasurable anticipation of the beneficial effect of the medication, the physiological reality of treatment remains unchanged. Drug therapy is the administration of a known toxic substance to the body. It is done on the premise that the toxicity of the disease is more damaging to the system than the toxicity of the drug. Radiation, drug therapy, and surgery can all be lethal.

The body responds to the medication/food as though it were undigestible. Spitting is the body's instinctive response to bad food. The common side effects of the treatments are attempts by the body to reject or eliminate toxic material.[40] Thus, awareness is dual. The conscious agreement to ingest a poison violates the body's awareness that it is being fed bad food and impedes its instinctive reach for nutritional substances.

The body's response to these toxins activates unconscious feelings around the digestion and elimination of food which may have long since been mastered. For the adult whose childhood history showed no significant feeding disturbances, the inability to take in and release food in socially appropriate ways will introduce new fears, accompanied by shame.

Despite the fact that it is the physician who is feeding the patient these toxic foods, this awareness is generally kept from conscious knowledge. In the service of protecting the omnipotent figure, the patient acknowledges only gratitude for the physician's persistence in treatment and professional skill in applying his techniques. The patient does not acknowledge feelings of aggression toward the object, despite the fact that the physician is the source of the toxic food.

The patient is able to effectively protect the physician from his aggression by resorting to the mechanism of splitting. Good and bad breast are perceived by the infant as separate and unconnected entities. Similarly, the patient who needs to maintain a good/bad object split is unable to integrate the fact that a good doctor is giving bad food.

The relationship to the doctor/food-giver may now become highly charged with ambivalence. On the one hand, he is the hoped-for sustainer of life; on the other hand, his food/medicine is poison to the body. This situation replicates the early love/hate relationship to the mother. Dependence on the nurturing object makes discharge toward the object an impossible solution. The repression of aggression becomes psychologically toxic, just as the medicine is physiologically toxic. While the body may retain instinctive power to attempt discharge of toxicity, the mind may not. The build-up of psychological toxicity may mean that the relationship to the physician/food-giver may, in time, become as toxic to the patient as the treatment.

The fantasy of omnipotence and omniscience is doomed to failure, then. The food turns out to be not only bad tasting, but turns against the body. Further, the power of the disease more often than not proves stronger than the power of the medicine: the disease continues, and the patient is left with the ravages of the disease and of the treatment. As the power of the food/medicine diminishes, so too is the omnipotent position of the physician in jeopardy. Franz Alexander noted that it is only in the dark that we see ghosts.[41] Many patients become familiar with the various aspects of their disease. They become proficient as demythologizing the very particular language of the medical profession. They become acquainted with the statistics predicting the probable course of the disease. They learn lessons in the physiology of their own bodies. In addition, the physician comes to be seen in a more humanized fashion. He is revealed to be vulnerable and mortal.

Concomitant to the demythologizing of the physician's power is a consequent evocation of aggression. The aggression is aroused by the thwarting of dependency needs.[42] Patients who have stripped away their own omnipotent projections from the physician may blame him for anything from poor diagnostic procedures, unforeseen complications, the inability to find effective medication—to the imminent death itself.

The Feeding Paradigm in Psychoanalysis: Words As Food

The effectiveness of psychoanalytic technique depends on the analyst's ability to aid in transferring to the analyst early feelings from unresolved conflicts. Once this transference has occurred, the patient has the chance to relive early developmental sequences with a new parent object. Inadequately mastered phases can now be successfully mastered under the more sensitive and therapeutic parenting. The psychoanalyst is sensitive to the maturational needs of the patient, and times his interventions so that they help to move the patient along the developmental process.[43]

The analyst's words to the patient are experienced by the patient as food. Insofar as his interventions are successful in enabling the patient to grow (the growth now is emotional rather than physical), his words are, indeed, symbolic food. The analyst, like the good mother, is careful to dole out his food, achieving a delicate balance between frustration and gratification.

The ideal maturational process in psychoanalysis would be consistent with the ideal maturational process in infancy. The patient moves from a position of dependence to independence, where he learns the proper amount of food he can contain, and can even instruct the analyst as to what this proper amount is (self-dosing). He learns appropriate and constructive release of impulses, both positive and negative, and learns that the communication of negative impulses can be used as a gift rather than as a weapon.

As with the original maturational process, so too in psychoanalysis is this ideal sequence rarely, if ever, achieved. Resistance to growth is witnessed. Within the context of the transference, the resistance to change is worked through.

Curing Oneself: Food As Medicine

Patients using biological treatments of disease seek cure through the careful, selective use of food. Here the symbolic meaning of food, as in medical or psychological treatments, is bypassed. The notion that food itself promotes natural, healthy growth is a literal return to the paradigm of mother/food as physiological nourishment for the growing child. The memory of parental care in providing food for proper nurturance is evoked. Food is no longer chosen purely for taste or convenience, but is selected for health-giving properties.

The patient who believes that proper nourishment from food will be palliative is reinstituting the movement from maternal nourishment to self-nourishment. Food, insofar as it is thought to have curative powers, comes to be understood and experienced as medicine.

The practical aspects of following a treatment regimen that depends on active participation by the patient are very different from a program of submission to pills or instruments of medicine. This active and independent patient quickly learns that food is a kind of medicine that he must do some work for.

Curing oneself means that the patient has moved from his initial, helpless position to a profound understanding of his role in creating and perpetuating the circumstances of his life that led to his disease, and to his newly found ability to be able to move actively and constructively toward health. He has learned to "feed" himself. He has learned to regulate his own food intake and elimination rationally, on the basis of his physiological needs, independently of his conscious and unconscious fantasies about food, and irrespective of his relationship to the provider of the food.

Feeling As Food

Feelings, like food, have nutrient value. Feelings are the expression of our particular psychological makeup, and the urge to feel comes to us as naturally and automatically as the urge to eat. Just as our body tells us when it needs nourishment by signaling hunger to us, the psyche calls out its need for psychological nourishment by giving us feelings. When we feel hurt, we need reassurance; when we feel angry, we need soothing. Always, we need understanding.

When there is emotional understanding—and this can be between two people, or between parts of or within oneself—something magical happens. It is as though all boundaries, separating an "I" from an "other," or, a "bad me" from a "good me," have been dissolved. There is a noticeable physiological effect: breathing is deeper, muscles are more relaxed, heart rate slows down, and color is brought to the face; the body exudes a natural warmth and glow, and the psyche seems open and accessible. Both body and mind feel lighter.

Medicines of any kind work only because they meet an essential need. Physical agents of healing have responded to some essential need in the body. Food is able to be used medicinally precisely because its nutrient value is a requirement for healthy biological functioning. Feelings, like food, are not a luxury. Rather, a well-oiled psyche needs (not wants) a full range of feelings. Emotional understanding is the medicine of the psyche that permits healing in that it fosters the essential need of allowing feelings into consciousness.

At times we attempt to interfere with the spontaneous arousal of the feeling process. Some feelings are painful, and we interpret this as meaning that they are bad. Once relegated to this evaluative category of "bad," we try to eject any feelings which fall under its domain.

The emotional system functions like the digestive system. Feelings, like food, need digesting and they need elimination. We can't get rid of a feeling by simply not wanting to have it; we can only not digest it. When we don't digest food, we suffer consequences. The nutrients are not absorbed, and we become malnourished. In not being able to go through its natural process of passing through the body, undigested food remains within the body. Toxic waste material that should have been properly discharged, instead putrefies, and finally, will systemically poison the body.

This is what happens to feelings when they're not digested. They lodge somewhere. We may hope and pretend that they're not there, but they have their way of making their appearances known. They may show up in disturbing dreams. Or, we may find ourselves unexpectedly upset, supersensitive to seemingly innocuous communications from others, or, to rather ordinary events. Or, we may develop a physical reaction which, in continuing without abatement for a long enough period of time, can develop into a physical disease. Because the feelings haven't been digested, they can't be eliminated. A process of psychological putrefaction has begun.

Food is a foreign body that, during the course of digestion, we make briefly our own. Feelings, too must become a part of us before we can begin the process of letting them go. When we interpret feelings as "bad," we don't want to welcome them into our bodies and our minds. They remain phenomonologically foreign to us, and are neither digested nor eliminated. Like undigested food, they get stuck inside of us. We become unable to shake them.

Freud's great discovery was that the process of digesting feelings is the process of verbalization; talking, or putting everything that one thinks and feels into words. Through verbalization, we gain mastery over powerful internal forces which, uncontrolled, threaten our destruction. In putting thoughts and feelings into words, proper absorption of psychological nutrients and discharge of psychological waste is accomplished. As one patient said, "As I talk, my symptoms go away, and I begin to feel very sad."

Notes

1. J. Gorman, "The Hugs of A. M. Rosenthal and the Fear of God," *Discover* (May 1987).
2. Research reported in *American Institute for Cancer Research Newsletter*, 6 (winter 1984).
3. S. Freud, "The Dynamics of Transference," *S. E.* (1924).
4. O. Fenichel, *The Psychoanalytic Theory of Neurosis*, (NY: W. W. Norton, 1945).
5. W. Hoffer, "The Mutual Influences in the Development of Ego and Id: Earlier States," *The Psychoanalytic Study of The Child*, 7 (1952): 31–41.
6. S. Ferenczi, "The Problem of the Acceptance of Unpleasant Ideas," *Further Contributions to the Theory and Technique of Psychoanalysis*, (London: Institute of Psychoanalysis, Hogarth Press, 1926).
7. A. Freud, *The Writings of Anna Freud, Vo. VI: Normality and Pathology in Childhood and Assessments of Development*, (NY: International Universities Press, 1965) 70–71.
8. S. Ferenczi, *"The Problem of Acceptance."*
9. S. Freud, "On Negation," *International Journal of Psychoanalysis*, 6 (1923).
10. O. Fenichel, *The Psychoanalytic Theory* 38.
11. Ibid.
12. Ibid.
13. S. Escalona, "Emotional Development in the First Year of Life," in Smilton Senn, *Problems of Infancy and Childhood*, Transactions of the Sixth (1952) Conference, Josiah Macy, Jr., Foundation (Ann Arbor, MI).
14. O. Fenichel, *The Psychoanalytic Theory* 65–6.

15. O. Fenichel, "The Dread of being Eaten," *International Journal of Psychoanalysis* 10 (1929).
16. S. Freud, *The Problems of Anxiety* (NY: W. W. Norton, 1936).
17. O. Fenichel, *The Psychoanalytic Theory* 64.
18. G. H. Grabor, "Die Zweisrlei Mechonismor der Identifizierung," *Imago* 23 (1937).
19. O. Fenichel, *The Psychoanalytic Theory* 62–63.
20. Ibid.
21. S. Freud, "Splitting of the Ego in the Defensive Process," *International Journal of Psychoanalysis* 22 (1941).
22. O. Kernberg, *Borderline Conditions and Pathological Narcissism* (NY: Jason Aronson, 1975).
23. M. Klein, "The Origins of Transference," *International Journal of Psychoanalysis* 33 (1952): 433–8.
24. O. Fenichel, *The Psychoanalytic Theory* pp. 62–3.
25. Ibid., 49.
26. A. Freud, *The Writings of Anna Freud* 75–7.
27. Ibid., 71.
28. Ibid., 72.
29. R. D. Abrams, and J. E. Finesinger, "Guilt Reactions in Patients with Cancer," *Cancer* 31 (1951): 474–82.
30. N. S. Kline, and J. Sobin, "The Psychological Management of Cancer Cases," *Journal of American Medical Association* 146 (1951): 1547.
31. H. E. Simmons, *The Psychogenic Theory of Disease: A New Approach to Cancer Research* (Sacramento, CA: General Welfare Publications, 1966).
32. A. H. Schmale, and H. Iker, "Hopelessness as a Prediction of Cervical Cancer," *Social Science and Medicine* 5 (England; Pergamon Press, 1951) 95–100.
33. O. Fenichel, *The Psychoanalytic Theory* 64.
34. O. Fenichel, "Ueber Respiratorische Introjecktion," *International Zeitschrift fuer Psychoanalyse* 17 (1931).
35. O. Fenichel, "The Scoptophilic Instinct and Identification," *International Journal of Psychoanalysis* (1937).
36. O. Fenichel, "The Psychoanalytic Theory of Neurosis" (1945) 63.
37. P. Slater, *Microcosm* (NY: John Wiley, 1966), 62–3.
38. Ibid.
39. J. G. Frazer, *The New Golden Bough* ed. J. H. Gaston, (NY: Criterion Books, 1959).
40. L. Roy, personal communication, 1985.
41. F. Alexander, and T. M. French, *Psychoanalytic Therapy*, (NY: Ronald, 1946).
42. T. M. Mills, "Authority and Group Emotion," in *Interpersonal Dynamics*, ed. W. G. Bennis, et al., (Homewood, IL: Dorsey, 1964).
43. H. Spotnitz, *Modern Psychoanalysis of a Schizophrenic Patient* (NY: Greene & Stratton, 1969), 104.

15

The Eye of the "I"

Freud was not the first to emphasize that aspect of being human that leads to death and destruction. In a piece of writing that predates Freud by about 5,000 years, we are told about Cain, the murderer who slew his brother, Abel. And, like Freud, who remains convinced that some positive benefit could come out of this aggression innate to man, Genesis, too, concludes that murder can result in good. It is out of Cain, the murderer, that civilization itself arises. Cain constructed the first city and invented agriculture; his descendents, the sons of Lamech, invented "artifices in brass and iron" and musical instruments—technology and art.[1]

We began this book, too, with a story of murder. Pearl Pizzamiglio tragically died after a holdup, and Michael Stewart, her assailant, is now in jail for her murder. We have seen, throughout the book, that all the world—around us and in us—can work either to our benefit or to our detriment. Somehow, that night in April 1984, Pearl Pizzamiglio was unable to find a way to utilize any constructive solutions— solutions that might have saved her life—to her advantage.

The issue between Pearl Pizzamiglio and Michael Stewart that ultimately killed her was not purely one of aggression. Yes, there certainly was aggression in Michael Stewart's act of not caring about his threatening effect on another human being. And, certainly, there must have been some stimulation of aggression in Pearl Pizzamiglio, some voice inside, screaming out, but not to be heard, "Why is this man doing this to me? Damn him." Maybe even, "May he rot in hell." But none of that is what killed her. What killed Pearl Pizzamiglio was her own body turning against itself, he own body following its own plan, without her conscious consent or willingness. Somehow, Pearl Pizzamiglio's "I," that part of her that should remain in control and be able to make rational decisions (and surely that part of her from which she normally functioned), had become inactivated. That night, there seemed to be no wakeful, vigilant "eye" for her "I."

Such an absence is not the way the human system was designed to operate. Our bodies and minds are brilliantly designed to maintain a functional status quo. When we treat them with care, they reward us with a state of health and well being. It takes some effort to interfere with these health-giving processes. It takes effort to put to sleep those processes which oversee our functionings, and which respond with ingenious lock-key precision to rebalance and reregulate any momentary disturbances. If our temperature goes up, our sweat glands leap into action to relieve the pressure. If our temperature goes down, our overall circulation decreases so that the all important heart is saved from the kind of stress that would make it stop. It is all quite miraculous.

Recent work on the autoimmune diseases has provided clues to a revolutionary understanding of health and disease that disrupts our most accepted notions of how our bodies work. The autoimmune diseases, next to cancer and heart disease, are our most compelling health problems. The list of such diseases is long, and the diseases are catastrophic, when not outright life threatening. These diseases include multiple sclerosis, myasthenia gravis, rheumatoid arthritis, type one (juvenile) diabetes mellitus, and systemic lupus erythematosus. Unlike cancer and AIDS, where there is an inactivation of key cells in the immune system, these diseases are characterized by an immunological response that is strong and well focused. The response, however, is directed against some essential component of the body: aggression against the self.

As has been delineated throughout this book, in diseases where the immune system is the culprit, what is crucial is the factor of recognition—self deciphering not-self.

Antigens—any substance foreign to the body, including viruses, bacteria, fungi parasites, and transplanted tissues or cells—are recognized by receptor cells. Each receptor cell is specific to an antigen, or to just a small part of the antigen called epitope. For the immune system to work effectively, it must be able to recognize a wide range of pathogens—all the kinds that are out there. There must be a great diversity of receptors—millions of receptors to recognize millions of epitopes. It is this very flexibility that holds the key to our most recent understanding of the immune system.

The capacity of millions of receptors binding to millions of epitopes enlarges the repertoire of the immune system so greatly that it seems unlikely that a single molecule could escape detection—including the molecules of the self. On this biological level, is it possible that self sees self? Recent work on rheumatoid arthritis suggests that the immune system receptors that perform the work of recognition can, themselves, be recognized by other receptors.[2] It is precisely this self-recognition that appears to be disturbed in the autoimmune diseases.

Once again, the precise parallels between the functioning of mind and body are astonishing. The discovery from the study of the autoimmune diseases that the body can attack itself finds its psychological equivalent in Spotnitz's theory of narcissistic defense: pathogens, emotional or biological, are ignored and the body, or mind, ill-fatedly turned its aggression on itself.

If it is, as research data suggests, the failure of the process of self-recognition that can result in disease, then clearly adequate self-recognition is the key to health. Pathogens—foreign substances—are only half the problem. Self, too, now must be clearly seen by itself for health to reign. Freud's therapy, as an attempt to uncover all hidden aspects of self, and Selye's agreement with him to "know thyself" have become biological necessities.

Freud saw that his purely psychological theory and therapy—knowing one's psyche—was only a half-step toward the understanding of mental functioning. Ever the biologist at heart, Freud looked forward to how the future would unfold in its conceptualization and treatment of disease. In the closest he came to an apology for the limitations of psychoanalysis, he stated in 1909 that ultimately, the treatment of choice for the nervous disorders would be biochemical. Such a treatment approach, however, would depend upon a much more thorough understanding of the brain, nervous system, and chemical components of the human organism than we had then, and that was even possible then.

One hundred years later, we are much closer to Freud's vision. We have a wealth of genetic data to show the biological origins of the two major mental disturbances. Studies on twins separated at birth, but manifesting the same kind of psychotic disturbance years later, are convincing evidence of the biological and genetic contributions of schizophrenia.[3] As well, cells from the hippocampus, that part of the brain thought to be a center for emotions and the perception of reality, have been found to be wildly disorganized in schizophrenic patients. Manic depression, a mental disorder evidencing wild mood swings, is now also considered to be largely genetic. With the 1987 identification of a manic-depression marker on human chromosome 11, Dr. Darrel Regier, Director of the Division of Clinical Research at the National Institute of Mental Health, remarked: "The study ushers in a new era of psychiatric research."[4] And a biological basis for some of the less frequent mental disorders has been found. Four abnormal proteins were found in the cerebrospinal fluid of patients with Creutzfeldt-Jakob, a form of dementia often confused with both Alzheimer's Disease and Huntington's Disease.[5] The protein amyloid has been known, for some years, to appear in large concentrations of victims of Alzheimer's, but recently scientists have identified a gene that produces a major protein component of amyloid.[6]

Of course, it was from the groundwork of psychic functioning that Freud laid that we have come to revise our opinions about physical diseases. Stress—that catch-all phrase coined by Selye, which simply means more than a system can handle—contributes to the causation of disease, and not the least of the stresses that we feel is psychological in nature.

We now understand, as we did at so many other junctures in history but lost sight of for the last one hundred years, that the division between mind and body exists only in abstract thinking. Such a split reflects nothing of the nature of the functioning of the human organism.

To end, let us return to the beginning—as medicine itself has done. Let us consider, for yet another moment, Pearl Pizzamiglio and her fate at the moment in her precarious life when Michael Stewart entered it. A different outcome is easily imagined.

Pearl Pizzamiglio was married, and statistical data on longevity show that certain health benefits accrue to married people. Let us suppose that she had taken greater advantage of her married state.

Let us suppose that Mrs. Pizzamiglio had allowed her husband to play a larger part in how the evening unfolded. Agitated and upset by Michael Stewart's act of terrorizing her, she might have called her husband *before* she called the police. The police report shows that she had quite an extensive conversation with the dispatch, and was beginning to repeat her story to the officer who arrived on the scene—all this before she finally called her husband, sleeping just seconds away, in Room 133 of the motel.

She said to him finally, "Honey, I've been held up. Hurry up—you better come here. I don't feel too good." By the time Mr. Pizzamiglio arrived, his wife was already having trouble breathing, and was holding her chest in pain.

But let us imagine that Mr. Pizzamiglio had, instead, been present during the police questioning of his wife. This interrogation was, as it always necessarily is, clinically cold and objective. Mrs. Pizzamiglio had panicked during the robbery, she told the police; surely only minutes later when she was being questioned much of this feeling was still present—fear for one's life ebbs away only slowly. But this highly charged condition had no appropriate moment for expression in this colloquy.

Her husband's presence in such circumstances would have been for a very different situation from the one she found herself in— surrounded by strangers interested only in facts. Depending on his style and the style of their relationship, he might have accepted her venting of this emotional pressure in any of a variety of helpful ways. Instead of having to contain her emotions, as the decorum of the official situation was demanding that she do, Mrs. Pizzamiglio would have had the welcoming outlet of her husband's concern for just this aspect of her situation—how she felt about it.

She might then have allowed her feelings freer rein; might have cried on his shoulder, or raged about the feeling of violation. She might even have complained about the objectification of herself that she felt from the police interrogation.

All these feelings (and whatever else she felt) would have been appropriate to communicate to a man committed specifically to her personal, emotional well-being. And such a release of feeling would have served to return her whole system to a state more closely approximating normality. The condition of biological overstimulation might have been relieved without catastrophically overtaxing her own body's means of discharge. In effect, her husband would have provided a second system (nervous system, psychic structure) to contain and process the stimulation.

Mrs. Pizzamilgio might in that event have returned to her home that night a badly shaken but nevertheless still living woman.

Mrs. Pizzamiglio died a premature death. Even had she lived to be the average age of morbidity for most Americans, she still would have died long before her body had the capacity to endure. It is now thought that the human body is biologically programmed to survive 120 years. It is only through the extraordinary wear and tear of unnatural circumstances that we have shortened our lifespan to roughly half the time of its innate capacity.

The human organism has developed a flexibility in dealing with and adapting to its nonhuman environment unsurpassed by any living species. We have exceeded the bounds of our bodies, and through the aid of technology, we can now live with a reasonable amount of comfort on virtually any part of earth, hot or cold, below ground or high above. We also survive under a broad range of emotional circumstances, with love, with indifference, or abuse.

This gift for adaptability is not usual in living species. For all other organisms, the limits of their bodies define where, how, and for how long they live.

Yet, in spite of the incomparable potential that we have demonstrated in our ability to be adaptable, we are failing in the effort. Our health data reflect this fact.

As good a definition as any of health is the ability to adapt to demands, demands from without and from within. Therapy, whether it be psychologic or biologic in approach, makes it possible to change specific defenses, or responses, to stimuli. Any good treatment augments or mobilizes the natural defenses or the organism. Responses are then rendered neither excessive nor inactive, but rather appropriate in intensity and duration to both the provoking stimulus and sensitive to the constitutional strength of the organism to tolerate the stimulation. Symptom alleviation occurs as a secondary byproduct of the organism's overall improved functioning.

Psychoanalysis has shown us for one hundred years that with a vigilant ego—the psychic eye of the "I"—rationality and reasonableness can override the automaticity of the unconscious. Pavlov, in 1924, showed that guinea pigs could learn to produce specific antibodies. Fifty year later, Robert Ader made the same discovery, and scientists have been demonstrating ever since that the immune system is not, or need not be, an automatic system.[7] Our physiological defense system, like our psychological defense system, can learn. The immune system, like the psyche, has, in a very literal sense, its own mind and its own decision-making capacity. It, too, has an eye for the "I."

Allowing our bodies and minds to use all the eyes they have at their disposal is surely the key to good health and long life.

Notes

1. C. Sagan, *The Dragons of Eden* (New York: Ballantine Books, 1977), 98.
2. I. R. Cohen, "The Self, the World, and Autoimmunity," *Scientific Amercican* (April 1988): 52.
3. J. Kovelman, and A. Scheibel, "Biological Substrates of Schizophrenia," *Acta Neurol. Scand.* 73:1 (1986): 1–32.
4. J. Egeland, *Nature* (March 1, 1987).
5. M. Harring, C. Merril, D. Asher, and C. Gajdusek, "Abnormal Proteins in the Cerebrospinal Fluid of Patients with Creutzfeldt-Jakob Disease," *New England Journal of Medicine* 315:5 (July 31, 1986): 279–83.
6. D. Selkoe, *Science* (Feb. 1987).
7. R. Ader, and N. Cohen, "Behaviorally Conditioned Immunosuppression," *Psychosomatic Medicine* 37 (1975): 333–40.

Index

293